Que's Computer Buyer's Guide

Joseph Desposito

Contributing Authors
Scott Foerster
Timothy S. Stanley

Que's Computer Buyer's Guide

Copyright © 1991 by Que® Corporation

All rights reserved. Printed in the United States of America. No part of this book may be used or reproduced in any form or by any means, or stored in a database or retrieval system, without prior written permission of the publisher except in the case of brief quotations embodied in critical articles and reviews. Making copies of any part of this book for any purpose other than your own personal use is a violation of United States copyright laws. For information, address Que Corporation, 11711 N. College Ave., Carmel, IN 46032.

Library of Congress Catalog No. 90-63259

ISBN 0-88022-659-5

This book is sold *as is*, without warranty of any kind, either express or implied, respecting the contents of this book, including but not limited to implied warranties for the book's quality, performance, merchantability, or fitness for any particular purpose. Neither Que Corporation nor its dealers or distributors shall be liable to the purchaser or any other person or entity with respect to any liability, loss, or damage caused or alleged to be caused directly or indirectly by this book.

94 93 92 91   4 3 2 1

Interpretation of the printing code: the rightmost double-digit number is the year of the book's printing; the rightmost single-digit number, the number of the book's printing. For example, a printing code of 91-1 shows that the first printing of the book occurred in 1991.

DEDICATION

To Madonna Butler, my lovely sister-in-law, who succumbed to cancer during the writing of this book.

Publisher
Lloyd J. Short

Acquisitions Manager
Terrie Lynn Solomon

Product Director
Shelley O'Hara

Production Editor
Kelly D. Dobbs

Editors
H. Leigh Davis
Don Eamon
Daniel Schnake
Laura Wirthlin

Technical Editor
Douglass G. High, Jr.

Book Design
Scott Cook

Indexers
Hilary Adams
Jill D. Bomaster

Production Team
Jeff Baker
Claudia Bell
Scott Boucher
Martin Coleman
Sandy Grieshop
Bob LaRoche
Michele Laseau
Sarah Leatherman
Howard Peirce
Cindy Phipps
Tad Ringo
Bruce Steed
Suzanne Tully
Johnna VanHoose
Lisa Wilson
Christine Young

Composed in Garamond and Macmillan
by Que Corporation

About the Author

Joseph Desposito

Joseph Desposito has a degree in electronic engineering from Manhattan College. He is a microcomputer consultant and free-lance writer specializing in microcomputer topics. Currently, he is a contributing editor at *Computer Craft* magazine.

Mr. Desposito has held the position of editor-in-chief of *PC Clones* magazine and has worked as senior project leader at *PC Magazine's* PC Labs. He also has served as a technical editor for several magazines, including *Creative Computing, Computers and Electronics,* and *Popular Electronics.* Mr. Desposito is the revision author for *Using 1-2-3 Release 2.3, 1-2-3 Quick Reference for Release 3.1, Using 1-2-3 Release 3.1, 1-2-3 Macro Library,* 3rd Edition, and *Using 1-2-3 Release 2.2.*

ACKNOWLEDGMENTS

My thanks to Shelley O'Hara for providing me with the groundwork for this book and for her excellent comments on each chapter. My thanks also to the following editors for their comments on the text: Kelly D. Dobbs, Dan Schnake, Tim Stanley, Doug High, Leigh Davis, Don Eamon, and Laura Wirthlin. Finally, my thanks to Scott Foerster for his initial input into this project.

Trademark Acknowledgments

Que Corporation has made every effort to supply trademark information about company names, products, and services mentioned in this book. Trademarks indicated below were derived from various sources. Que Corporation cannot attest to the accuracy of this information.

1-2-3 and Lotus are registered trademarks of Lotus Development Corporation.

Amiga is a registered trademark of Commodore-Amiga, Inc.

Apple, Apple II, Apple IIc, Apple IIe, Apple II+, Apple Font/DA Mover Utility, AppleTalk, AppleWorks, ImageWriter, LaserWriter, LaserWriter Plus, LaserWriter II NT, LaserWriter IISC, Mac, Macintosh, Macintosh Plus, Macintosh SE, Macintosh SE/30, and MacWrite II are registered trademarks and ImageWriter 2, Macintosh System, and MultiFinder are trademarks of Apple Computer, Inc.

Atari is a registered trademark and ST is a trademark of Atari Corporation.

Bitstream is a registered trademark of Bitstream, Inc.

Centronics is a registered trademark of Centronics Data Computer Corporation.

Commodore is a registered trademark of Commodore Electronics Limited.

COMPAQ is a registered trademark of COMPAQ Computer Corporation.

CompuServe Information Service is a registered trademark of CompuServe Incorporated and H&R Block, Inc.

dBASE is a registered trademark of Ashton-Tate Corporation.

EPSON is a registered trademark and Epson Equity I+ and Epson FX-1050 are trademarks of Epson Corporation.

HP is a registered trademark and HP DeskJet and LaserJet are trademarks of Hewlett-Packard Co.

IBM, IBM PC, IBM AT, OS/2, IBM Personal PagePrinter, Quietwriter, and PS/2 Model 30 are registered trademarks and IBM PC XT, IBM ProPrinter, and PS/2 are trademarks of International Business Machines Corporation.

InSet is a registered trademark of INSET Systems, Inc.

Intel is a registered trademark of Intel Corporation.

MCI Mail, Microsoft, Microsoft Windows, Microsoft Word, and MS-DOS are registered trademarks of Microsoft Corporation.

Motorola is a registered trademark of Motorola, Inc.

NEC is a registered trademark of MultiMate International, an Ashton-Tate Corporation.

OKIDATA is a registered trademark of Oki America, Inc.

PageMaker is a registered trademark of Aldus Corporation.

Paradox, Quattro, and Quattro Pro are registered trademarks of Borland/Ansa Software.

PC Paintbrush is a registered trademark of ZSoft Corporation.

PFS is a registered trademark and First Publisher is a trademark of Software Publishing Corporation.

PostScript and Encapsulated PostScript are registered trademarks and Adobe Illustrator is a trademark of Adobe Systems, Inc.

QuarkXPress is a trademark of Quark, Inc.

Unix is a trademark of AT&T.

WordPerfect is a registered trademark of WordPerfect Corporation.

WriteNow is a trademark licensed to T/Maker Company.

Xerox is a registered trademark of Xerox Corporation.

Trademarks of other products mentioned in this book are held by the companies producing them.

Table of Contents

Introduction 1

1 What Can a Personal Computer Do? 5
   Benefiting from a Personal Computer 6
      Saving Time and Money 6
      Handling Repetitive Work 7
      Increasing Accuracy 7
      Opening Up New Avenues of Opportunity 8
   Using a Personal Computer 8
      Working with Words 9
      Working with Numbers 10
      Working with Information 11
      Working with Finances 11
      Communicating with Other Computers 11
      Working with Symbols and Images 12
      Working with Sound 13
      Playing Games 13
      Enhancing Education 14
      Creating Programs 14
   Making a Decision 14
   Chapter Summary 17
   In the Next Chapter 17

2 How Does a Computer Work? 19
   Defining PC Components 19
      System Unit 21
      Monitor 25
      Keyboard and Mouse 27
      Floppy Disk Drive 29
      Hard Disk Drive 32
   Defining Software Types 33
      ROM 33
      Operating System Software 34
      Application Software 36

Chapter Summary 37
In the Next Chapter 37

3 What Components Do I Need? 39

Central Processing Unit 39
   Speed 40
   8, 16, and 32 Bits 40
   CPU Compatibility 41
   Intel CPUs 41
      8088 and 8086 42
      80286 43
      80386SX and 80386 44
      80486 46
   Motorola CPUs 46
ROM 48
RAM 49
   IBM and Compatible Computers 50
   Macintosh, Amiga, and Atari Mega and ST Computers 51
System Unit Case 51
Keyboard and Mouse 52
Monitors and Video Adapters 54
   Monochrome Monitors 54
   Color Monitors 55
   Monitor Size 56
Floppy Disk Drives 58
Hard Disk Drives 58
   Size 58
   Performance 59
      Access Speed 60
      Transfer Rate 60
Hard Cards 61
Removable Hard Disks 61
Slots and Buses 61
Serial and Parallel Ports 63
Printers 64
Other Equipment 64
   Modems 64
   Scanners 66
   Surge Protectors 68
   Furniture 68

	Supplies	68
	Other	69
	Chapter Summary	69
	In the Next Chapter	69
4	**What Type of Computer Do I Want?**	**71**
	Comparing Manufacturers	72
	Software Availability	73
	Ease of Use	73
	Performance	75
	Price	76
	Reviewing Manufacturers	77
	IBM	77
	Apple Computer	78
	IBM Compatibles	78
	Acer	79
	ALR	79
	Altec	80
	AST	80
	AT&T	81
	Austin	81
	Compaq	81
	CompuAdd	82
	Dell	82
	DTK	83
	Epson	83
	Everex	84
	Gateway 2000	84
	Hewlett-Packard	85
	Kaypro	85
	Leading Edge	85
	NEC	86
	Northgate	86
	Packard Bell	87
	PC Brand	87
	Swan	87
	Tandon	87
	Tandy	88
	Texas Instrument	89
	Toshiba	89

Wyse	90
Zenith	90
ZEOS	90
The Rest	91
Commodore	91
Atari ST or Mega	92
Reviewing Your Choices	93
Selecting a Video Adapter	94
Deciding How Much Memory	95
Selecting a Hard Drive	96
Selecting a Manufacturer	96
Selecting a Model	97
IBM Models	97
IBM-Compatible Models	99
Macintosh Models	99
Chapter Summary	100
In the Next Chapter	101

5 What Computer Model Do I Want? 103

Selecting a Model Based on an Application	103
Word Processing	104
Low-End Word Processing	105
High-End Word Processing	106
Spreadsheets	107
Low-End Spreadsheets	107
High-End Spreadsheets	108
Databases	109
Low-End Databases	110
High-End Databases	111
Graphics	112
Electronic Communications	113
Desktop Publishing	114
Low-End Desktop Publishing	114
High-End Desktop Publishing	115
Education	116
Accounting	117
Building a General-Purpose PC	117
IBM General-Purpose Computer	117
IBM-Compatible General-Purpose Computer	118
Macintosh General-Purpose Computer	119

    Buying a Portable Computer 119
        Luggables 120
        Laptops 122
        Notebooks 122
    Buying a Used Computer 123
        Purchasing a Used IBM Computer 124
            IBM PC 125
            IBM PC XT 125
            IBM AT 125
            IBM PS/2 125
        Purchasing a Used IBM Compatible 126
        Purchasing a Used Macintosh 126
        Purchasing a Used Amiga, ST, or Mega 127
        Purchasing Some Other Kind of Used Computer 127
        Evaluating a Used Computer 128
        Finding a Used Computer 128
    Chapter Summary 129
    In the Next Chapter 129

6 What Printer Do I Want? 131

    Printing 131
    Understanding Printer Technology 132
        Dot-Matrix Printers 133
            Dot-Matrix Print Quality 133
            Dot-Matrix Printer Features 135
            Dot-Matrix Printer Manufacturers 136
        Inkjet and Thermal Transfer Printers 136
            Inkjet and Thermal Printer Fonts 137
            Inkjet and Thermal Printer Features 137
            Inkjet and Thermal Printer Manufacturers 137
        Daisywheel Printers 137
        Laser Printers 138
            Laser Print Quality 138
            Laser Printer Language 139
            Laser Printer Features 140
            Laser Printer Manufacturers 141
    Considering Printer Features 142
        Print Quality 142
        Ports 143
        Memory 144

  Resolution 145
  Speed 146
  Paper Size 147
  Operating Costs 147
 Determining Your Required Output 148
  Printing Internal Reports 148
  Printing Letters, Resumes, and Papers 149
  Printing Mailing Labels 149
  Printing Banners 149
  Printing Wide Spreadsheets 150
  Printing Forms 150
  Printing Newsletters, Brochures, and Other High-Quality
  Documents 151
 Determining the Right Printer for Your Applications 151
  Spreadsheet Applications 151
  Database Applications 152
  Word Processing Applications 152
  Desktop Publishing Applications 153
  Accounting Applications 153
  Graphics and Drawing Applications 154
  Educational Applications 154
 Determining the Printer You Need 154
  9-Pin Dot-Matrix Printers 155
  24-Pin Dot-Matrix Printers 155
  Inkjet Printers 155
  Laser Printers 156
  PostScript Laser Printers 156
  QuickDraw Page Printers 156
  Color Printers 157
 Chapter Summary 157
 In the Next Chapter 157

7 How Do I Purchase a Computer System? 159
 Where Do I Purchase a Computer? 159
  Computer Stores 160
  Superstores 161
  Electronics Stores 161
  Department Stores 162
  Mail Order 162
 How Do I Find a Vendor? 164

What Questions Should I Ask? 164
Who Does Setup and Training? 166
How Do I Make the Big Purchase? 166
Chapter Summary 169
In the Next Chapter 170

8 What Software Do I Need? 171

Analyzing Your Needs 171
    Setting Your Software Goals 172
    Setting Software Requirements 173
    Choosing a Software Environment 175
        Single-Task Operating Systems and Environments 175
            Text-Based DOS 176
            System and Finder 177
        Multiple-Task Environments 177
            Microsoft Windows 178
            DESQview 179
            Other IBM-Compatible Operating Environments 179
            Multifinder 180
        Multitasking Operating Systems 180
            OS/2 181
            Macintosh System 7 182
    Considering Training and Support 182
    Determining Your Hardware Configuration 183
Selecting Application Software 185
    Word Processors 185
    Spreadsheet Programs 188
    Database Programs 191
    Financial Programs 194
        Low-End Accounting Software 194
        Personal Finance Software 195
    Desktop Publishing Packages 198
    Communications Software 200
    Integrated Programs 203
    Paint and Drawing Programs 206
    Music Sequencing and Notation Software 208
    Education and Game Programs 212
    Shareware 214
Chapter Summary 215
In the Next Chapter 216

9 How Do I Install and Maintain My Computer? 217

Preparing for Your New Computer 218
    Ensuring Proper AC Power 218
    Ensuring Proper Ventilation 219
    Working Environment 219
    Avoiding Static Electricity 220
    Avoiding Magnets 221
    Installing a Phone Line 221
Setting Up Your Computer 222
    Unpacking Your Equipment 222
    Setting Up Your System 223
Maintaining Your Computer 224
    System Unit Maintenance 225
    Disk Drive Maintenance 225
        Floppy Disk Drives 225
        Hard Disk Drives 226
    Keyboard, Mouse, and Video Monitor Maintenance 228
    Printer Maintenance 228
Troubleshooting 228
    Troubleshooting the Initial Setup 229
    Long-Term Troubleshooting Strategies 230
Chapter Summary 231
In the Next Chapter 231

10 How Do I Plan for the Future? 233

Repairing a Personal Computer System 233
    In-Warranty Repairs 234
    Out-of-Warranty Repairs 235
        Finding a Reliable Repair Center 235
        Repairing Your Computer Yourself 236
Upgrading a Personal Computer System 237
    Manufacturer's Hardware Upgrades 237
    Manufacturer's Software Upgrades 237
    Other Upgrades 238
        Memory 238
        Hard Disk 239
        Monitor/Graphics Adapter 239
        System Board 240
        Math Coprocessor 241

Printers	241
Keeping Pace with New Developments	242
Subscribing to Computer Magazines	242
Joining an On-Line Service	243
Chapter Summary	243

Index 245

Introduction

Buying a personal computer for the first time can be a daunting experience. Not only do you have many different brands to choose from, but after you decide on a particular brand, you have to figure out which model to buy. After you select a personal computer, you need to make decisions about what kinds of equipment to connect to the computer. You have to figure out which monitor, printer, and modem suits your needs. When you decide on the equipment, you need to choose software, or the programs you need to accomplish your personal computing goals. Choosing the right software takes as much thought as choosing the right hardware.

Designed to guide you through all the steps necessary to reach a purchasing decision, *Que's Computer Buyer's Guide* covers all the computer hardware and software you may need to get you started. This book provides you with the background necessary to make intelligent purchasing decisions and offers advice about what to buy and what not to buy.

Rarely has the information required to make the right decisions about purchasing a computer, peripherals, and software been put in one place as is in this book; usually the information is scattered around in various books, magazines, and other sources. This book is not specific to one brand of personal computer like many other computer books and magazines are. This book deals with a wide spectrum of personal computers—computers powerful enough to meet your business and personal computing needs.

Unlike buyer's guides that appear in computer magazines (or in other consumer magazines), *Que's Computer Buyer's Guide* does not include long lists of features so that you can compare dozens of products in the same category. Instead, this book explains to you, in a nontechnical way, what different types of products can do and which type of products are best for a particular application. This book then recommends one or more products in a category—recommendations based on years of experience using these products.

Que's Computer Buyer's Guide provides you with the information you need to make intelligent purchasing decisions about computers, peripherals, and software. This book helps you select a computer manufacturer and model, a printer, and a software program appropriate for your needs and gives you tips on buying, maintaining, and upgrading your system.

Who Should Read This Book

Anyone planning to buy a personal computer for the first time, whether for use in a business or at home, should read *Que's Computer Buyer's Guide*. If you are interested in an IBM or compatible, Apple Macintosh, Commodore Amiga, or Atari Mega or ST computer, this book will help you understand—without inundating you with the technical details—how to select a model appropriate for your needs.

Que's Computer Buyer's Guide also is helpful to anyone new to personal computing—maybe you are working with computers for the first time at your job or in school. This book provides the information you need to understand the equipment you are working on and what alternatives are available. The information contained in the book helps to put your computing system into perspective and lays the groundwork for any purchase you may make: a computer, a peripheral (such as a printer), or a software program.

Finally, *Que's Computer Buyer's Guide* is appropriate for anyone who already owns a computer but who wants to understand more about peripherals and software. Chapter 6, for example, is dedicated to printers, and Chapter 8 covers many popular software programs.

How This Book Is Organized

Que's Computer Buyer's Guide is logically structured so that information about what you want to do proceeds recommendations on what is needed to accomplish your goals. The first five chapters are dedicated to helping you choose the computer that is right for you. Subsequent chapters deal with printer, purchasing, software, maintenance, and planning for the future. An overview of each chapter follows.

Chapter 1, "What Can a Personal Computer Do?," describes the benefits of using a computer. The intent of this chapter is to help you decide what you want your computer to do.

Chapter 2, "How Does a Computer Work?," provides a basic overview of the major parts of a computer system and shows how the parts work together. Definitions of basic terms are included in this chapter. The material is presented in a nontechnical way so that you get the information you need to help you make a purchase decision.

Chapter 3, "What Components Do I Need?," builds on the information in Chapter 2, covering features in more detail. This chapter describes similarities and differences among various components and makes recommendations based on what those components are best suited to do.

Chapter 4, "What Type of Computer Do I Want?," helps you select a particular manufacturer. This chapter deals with issues such as software availability, compatibility, performance, price, support, upgrade, warranties, service, and so on.

Chapter 5, "What Computer Model Do I Want?," helps you decide on a particular model from a particular manufacturer. The chapter provides real-world examples of applications for different types of environments: a home office, a small business, and so on.

Chapter 6, "What Printer Do I Want?," helps you decide which printer to purchase. This chapter describes the features of different types of printers in a nontechnical way and provides recommendations based on specific applications.

Chapter 7, "How Do I Purchase a Computer System?," explains how to research different systems and needs and provides you with questions to ask prior to making a purchase. This chapter also describes various places to shop for a computer and offers tips on where to get the best deal.

Chapter 8, "What Software Do I Need?," defines the various types of software programs and explains what these programs can do. The chapter describes the differences among programs and helps you decide what features you need. Finally, the chapter provides specific software recommendations.

Chapter 9, "How Do I Install and Maintain My Computer," explains how to set up a computer system and describes different kinds of easy-to-perform maintenance procedures. The chapter also explains where to get help if you need it.

Chapter 10, "How Do I Plan for the Future?," helps you prepare for future upgrades to your system—for hardware and software.

Other Reference Sources

Although *Que's Computer Buyer's Guide* tells you what you need to know to make an intelligent computer purchase, no book can fill all your personal computing needs. Que Corporation publishes a full line of microcomputer books that complement this one.

If you want more information about computing fundamentals, you should try other Que books. For general information, look through *Introduction to Personal Computers* and *Que's Computer User's Dictionary*. For IBM and compatible computers, *Using DOS* and *Using Microsoft Windows 3* provide information about the most popular operating systems. For Macintosh computers, *The Big Mac Book* is an all-in-one reference source.

If you are interested in finding out more about how to use a particular software application, many Que books are available for you to choose from—for IBM and compatible and Macintosh computers. Que books on some of the more popular applications include *Using 1-2-3 Release 2.2*, *Using WordPerfect 5.1*, and *Using dBASE IV* (for IBM and compatibles) and *Using Excel*, *Using Microsoft Word 4*, and *Using FileMaker* (for Macintosh computers).

If you are interested in further technical details about computer hardware, examine Que's *Upgrading and Repairing PCs*. This informative text shows you how to get the most from your current hardware and how to upgrade your system to achieve better performance from your software.

1

What Can a Personal Computer Do?

When you think of all the possible purchases you can make in your lifetime, a personal computer has to be one of the most mystifying and frustrating. First of all, a computer costs a significant amount of money, more than you probably would spend for a good stereo sound system and sometimes as much as you would spend for a low-priced automobile. Because a computer costs so much, you want to make the right decision the first time. This objective pressures you to collect and assimilate all the information you can about the purchase.

As you collect the information, the purchase decision becomes even more confusing and intimidating. You have many types of computers with many different features to choose from. You are bombarded with advertisements and reviews comparing the types and features, but it is difficult to make sense out of the material. What is RAM? What does MHz stand for? What is a 80386 CPU? All you want to know is the bottom line—what computer do you need to get the job done (if you need one at all)?

A personal computer purchase is just the beginning of a series of purchases you must make to do a particular job. Besides the computer, you need programs to run the computer and connected equipment (for example, a printer).

This book hopes to take some of the mystery out of purchasing a personal computer and the accessories. The book explains what computers are and guides you through making an intelligent purchasing decision. Terms are defined and related to performance. For example, how does the amount of RAM affect how you use the computer to track real estate clients? By understanding the different features, you can make an informed purchasing decision.

The first step in making that decision is deciding what you want the computer to do. A person who uses a computer to do financial forecasting may need a different computer than someone who uses the computer to type letters. You need to define in specific terms the tasks you want the computer to do.

This chapter begins by explaining some of the benefits of using a personal computer. (Note that this book uses PC generically to refer to any type of personal computer.) This book also shows you some of the tasks you can accomplish with your computer. Today, you may want the computer to do a home budget, but tomorrow you may want to use the computer to publish a neighborhood newsletter. As you make up your list of what the computer should do for you, consider all possibilities. This chapter helps you determine specifically what you need the computer to do.

Benefiting from a Personal Computer

A personal computer may be expensive, but it often pays for itself. These benefits can be seen in many ways. A PC can save you time and money; it can help you do repetitive work; it can increase accuracy in your work; and it can open up new avenues of opportunity for you.

Saving Time and Money

Computers can save you time and money. Any project that involves the calculation of numbers is improved on a computer because a computer can calculate much faster than the human mind. If you enter numbers erroneously, such as on a simple list of expenses added together for a total, the corrections can be made, and the total can be recalculated in a matter of seconds.

More complex tasks also are simplified. For example, in business, you may want to make a five-year projection of sales versus expenses and develop graphs that highlight important areas of interest. Doing this task manually—gathering the figures, performing the calculations with a calculator, typing them into a report, drawing a graph—takes a good deal of time. Using a computer greatly simplifies the tasks. With the right program, you enter the figures once, and the program calculates the results and creates a graph.

Redundancy is eliminated because information (numbers, text, pictures) can be entered once and then stored permanently on a disk for future reference. You can access any saved information and change, rearrange, remove, or add to the existing information. This flexibility also speeds up your work.

Besides saving time, a personal computer can save you money. One way is by helping you avoid mistakes. Depending on what you are doing—for example, adding a long list of figures—one mistake can cost you hundreds or even thousands of dollars. Computers can help you avoid errors like this by doing calculations quickly and correctly. Of course, if you type numbers incorrectly to begin with, a computer is not likely to catch the mistake.

Another way in which a personal computer can help you save money is by providing you with alternative ways to do a job. For example, you may be using outside sources to typeset and print your company newsletter. With a PC and the right program, you can publish the newsletter yourself.

Handling Repetitive Work

If you have been stuck with a punishment such as writing "I will not talk in class" 100 times, you know how boring a task like this one can be. Although you may not like it, a computer does not mind this task. A PC performs a routine task like this one quickly and without making errors (even if you increase the punishment to 1,000 or 10,000 times).

Computers are perfect for tasks such as typing the same letter to 10,000 people (and even personalizing it). A PC also is perfect for doing math problems that involve numerous repetitive calculations.

Quality can be improved because the time saved on mundane tasks such as retyping or recalculating gives you more time to concentrate on the content of the task.

Increasing Accuracy

A computer can help you do your work more accurately. If you work with words, a spelling checker can help you weed out most or all spelling mistakes, and a grammar checker can alert you to inaccuracies in grammar. If you work with numbers, a spreadsheet program can improve the accuracy of your results. For example, a change to one or more numbers of a budget forecast usually affects many numbers throughout the budget. A spreadsheet program can recalculate the entire budget quickly and accurately.

Opening Up New Avenues of Opportunity

No matter what career path you currently pursue, owning a personal computer can open up new avenues of opportunity for you. With the proper training and qualifications, you can write a book or a magazine article with a PC; you can design ads or newsletters with a PC; or you can connect your electronic music keyboard to your PC.

You may be thinking about a career change. You may want to pursue computer-specific areas such as PC consulting, programming, training, or technical repair. Maybe your dream is to design and program the next great computer game. These kinds of opportunities and more are available in personal computing.

Using a Personal Computer

For a computer to save you time and money, you must know what you want the computer to do. What tasks do you want to automate? What types of items do you want the computer to create—letters, graphs, reports, mailing lists? The following list describes many tasks you may want to do with a personal computer:

- Working with words
- Working with numbers
- Working with information
- Handling finances
- Communicating with other computers
- Working with symbols and images
- Working with sound

- Playing games
- Enhancing education
- Creating programs

To do each of these tasks on a computer you need an application program often referred to as *software*. Software gives the computer the instructions it needs to perform a task. A large variety of application software is available in each of these categories. (Chapter 8 addresses the world of software.) Use this material to first understand the range of capabilities a computer provides and then to determine what you want your computer to do now and in the future.

Working with Words

You can use your computer to type letters, reports, manuscripts, or term papers. To do so, you need a program called a *word processor*. In many ways, you use a word processor like you use a typewriter, but a word processor offers significant advantages.

If you often make mistakes when you type, a word processor increases accuracy. You see on-screen what you type. As characters appear on-screen, you can check them for accuracy. If a character is not correct, you can delete and replace the incorrect character with the correct character—no white out is needed.

If you have to make changes to the text you type, a word processor can help. With a word processor, you can rearrange text. If you type a paragraph with a typewriter and then decide later to move the paragraph to a different page in the document, you have to cut out the paragraph with a pair of scissors and paste it with glue or tape in the appropriate place on another page. You need to retype the affected pages. With a word processor, you indicate the paragraph to be moved and then indicate the place to where you want it moved. This method is simple and neat, and no retyping is needed.

Most quality word processors also spell check your work when you ask—either at the end of the manuscript or when you are stumped on a word. You can correct spelling errors—or any other type of error—*before* you print the document. If the printed document contains errors, you can return to the program, make the necessary changes, and print the document again.

You can use a word processor to create documents from simple letters to complex manuals. Depending on the word processing program you select, other features are available that enable you to create document headers, page numbers, footnotes, and so on. Your word processor, for example, may have a built-in thesaurus that enables you to find just the right word. Your word processor also may enable you to insert graphics into the document.

If you need presentation-quality output, you may need a desktop publishing program in addition to a word processor. With this type of program, you can create brochures, reports, newsletters, and so on. You can place text in one or more columns, add pictures, and use different typefaces for headlines, initial capitals, and captions. A document created with a desktop publishing program can look professional—as if you had the job printed at a print shop. All of these capabilities are available to you with the right computer and software combinations.

Working with Numbers

You also can use your computer to work with numbers such as those in financial statements, budgets, and cash reports. To do so, you need a software program called a *spreadsheet*. A spreadsheet program is the electronic representation of a page in an accountant's pad. The difference, however, is that a spreadsheet program usually contains 8,196 rows and 256 columns. These dimensions give you enough room to enter data for even the most complex financial reports.

To perform mathematical operations on data, you enter the appropriate formulas. When you enter a new figure in your spreadsheet, the program recalculates all of the formulas. If you make a change, you do not have to redo any of the calculations by hand—the program does it for you.

If you are interested in figuring out different financial scenarios, you can enter different numbers and then recalculate the spreadsheet. This *what-if* feature of a spreadsheet gives it a tremendous edge over other calculating tools.

If you are interested in seeing a graph of the numbers, you easily can create line, bar, pie, and other types of graphs. The spreadsheet uses the numbers you already have entered to create graphs for you.

If you are interested in entering data such as names, addresses, and phone numbers into a spreadsheet, you easily can sort the data, create reports, and perform statistical calculations on the data.

Working with Information

If you are interested in a program that helps you track names, inventory, or any other kind of data, you need a database program for your personal computer. You can use a database to perform simple tasks such as managing your Christmas card list to complex tasks such as developing a complete order-entry system.

A database enables you to find information quickly and easily. Rather than searching through your filing cabinet, you can type a command and have the database program find and display the record on-screen.

A database program enables you to extract information from the database file in many ways. For example, you can print a report that contains information on all the people in the file who live in the state of New York, or you may want information on New Yorkers between the ages of 21 and 29. Whatever your needs, a database program can help you prepare reports quickly and easily.

Working with Finances

Because PCs are adept at working with numbers, they are excellent at tracking business and personal finances. For businesses, many accounting programs are available to manage your company's books. Some accounting programs are very powerful, meant to handle a good-sized business. Others are less powerful, specifically designed to help a small-business owner track his finances. For personal finances, programs are available to help you track your assets and debits.

Communicating with Other Computers

Communications programs enable you to connect to other personal computers or to much larger computers called *mainframes*. If you connect to another personal computer, you can exchange messages and files. When you connect to a mainframe computer, you usually are connecting to an on-line service. On-line services contain information on many subjects that you can access with your personal computer. For example, you can shop or make plane reservations through this service.

Some services, such as MCI Mail, are dedicated to electronic mail. Anyone who is a member of a service like this one can send an electronic letter to any other member. Other services, such as Dow Jones News and Retrieval, are dedicated to providing business users with up-to-date news and financial information.

You also can use a personal computer to communicate with business locations that have fax machines. By adding the appropriate fax product to your PC, you can send or receive faxes.

Working with Symbols and Images

If you often display information in graphical form, you need presentation graphics software for your personal computer. Presentation graphics software enables you to create high-quality charts and graphs for documents, slides, and transparencies.

Presentation graphics programs give you a wide variety of graph types to choose from including line, bar, stacked bar, pie, high-low, and others. With these programs, you can put special effects into your graphs (such as arrows or comments) or create graphs with symbols. For example, you may create a bar graph with five little cars stacked on top of each other to represent 500 cars sold.

Using a presentation graphics program is just one way to manipulate symbols and images with a PC. You also can use paint programs, draw programs, animation programs, and computer aided design (CAD) programs.

If you are artistically inclined, you can create quite sophisticated electronic paintings with a paint program. If not, you can modify pictures that the program provides.

If a particular paint program doesn't provide a large assortment of pictures, you can enter pictures into a computer yourself. With the aid of video frame grabber circuitry connected to your PC, you can capture video off of a television or VCR, bring the video image(s) into your PC, and modify the image with your paint program.

Another way to enter pictures into your computer is by connecting a scanner to your PC. You run the picture through the scanner as you would run a sheet of paper through a fax machine. The scanner sends a copy of the picture to the computer where you can modify the image with your paint program.

Computer aided design programs generally are directed at technical professionals such as mechanical engineers, electrical engineers, architects, and industrial designers. With these programs, you can create any kind of drawing that you can do by hand with drafting tools. Additionally, you can create 3-D technical drawings.

Working with Sound

With the proper combination of software and hardware, personal computers can talk, listen, or even play music. PCs talk through electronic speech circuits, built-in or added to the computer, connected to a decent speaker. Some people use a PC as a telephone answering machine. Not only can the PC answer the calls and store messages, but the computer also can route a call based on the caller's preferences (indicated by responses on a touch-tone phone). Products such as The Complete Communicator provide the software and hardware necessary to perform these functions.

Most people communicate with a PC through a keyboard or mouse, but a PC equipped with the appropriate voice recognition software and hardware can accept voice commands. Instead of typing or pointing to commands, you can issue them into a microphone. A product such as the Voice Master Key System provides the software and hardware needed to implement voice recognition on a PC. The use of voice recognition software and hardware is not common, but it will be in the future.

Working with sound on a personal computer often means working with music. You can write and play music with a personal computer if you have the right equipment. A common configuration is a personal computer connected to a keyboard synthesizer through MIDI. More information on this topic is given later.

Playing Games

If you are the kind of person who enjoys arcade games, you can use your PC to bring the arcade home. A PC equipped with a joystick or a mouse can provide you with some of the finest arcade action available.

PCs, however, can entertain you with much more than arcade games. For example, you can try simulations. Do you want to see what its like to be in the cockpit of a plane? Would you like to see what its like to deal with problems concerning the earth's environment? Would you like to try to run a business—without having to invest your own money?

A wide selection of adventure games for PCs also is available. Whatever your interest—knights of the round table, the old West, outer space—you can become involved in the life and times of some fictional characters as you try to ward off danger and achieve your goals.

Enhancing Education

A PC is an excellent educational tool for all ages. From preschool to adult levels, you can find software that helps individuals learn a particular subject area. Preschoolers can learn how to count or add with games that feature syndicated cartoon characters such as Charlie Brown, Bert and Ernie, and Mickey Mouse. School-age children can learn about chemistry or electronics by working with computer simulations of technical labs. Adults can learn to type through practice and feedback about errors or to understand popular computer programs through tutorials.

No matter what the instructional method—games, simulations, practice, or tutorials—thousands of educational software programs are available to enhance your learning experience, and most require just a standard PC and an inquisitive mind.

Creating Programs

Every computer software program that ever existed was created by a person who knew how to write in a language that the computer could understand. You can learn a large variety of languages that a PC can understand. If you have a great idea for a computer software program, you may want to spend the time and effort needed to learn a programming language.

Making a Decision

Now that you have a basic knowledge of what a computer can do for you, you need to determine your requirements. To do this, follow these steps:

1. Make a checklist. What do you want the computer to do? Define your objective with focused statements—for example, "To improve the corporate image when producing proposals by incorporating graphics and other illustrations."

2. Collect data about your current way of doing things. You may want to computerize a small business or a home office, or you may want to use a computer for personal improvement or for entertainment. If you want to use a PC in a business or home office environment, the first thing to think about is the way you do things now. Think about the reports, forms, and invoices you create. Are you dealing with text, numbers, or graphics? How do these reports, forms, invoices, and so on look now? Do you use color? You should collect samples of what you are doing now or what you would like to do. If you don't have samples available, try to create by hand the kinds of things you would like the computer to do for you.

3. Do a little brainstorming based on what you know computers can do. How could your work be done better on a computer?

After these three steps, you should have a detailed list of what you want the computer to do. This list gives you a head start in finding a computer best suited to your needs. To fine-tune the list, you should consider other issues before you make a purchase decision:

- Set priorities. If you haven't already done so, look around in computer stores to get a general idea of what is available. What features seem most important? What do you think you will need immediately? What can you buy later? For example, you may want to purchase a printer right away but purchase an item such as a modem (used for communication with other computers) later.

- Think of the users. Who will be using the computer? Users may have different skill levels, and a program should be able to accommodate the needs of beginners and more advanced users.

- Consider compatibility issues. Do you need to share your data with anyone else? If so, you need to gather information about their computing environment.

- Take into consideration your experience. What are your abilities? What is your previous experience and typing ability? Have you used a computer before?

- Determine your working environment. Where will the computer be used?

- Establish a budget. How much money can you spend?

- Plan for the future. What should the computer be able to do in one year and three years? For example, do you want the system you purchase now to be able to run the more advanced graphics software coming out in the market? If so, you may need to purchase more advanced hardware or hardware that can be changed easily.

The following checklist summarizes these issues. This list can start you on your way to making the right purchasing decisions.

What do you want the computer to do?

>   Help run a business
>   Help manage a home office
>   Enable you to do at home what you do on the PC at work
>   Help with schoolwork
>   Entertain
>   Other:

How will you use the computer?

>   Only for business-related work
>   Only for pleasure
>   For business and pleasure
>   Other:

Where will you use the computer?

>   At the office
>   At home
>   At home and office
>   At school
>   On the road
>   Other:

Who else will use the computer?

>   Employees
>   Family members
>   Friends
>   Other:

What do you want a computer to do several years from now?

How much can you spend?

>   Under $1,000
>   Between $1,000 and $3,000
>   Between $3,000 and $5,000
>   Between $5,000 and $10,000
>   Over $10,000

What features are most important?

Chapter Summary

In this chapter, you learned some of the benefits of personal computers. You learned that personal computers can open up new opportunities for you, save you time and money, and do repetitive work for you. You also learned some basic information about working with words, numbers, information, finances, other computers, symbols and images, sound, games, education, and programs. Finally, you learned how to lay the groundwork for making an informed purchasing decision.

In the Next Chapter

The next chapter provides you with an overview of the major parts of a computer system in terms that you can understand. The chapter defines each part and shows you how the parts work together.

2

How Does a Computer Work?

Understanding how a computer works is often just a matter of understanding the function of the individual components such as the system unit, keyboard, mouse, monitor, floppy disk drive, and hard disk drive. This chapter defines each of these components and describes how each works as part of a computer system. This chapter also defines software types such as ROM software, operating system software, and application software so that you begin to understand how each of these components plays a role in the operation of a computer.

The contents of this chapter are meant to provide an overview of a computer system and lay the groundwork for the following chapter, which describes the features of different kinds of computers in more detail. Knowing how a computer works eventually will help you to purchase appropriate components for your system.

Defining PC Components

A typical computer system contains the following components:

- System unit
- Keyboard

- Mouse
- Monitor (display)
- Floppy disk drive
- Hard disk drive

With many computer systems, all of these components can be purchased separately. As shown in figure 2.1, these components fit together to make up a computer system. The keyboard sits in front of the system unit; the mouse sits to the right side of the unit (for right-handed users); and the monitor sits on top. Inside the system unit is the floppy disk drive and the hard disk drive. In the figure, the slot for the floppy disk drive is visible, but you cannot see the hard disk drive. Some systems, like laptop computers for example, squeeze all of these components into one unit.

You need to be aware of the different components that make up a computer system and how each relates to the other. The more you know about these components, the better decisions you can make about which ones to buy when you decide to purchase a computer system. The following sections explain all of these components in detail.

Fig. 2.1. A typical personal computer system showing the system unit, a monitor on top of the unit, and a keyboard in front.

Chapter 2: How Does a Computer Work? **21**

System Unit

The system unit of many personal computers is a rectangular case that sits on a desk or stands on the floor (see fig. 2.2). To succeed at operating a personal computer, you have to understand a little about the system unit. Among other things, the system unit usually has a switch to turn the computer on, holds the disk drives that store information, and has connectors that enable you to attach other components to the system. If you don't know anything about the system unit, you may not be able to turn the computer on.

Fig. 2.2. This system unit is a floor standing or tower model.

There are some simple facts you should know about the system unit. Almost all system units have a power switch for turning the computer on and off. The system unit shown in figure 2.1 has the power switch in the front, but some units have the switch at the side or in the back.

Many system units have a lock, like the one shown in figure 2.3. Locking the system unit does not prevent anyone from stealing the unit, but it can stop someone from taking the cover off (and possibly stealing a hard disk drive). Locking the system unit also prevents people from entering information into the computer through the keyboard. If no one else has access to your computer, the lock is superfluous; but if you are worried about someone tampering with your system, it provides some degree of data security.

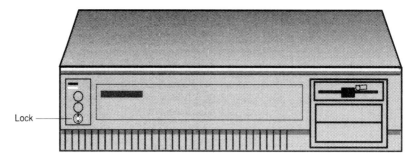

Fig. 2.3. The lock on the system unit disables the keyboard.

The front of the system unit provides access to the floppy disk drive(s) and a tape drive, if you have one. In figure 2.1, you can see the slot where you insert a 3 1/2-inch floppy disk. Notice the button on the disk drive. The button is used to eject the disk from the drive. Some system units have 5 1/4-inch drives. These floppy drives usually have a latch or a lever used to close and open the drive after a disk has been inserted. (See the section on floppy disk drives.)

Although many system units have hard disk drives inside of them, all you can see from the outside are one or two indicator lights (if anything). Often, a light indicates that the power is on. Most of the time, another light can be seen that flashes as the hard disk is used.

If you look at the back of a system unit, such as the one shown in figure 2.4, you see many connectors. Most input and output devices are connected to the back of the system unit (the keyboard sometimes is connected in the front). The power cord also is connected at the back. The connectors you are most likely to see at the back of the system unit are those for the keyboard, the video monitor, the modem, the mouse, the printer, and some other types of auxiliary connectors.

The keyboard connector is often a round connector with five pinholes. The connector for the monitor usually has 9 or 15 pinholes. The connector for the modem, called the *serial port*, usually has 9 or 25 pins. (Other devices such as a mouse or a printer also can be connected to a serial port.) The connector for the mouse is sometimes a small circular connector with 9 pinholes (a mouse also can be connected to a serial port). The connector for a printer, a Centronics *parallel port*, usually has 25 pinholes. Each of these connectors is shown in figure 2.5.

Different types of computers have different connectors. For example, the Macintosh computer does not have a parallel port because printers connect to the serial port on this computer. Make sure that the computer you purchase has connectors for each of the devices you want to attach.

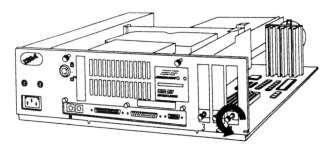

Fig. 2.4. Connectors at the back of the system unit.

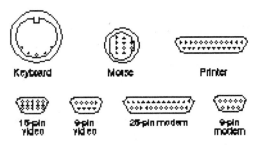

Fig. 2.5. Typical connectors for keyboard, video monitor, modem, mouse, and printer.

The only other items of interest at the back of the system unit are the slots shown in figure 2.4. These slots are reserved for electronic circuit boards that expand the capabilities of the computer. The boards are placed inside the system unit, and the connectors and some switches on the board are designed to poke out of the slot opening as shown in figure 2.6. The connector may be for a video monitor, a modem, a printer, or some other kind of input or output device. The switches may be used to enable or disable a feature of the board. Some circuit boards have neither a connector nor switches showing through the slots. Although the slots are oriented vertically in figure 2.4, they can be horizontal on some computers.

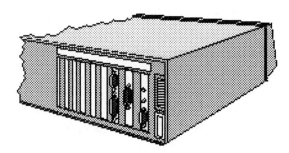

Fig. 2.6. Expansion boards placed inside the system unit often have connectors that can be seen at the rear of the unit.

Unlike other electronic products that warn you against opening the case, it's common to take the cover off of a computer's system unit. (If you plan on doing this, consult the unit's documentation for safety procedures.) Usually, the cover is removed only to place additional circuit boards inside the computer. Whether or not you plan on doing this operation yourself, you need to know what is inside the system unit, because that is where components crucial to the operation of the system are housed.

Inside the system unit resides a large circuit board, among other things. This board is the *system board* or the *motherboard*. The black rectangular components on the board are the electronic devices that make up the computer. Collectively, these devices are called *chips*. One of these chips, usually the largest on the motherboard, is the central processing unit (CPU). Other important chips on the board are the RAM (random-access memory) and ROM (read-only memory) chips. When you purchase a computer, you need to know the type of CPU, the amount of RAM, and the version of the ROM. The CPU, RAM, and ROM are explained in more detail in Chapter 3.

A chip almost as large as the CPU (or an empty socket for the chip) often is found on the system board; this chip is the math coprocessor (or socket for the chip). The math coprocessor speeds up the computer's capability to do floating-point arithmetic operations. Some of the more powerful computers don't need a separate chip for a math coprocessor, because the coprocessor is built into the CPU chip.

Other important parts of the system board are the expansion slots. These slots hold additional circuit boards that expand the capabilities of the computer. You need to know the number of slots on the system board. The more slots, the more you can expand your computer. You also need to know what type of slot is on the system board. (The reasons why you need this information are covered in Chapter 3.) The type of expansion slot is an important factor in most personal computer purchasing decisions.

Besides the motherboard with its chips and slots, the system unit contains the disk drives. The floppy drive, which you can see from outside the system unit, connects to the system board or to an expansion board. Either method works, but the latter uses up one of the expansion slots.

The hard disk also resides in the system unit. Like floppy disks, a hard disk can connect to the system board or an expansion board.

One more important component resides in the system unit—the power supply. The power supply in many computers is on the right rear side of the system unit (looking at the unit from the front). The power switch that you can see from outside of the system unit is an integral part of the power supply.

By now, you should have some understanding of a personal computer's system unit. However, remember that not all system units are exactly alike, and not all PCs have a separate system unit.

The following sections describe other components of a computer system. An overview is given in this chapter, and each component is covered in more detail in Chapter 3. This discussion should help you understand what type of equipment to consider and what you can ignore.

Monitor

A video monitor is the main device in a personal computer system for displaying information to the user. A video monitor is classified as an output device because it displays information only after the information has been processed. In a personal computer system with separate components, a cable from the video monitor connects to a video connector (such as the 9- or 15-pin connector shown in fig. 2.5) at the back of the system unit (see fig. 2.7). Some personal computers have video circuits built into the system board; others don't. If video circuits are not built in, you need to purchase a video adapter—an expansion board that contains video circuitry.

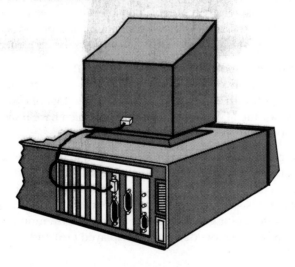

***Fig. 2.7.** The video monitor connects to the back of the system unit.*

Monitors can differ in size, in resolution (a term defined later), in the colors they display, and in the way they display information.

Most personal computer systems use a video monitor with a 14-inch diagonal screen. The size of a monitor can vary dramatically, however, from very small (5 inches diagonally) to very large (more than 20 inches diagonally). Small monitors usually are built into compact computers, meant to be carried from place to place. Large screen monitors are used for applications such as desktop publishing to display the entire page (or two pages) of a publication in readable form and for group presentations. Unless you have a special application in mind, you should choose a standard-size monitor.

For monitors, *resolution* is the maximum number of individual dots that can be placed on-screen. A monitor has horizontal resolution (number of dots across the display) and vertical resolution (number of dots down the display); the resolution is given as a set of numbers such as 640 x 480. The first number always refers to the horizontal resolution, and the second number specifies the vertical resolution. Generally, the higher the resolution, the sharper the display.

Monitors generally are classified as monochrome or color. Monochrome monitors usually have amber and black, green and black, or white and black displays. If you intend to use a monochrome monitor with an IBM-compatible computer that lacks built-in video circuits, you can do one of two things: purchase a standard monochrome monitor and a Hercules (or compatible) monochrome graphics adapter; or you can purchase a VGA monochrome monitor and a VGA adapter (VGA is explained later in this section). The adapter fits into one of the expansion slots in the system unit and provides a 9- or 15-pin video connector for your monitor.

If you intend to use a monochrome monitor with an IBM PS/2 or PS/1 computer that has built-in VGA, all you need is a VGA monochrome monitor. If you want a Macintosh with a monochrome display, the logical choices are the Macintosh Classic or the Macintosh SE/30, both of which have built-in monochrome monitors.

If you intend to purchase a color monitor for your system, you need to know something about color standards. IBM has set the standards for displaying color on IBM and compatible computers. Over the past decade, three IBM color display standards have emerged. The first of these display standards is CGA, which stands for color graphics adapter. Typical CGA monitors are limited in the number of colors that can be displayed (16) and the number of dots (640 x 200).

Another IBM display standard is EGA, which stands for enhanced graphics adapter. Monitors designed for this standard can display more colors (64) and have better resolution (640 x 350) than CGA monitors. A comparison of EGA and CGA displays shows that the alphanumeric characters on an EGA monitor are much sharper than the characters on a CGA monitor. This sharpness is a direct result of the increased resolution that EGA offers.

The current standard for IBM and compatible computers is VGA, which stands for video graphics array. The major difference between VGA and EGA monitors is the way in which each displays information electronically. EGA monitors use digital, or discrete, electronic signals to display information; VGA monitors use analog, or continuous, electronic signals to display information. A direct benefit of using analog signals is the number of colors that can be displayed on a monitor. An EGA monitor can display 64 different colors, but a VGA monitor can display an infinite number of colors. This difference translates into the capability to produce much more realistic images on the monitor. VGA monitors also have a higher resolution (640 x 480).

If you are considering color for an IBM-compatible computer, purchase a VGA multifrequency monitor, rather than CGA or EGA. A multifrequency monitor, often referred to as a multiscan monitor, can work with any of the display standards mentioned and with Apple Macintosh and Commodore Amiga computers. Multiscan monitors can display an infinite number of colors and typically have a maximum resolution of 800 x 600, although some of the better models go as high as 1,024 x 768. If you want flexibility and high resolution, a multiscan monitor is your best choice.

IBM-compatible computers usually need a video adapter. For a VGA monitor, you need a VGA adapter. For a multifrequency monitor, you can use any kind of video adapter including super VGA.

Apple Macintosh, Commodore Amiga, and Atari ST and Mega computers do not follow the IBM standards. Apple Macintosh computers have built-in color circuitry or use color video adapters that provide 8-bit, 16-bit, or 24-bit color (these numbers relate to the number of colors that can be displayed). A typical 13-inch monitor for a Macintosh color computer has 640 x 480 resolution and can display over 16 million colors.

Amiga computers with color circuitry built in typically connect to a multiscan monitor. The best monitor for the Amiga is the Amiga RGB monitor, although the multiscan monitor is *not* necessary. Atari computers also have built-in color circuitry. If you decide to buy one of the computers this company offers, purchase an Atari monitor for the best results.

Keyboard and Mouse

Entering information into a PC most often is done with a keyboard, although more and more people are using a mouse. A keyboard is great for entering alphanumeric information, and a mouse excels at entering graphics into the computer. Both are input devices.

Keyboards vary according to the computer brand and model that you buy. If you were to purchase a personal computer today, however, you would likely get a keyboard that looks like the one shown in figure 2.8. This keyboard has 101 keys. When you buy a personal computer, you rarely get a chance to select the keyboard you want, except for certain Macintosh models. You may want to use the keyboard as the deciding factor between two similar computers. If you want a particular computer but hate the keyboard that comes with it, you can purchase a keyboard from another source. More information about keyboards is included in Chapter 3.

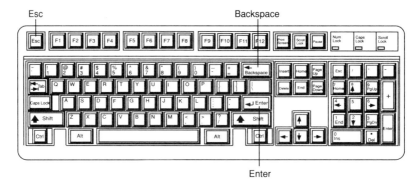

Fig. 2.8. A current model of a personal computer keyboard.

A mouse is a device with the look and feel of a bar of sculpted soap (see fig. 2.9). A ball is set into the bottom of the mouse, which makes it easy to move on a desktop. One or more buttons are located on the top; these buttons enable you to do certain kinds of things in an applications program. To use a mouse, you just move it around on the desk. When you move the mouse, the cursor on the video display moves in a corresponding way. A mouse is used to perform operations difficult to do with a keyboard, such as drawing on the computer display. Although drawing is difficult to do with a keyboard, it is relatively easy with a mouse. Moving a cursor quickly around the display by using the keyboard also is difficult; it's a cinch with the mouse. A mouse is usually an optional accessory for IBM and compatible computers, but a mouse is standard fare for Macintosh, Amiga, ST, and Mega computers.

Chapter 2: How Does a Computer Work? 29

Fig. 2.9. A two-button mouse.

The keyboard and mouse plug into connectors on the system unit. Keyboard connectors are various shapes and sizes depending on the brand of computer and can be found on the front or back of the system unit. The mouse can be attached to a mouse port or to a serial port. Some computers have labels or icons next to a connector to help you make the right connection.

Floppy Disk Drive

When you work with a PC, information that you type at the keyboard is placed in short-term memory or RAM. (You type information at the keyboard, and the CPU in the system unit processes and moves the information into the RAM chips.) As long as the power switch to the computer is on, the RAM chips continue to hold the information. When you turn off the power, the information is cleared from the RAM chips—you lose it. (You can lose information accidentally if power is interrupted even for a few seconds.)

To avoid losing your information, you can save it before you turn the computer off. A floppy disk drive and floppy disk can be used to save information. The drive also can send information back into the RAM chips. Because you can store information to and retrieve information from a floppy disk, the floppy drive is an input/output device.

Floppy disk drives for personal computers come in two popular sizes, 5 1/4 inch and 3 1/2 inch. These sizes reflect the size of the disk that you place in the drive. See figure 2.10 for a comparison of a 5 1/4-inch disk (sometimes referred to as a minifloppy) and a 3 1/2-inch disk (sometimes referred to as a microfloppy). A 5 1/4-inch disk has a flexible plastic jacket; a 3 1/2-inch disk has a hard plastic jacket. Both disk sizes contain a round flexible magnetic disk inside the plastic jacket.

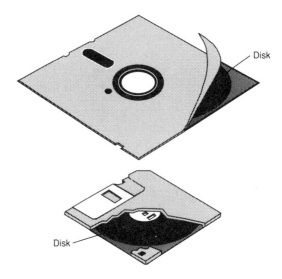

Fig. 2.10. *A 5 1/4-inch floppy disk has a flexible plastic jacket; a 3 1/2-inch floppy disk has a hard plastic jacket.*

A floppy disk drive can hold one disk at a time. Drives that hold the larger 5 1/4-inch floppy disks have a lever or latch that opens and closes the drive. Basically, you make sure that the latch or lever is in the open position, slide the disk into the drive, and then close the latch or lever. With the smaller 3 1/2-inch disks, you slide the disk all the way into the drive. To take the disk out, you push a button on the drive.

To save your information, you place a disk in the floppy disk drive and issue a save command to the computer. You hear a whirring noise; see the light on the drive go on for a few seconds; the noise stops; and the lights go off. To use the information again, make sure that the proper disk is in the drive and issue an open command to the computer to retrieve the information. The disk drive whirrs, and the light goes on. After a few seconds, the whirring stops, the light goes off, and your information is back in the computer.

Floppy disk drives can be used to copy files from one floppy disk to another or from a floppy disk to the hard disk (and vice versa). Commercial software programs generally come on floppy disks and often are copied to a system's hard disk.

Floppy disk drives can be double density (often referred to as low density) or high density. A high-density drive can store more information on a floppy disk than a double-density drive. High-density floppy disks are designed for high-density floppy drives and cannot be used in double-density drives. Double-density disks, however, can be used in double-density and high-density floppy drives (with some reservations, as explained in the following chapter).

For IBM and compatible computers, a 5 1/4-inch double-density disk can store 360K (kilobytes) of information; a 5 1/4-inch high-density disk can store 1.2M (megabytes) of information; a 3 1/2-inch double-density disk can store 720K; and a 3 1/2-inch high-density disk can store 1.44M. (One *kilobyte* equals 1,024 bytes or characters of information; one *megabyte* equals 1,000 kilobytes.)

For Apple Macintosh computers, a 3 1/2-inch double-density disk stores 800K of information, and a 3 1/2-inch high-density disk stores 1.44M (older Macintosh computers use 3 1/2-inch disks that store only 400K.) Amiga computers use 3 1/2-inch disks that store 880K, and Atari computers use 3 1/2-inch disks that store 720K. Table 2.1 summarizes this information.

Table 2.1
Disk Storage Space

Floppy Disks (inches) Capacity	*Size*	*Double-Density Capacity*	*High-Density*
IBM & Compatible	5 1/4 3 1/2	360K 720K	1.2M 1.44M
Apple Macintosh	3 1/2	800K	1.44M
Commodore Amiga	3 1/2	880K	
Atari ST and Mega	3 1/2	720K	

When you buy a box of disks, no matter what the capacity, you cannot use the disks right away with your computer. You must format a disk before you can use it to store information or programs. On IBM and compatible computers, you format a disk by using a formatting command. The Apple Macintosh detects an unformatted disk as soon as you put the disk in the drive. A message appears on the display asking whether you want to format the disk. (You also can buy preformatted disks.)

Hard Disk Drive

A hard disk drive performs the same basic function as a floppy disk drive and works much the same way. Major differences exist between a hard disk drive and a floppy disk drive. With a hard disk drive, you do not have to insert and remove disks. The disks, or *platters*, are sealed inside a metal case. The only time you get to see these platters is when you look at a photo or a figure such as figure 2.11.

Fig. 2.11. The platters of a hard disk drive.

A hard disk drive is much faster than a floppy disk drive. Information that takes five seconds to save with a floppy disk drive may take less than a second to save with a hard disk drive. A hard disk drive has enormous storage capacity; a drive rated at 40M can store over 40 million characters. Typical floppy disks store up to 1.4 million characters. Note that floppy disks are removable, and you can accumulate piles of them and actually store more information than you can on the hard drive. You also can remove the floppy disk from a disk drive on one computer and place the disk in another computer. (Some hard disks have removable platters, but this type of hard disk drive is not common.)

Before you use a hard disk for the first time, you (or the dealer or manufacturer) must format and partition it. Information on these procedures can be found in the documentation that comes with your computer's operating system software.

Most personal computer systems need a hard disk drive and a floppy disk drive. The hard disk drive gives the system speed and storage space, and the floppy disk drive gives the system flexibility.

Defining Software Types

Although a personal computer has the potential to do a great deal of work, nothing happens unless a program is executed. A program is just a series of instructions that tells the CPU what to do. A program tells the CPU what to do with the characters typed at the keyboard, what to do with the information read from the disk drives, what to put on the display, and so on. Because a program is a series of instructions, programs are classified as software rather than hardware. (Hardware refers to physical components such as the system unit, monitor, keyboard, mouse, and disk drives.)

The following sections describe the following kinds of software: ROM software, operating system software, and application software. Each type serves a purpose in making your computer run as smoothly and efficiently as possible. You need to understand what different manufacturers offer so that you can select the proper software for the tasks you want to do.

ROM

All personal computers have some programs stored in the ROM chips on the system board. This ROM software is included with the computer and does not have to be purchased separately. These programs are used to start (or boot) the computer, perform diagnostic tests, send and receive information to and from the components connected to the computer, and do other jobs. These programs are a permanent fixture of the computer; they do not get erased when you turn off the power.

In IBM and compatible computers, an important set of programs stored in ROM is the BIOS (basic input/output system). If an IBM-compatible computer has a BIOS that duplicates the functions of the IBM BIOS, the compatible can run the same software that runs on an IBM personal computer.

Operating System Software

A personal computer's operating system software is a set of programs that perform essential computing tasks. Typical operating system tasks are to fetch information typed at the keyboard, to open and close data files, to terminate programs, to manage memory usage, to create files, to rename files, to delete files, and to format disks. The operating system, which usually is loaded into the computer from the disk drive, but which can be contained in ROM chips, acts as the interface between the person who uses the computer and the computer.

For IBM-compatible computers, the MS-DOS disk operating system is clearly the most popular. (IBM models use PC DOS, an almost identical operating system.) MS-DOS started with Version 1.0 but currently is up to Version 5.0. It is not imperative, but certainly recommended, to use the latest version of an operating system. (Definitely use a version of DOS greater than 3.0.) A direct competitor of MS-DOS is DR DOS. Although not widely used, the latest version of this operating system (Version 5.0) offers some advanced features. For example, DR DOS 5.0 can manage memory so that more memory is available to run software programs such as word processors and spreadsheets. DR DOS is compatible with MS-DOS. Other operating systems competing with MS-DOS are OS/2, UNIX, and XENIX. MS-DOS is designed for one user, but these other operating systems are designed for multiple users.

With MS-DOS, you have to memorize commands and type them in to perform a task. Although easy enough to learn, MS-DOS intimidates many beginners. Recognizing this fact, some computer software companies have developed graphical operating environments for MS-DOS. One of the most popular is Microsoft Windows. The latest version of Windows, Version 3.0, uses little pictures called icons, pull-down menus, and on-screen windows, to help people understand more easily how to perform particular computing tasks. Figure 2.12 shows the difference between a typical DOS screen and a typical Windows screen.

Another operating environment similar to Windows is GEM. GEM is available for IBM systems but is rarely used. GEM is the operating environment of choice for Atari ST and Mega computers.

Although Windows and GEM are the two best known graphical user interfaces for IBM and compatible computers, some others are available. One is PC/GEOS. This interface currently works with a software program called GEO Works Ensemble. Another interface is ViewMax. This is a graphical interface that works along with DR DOS 5.0. Not many software programs, however, use the conventions of the interface. Therefore, you lose consistency as you switch from program to program. For example, you may have to work one way with your word processor and another way with your personal finance program.

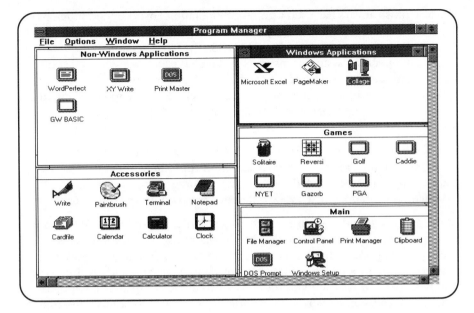

Fig. 2.12. *The Windows screen on the top shows icons arranged in several windows—you point to an icon to start a program. The MS-DOS screen on the bottom shows the DOS prompt—you type a command to start a program.*

The Macintosh always has used a graphical operating environment. Judging by the success of the Macintosh, many people find this kind of interface preferable to a command-line interface such as MS-DOS. The latest version of the Macintosh operating system software is System 7.0 (due to be released soon). This version is expected to include the Sound Manager, a program that enhances the sound input capabilities of the Macintosh, true multitasking (the capability to run more than one program at a time), and other advanced features.

The Commodore Amiga 3000 uses Amiga OS 2.0, the latest version of the operating system. Like the Macintosh and Atari computers, the Amiga uses a graphical user interface, called Workbench. *All* Amigas also have a CLI (command-line interface), a *major* difference between Amiga and Mac.

Of the many factors that go into purchasing a particular computer system, the user interface, which works closely with the operating system software, is one of the most important. If you feel more comfortable with a graphical user interface, any computer can supply you with one. You should know, however, that many of the most popular programs for IBM and compatible computers, including such favorites as Lotus 1-2-3 and WordPerfect, do not use this kind of interface.

Application Software

Application software is a program or set of programs stored on disk that you load into the computer to perform a specific task. Typical application programs are word processors, spreadsheets, paint programs, communications programs, and databases. Application software generally runs under a particular operating system such as MS-DOS. You have to load the operating system first (you do this one time when you first turn on the computer) and then load the application program. A vast number of application programs that run under MS-DOS are available for IBM and compatible computers.

When you work with an application program, you must spend time learning how to give the program commands and how to use the different features of the program. Unfortunately, learning how to work with one application is no guarantee that you will understand how to work with another. For every application, especially those that run under MS-DOS, you have to repeat the learning process.

Operating environments such as the one used by the Macintosh make learning to use a new application easier. Every Macintosh application presents the user with a similar interface so that the user is comfortable performing basic tasks, such as saving and retrieving information. The specifics of the application still need to be learned and understood, but many of the routine tasks of a Macintosh application are done the same way from program to program. Windows attempts to do this for personal computers that use MS-DOS. The problem, however, is that the most popular programs for IBM and compatible computers, such as WordPerfect Versions 5 and 5.1 and Lotus 1-2-3 Versions 2.01 to 3.1, do not use the Windows interface. Windows versions of these program will likely be developed in the near future, but they may not have the look and feel of the current versions.

Application software comes on a set of floppy disks. If a computer has a floppy and hard disk drive, the general procedure is to copy the application software onto the hard disk drive, where the software always is readily available for use. If you don't have a hard disk, using the application program can be difficult and sometimes impossible. If the program can be run from a floppy disk drive, you often have to switch disks many times during the operation of the program. Some applications do not run successfully from a floppy disk drive.

More information on application software with specific recommendations on what to buy is given in Chapter 8.

Chapter Summary

This chapter described the major parts of a personal computer system. It defined and gave some details about the components that make up a typical personal computer system: the system unit, the monitor, the keyboard, the mouse, the floppy disk drive, and the hard disk drive. The chapter described the system unit, inside and out, described different video standards for IBM and compatible computers and the monitors that work with them, and described different kinds of floppy disk drives available for PCs. This chapter also gave some reasons for the appeal of hard disks. Finally, the different kinds of software used in personal computers—ROM software, operating system software, and application software—were explained.

In the Next Chapter

The next chapter builds on the information presented in this chapter. Features are explained in more detail to help you make intelligent purchasing decisions. You learn what is available, the differences among various products, and how different products are suited to different applications.

3

What Components Do I Need?

The preceding chapter gives you an overview of a typical personal computer system. This chapter describes in more detail the components that make up a personal computer system. This chapter describes the differences among CPUs and explains how these differences affect computer performance. The text describes differences among the other components—RAM, ROM, keyboard, mouse, monitor, hard drive, floppy disk, expansion slots, buses, and ports. These differences relate to the types of tasks you perform with a computer system. This chapter shows how what you want to do with a personal computer affects what you should buy.

Central Processing Unit

The *central processing unit* (CPU) is the most important component of a personal computer. The CPU determines how well the computer performs and what software you can run. Because the CPU usually resides somewhere in the system unit, you must look at the computer's specifications to learn about the CPU. The following sections help you interpret these specifications and show you how CPUs differ.

Speed

Most people relate speed to the time necessary to go from one place to another. With a CPU, however, speed relates to the time necessary to perform program operations, such as adding two binary numbers. CPU speed is measured in *megahertz* (MHz), millions of cycles per second. Generally, the higher the megahertz rating, the faster the computer performs. The speed for personal computers described in this book ranges from 4.77 MHz (the slowest) to 40 MHz (the fastest).

Speed matters for personal computers. No matter what kind of software application you use, the computer takes time to process information, send and retrieve the information from disk drives, and perform other operations. Speed is especially important when a computer has a graphics user interface, which makes using the computer easier but slows the speed of operation. Whether you are thinking about the CPU or any other component of a personal computer system, consider how fast that component works. Unfortunately, the fastest computers usually cost the most. For example, the fastest IBM and Apple systems cost well over $10,000. Ultimately, most people have to make a trade-off between speed and price.

If you can spend around $2,000 for an IBM-compatible computer or $3,000 for an IBM or Apple computer, you can get a system that offers good performance. If you don't want to spend that much, you can get slower systems that cost about $1,000. Depending on what you plan to do with a computer, this kind of system may meet your needs.

8, 16, and 32 Bits

The performance of a personal computer also depends on the way the CPU processes information. CPUs send and receive information 8, 16, or 32 bits at a time. A *bit* is a binary digit—a 0 or a 1. Think of a highway. Some computers have 8 lanes to move data around; some have 16 lanes; and some have 32 lanes. More information can be processed at a time by the CPU and moved around to components such as RAM when a computer has 32 lanes than when it has 8 lanes or paths. Depending on the application, this greater processing capability can enhance computer performance.

In theory, a 16 MHz CPU moving data around 32 bits at a time should be able to outperform a 16 MHz CPU moving data around 16 bits at a time. In practice, however, these different CPUs often run the same software (originally designed for older CPUs with 8 data lanes), and therefore, neither CPU has a performance advantage over the other. As new versions of software products are developed, however, this situation should change.

Purchase a system with the maximum performance you can afford. Knowing the number of bits at which a processor moves data around the computer helps you make a smarter purchase today and prepares you to take advantage of new software designs in the future. In the sections that follow, notice the number of bits in the data path of each CPU.

CPU Compatibility

Personal computers generally use CPUs manufactured by Intel or Motorola. Intel makes CPUs for IBM and compatibles. Motorola CPUs are found in Apple Macintosh, Commodore Amiga, and Atari Mega and ST computers. Personal computers with Motorola CPUs are not compatible with computers that use Intel CPUs, and the different brands of computers that use Motorola CPUs are not compatible with each other. For example, you cannot run software for the Macintosh on an Amiga computer, even though the Macintosh and Amiga have identical CPUs. This fact is due to differences in system board design and in the programs stored in the ROM chips on the system board. (You can, however, use various ways to get one type of computer to run another computer's software. These methods often are costly and don't guarantee complete compatibility.)

Because of these differences, software plays a big role in the selection of a computer with a particular CPU. Software helps you choose between companies—Intel or Motorola—and among CPUs. Most companies produce software for only one type of CPU. You cannot buy Lotus 1-2-3, for example, for the Macintosh. Other spreadsheets can run on the Macintosh, but not that particular one. Some programs, such as Microsoft Excel, have versions for Macintoshes and IBM compatibles. You cannot take the Macintosh version of the software, however, and run it on an IBM compatible—you need the version for IBM and compatibles.

To make an intelligent CPU choice, therefore, you must have a clear idea of the kinds of applications you want to run on a personal computer. Throughout this chapter, guidelines are offered for selecting a CPU and other components based on your software requirements.

Intel CPUs

Introduced in 1981, the IBM PC used one of the most powerful CPUs available, the 8088 from Intel. The IBM PC quickly became the standard for business computing, and many sophisticated programs were developed to run on the IBM PC. As years passed, IBM came out with faster and more powerful personal computers—all using the latest model CPU from Intel. Other companies got on the bandwagon, manufacturing personal computers that used Intel CPUs. Each time a new computer was introduced, whether from IBM or another company, businesses expected the new computer to run the same software—only faster. Intel, in effect, was forced by its customers to improve its CPUs and keep them compatible with older units.

Intel succeeded in producing a line of compatible CPUs with ever-increasing speed and power. This family of CPUs, developed by Intel and used in IBM and compatible computers, includes the 8088, 8086, 80286, 80386SX, 80386, and 80486. With Intel CPUs and those from other companies, you can assume that the higher the number, the higher the performance.

Software that runs on personal computers with 8088 and 8086 CPUs also runs on computers using any other CPU from Intel. Some newer programs, however, do not run on computers with 8088 or 8086 CPUs.

You usually can spot programs that work only on 80286 through 80486 CPUs by reading the system requirements information on a software package or by taking note of the name of the program. Paradox/386 is one example.

8088 and 8086

The 8088 has an 8-bit data path. Originally, the 8088 worked at a speed of 4.77 MHz, but current models also have a speed option of 8, 10, or 12 MHz in addition to the 4.77 MHz standard. IBM used the 8088 in two computers: the IBM PC and the IBM PC XT. The 8088, although fast when first introduced, is slow by today's standards, even when running as fast as 12 MHz. The major attraction of a personal computer with an 8088 CPU is its low price. You usually can recognize these computers by the designation *XT*—for example, the Laser Turbo XT.

Personal computers with 8088 CPUs run many popular software packages, including best-sellers like WordPerfect 5.1 and Lotus 1-2-3 Release 2.2. Most MS-DOS programs run reasonably well on an 8088 computer, especially programs that deal mainly with text, such as word processors or spreadsheets. Programs that use graphics, such as paint programs, tend to operate slowly on an 8088 computer. Even a word processor takes a long time to complete certain tasks, such as checking the spelling of a long document.

Some of the newer programs, designed specifically for more powerful CPUs, do not run on a computer with an 8088 or 8086 CPU. Examples of these programs are Lotus 1-2-3 Release 3.1 and Paradox/386. Also, Windows 3.0, the popular graphical user interface for IBM and compatible computers, does not run well on these computers.

Although the 8088 and 8086 CPUs were designed by Intel at about the same time (1978), IBM did not use the 8086 in one of its computers until 1987, when IBM introduced the PS/2 Models 25 and 30. (Other companies, AT&T and Compaq for example, used this CPU before IBM did.) The 8088 and 8086 are similar in most respects, except that the 8088 has an 8-bit data path, and the 8086 has a 16-bit data path.

Two other CPUs, the V20 and V30, were manufactured by NEC to compete with Intel. These CPUs share the same limitations as the 8088 and 8086. Software that doesn't run or work fast enough on an 8088 doesn't improve much on computers with these other CPUs.

You should consider a personal computer that uses one of these CPUs only if cost is of critical concern. A complete system including monochrome monitor, hard drive, and printer costs around $1,000. You can use a system like this for word processing, spreadsheet analysis, and other tasks, and to run educational and game software. You may, however, experience long delays when working with these low-end systems.

The following table lists representative systems with 8088, 8086, and similar CPUs.

Table 3.1
8088 and 8086 Systems

CPU	Computer	Bits*	Speed
8088	IBM PC XT	8	4.77 MHz
8088	Epson Equity I+	8	4.77 and 8 MHz
V-20	CompuAdd 810	8	4.77 and 10 MHz
8086	Tandy 1000 RL	16	9.5 MHz

*CPU has an 8-bit or 16-bit data path.

80286

The first personal computer to use the Intel 80286 was the IBM AT, which had a speed of 6 MHz. Although an advanced CPU for its time (1984) and still a popular processor, the 80286 has become the black sheep of the Intel family. The 80286 has a 16-bit data path as well as advanced features not found in the 8088 or 8086. The 80286 can work at speeds up to 20 MHz. Computer programmers, however, had real difficulties trying to take advantage of the advanced features of the CPU. Thus, the only real advantage of an 80286 over an 8088 or 8086 is speed. Programs run significantly faster on a personal computer with an 80286 CPU than they run on computers with 8088 or 8086 CPUs. For this performance advantage, you have to spend more money. Consider a personal computer with one of the other high-performance CPUs of the Intel family.

The following table lists representative systems with 80286 CPUs.

Table 3.2
80286 Systems

CPU	Computer	Bits*	Speed
80286	IBM AT	16	8 MHz
80286	IBM PS/1	16	10 MHz
80286	Leading Edge D-2 Plus	16	12 MHz
80286	CompuAdd 220	16	20 MHz

*CPU has a 16-bit data path.

80386SX and 80386

Although IBM was the first personal computer maker to use the 80286 CPU, IBM was not the first to use the 80386. This honor went to COMPAQ, and the 80386 established that company's reputation as the leading supplier of high-performance computers. The 80386 (sometimes referred to as the 80386DX) has a 32-bit data path and runs at speeds as high as 33 MHz.

Speed is not the only feature of this CPU. It also is excellent at *multitasking*—the capability to perform several tasks at the same time. An operating environment, such as Windows, or an operating system, such as OS/2, can exploit multitasking. Using Windows on an 80386 computer enables you to load several programs into memory at one time and have them all readily available and working. While you are typing a letter, for example, you also may have your spreadsheet performing a long calculation. When the calculation is finished, you can move immediately from the word processor to the spreadsheet and then back again, without having to quit or close either program.

The 80386SX is less powerful than the 80386 but was introduced by Intel after the 80386. Like the 80286, the 80386SX has a 16-bit data path. Unlike the 80286, the 80386SX's advanced features run smoothly, like those of the 80386. If you compare the 80386SX to the 80386, you find some similarities—the most important being the capability of the 80386SX to run any software designed for the 80386. The 80386SX has a 16-bit data path; the 80386 has a 32-bit data path. The maximum speed of the 80386SX is currently 20 MHz; the top speed of the 80386 is currently 33 MHz.

Trying to choose between PCs with 80386SX and 80386 CPUs is usually a matter of price. A company's 80386SX computer can cost significantly less than its 80386 model. Because you can run the same software with both CPUs, the lower cost can be enticing. An 80386 computer usually has better all-around performance than an 80386SX computer.

When you compare the 80286 CPU to either 80386 CPU, the major difference is the software you can run. A computer with an 80286 CPU can run programs designed to run on 8088, 8086, and 80286 CPUs. A computer with an 80386SX or 80386 CPU can run all these programs plus programs specifically designed for these CPUs, such as Paradox/386, Q&A/386, AutoCAD/386, and Interleaf. These programs take advantage of the features of an 80386SX or 80386 CPU.

Another difference between the 80286 and 80386 CPUs is speed. Suppose that you have a computer with an 80286 CPU. If you are not satisfied with its performance, you may want to purchase a faster model. If the 80286 computer you have runs at 12 MHz, you can buy another 80286 that runs as fast as 20 MHz. Suppose that you want an even faster model. You cannot purchase an IBM-compatible computer that runs faster than 20 MHz unless you buy an 80386 computer. This limitation may change as CPU makers strive to improve their products. (Intel is not the only company producing 80286 CPUs.)

You may think that you don't need all this speed. To work with graphics-based programs, such as most desktop publishing programs or CAD programs, however, you need a fast computer. To run large applications, such as spreadsheets or databases, you need a fast computer. The alternative is spending a great deal of time waiting for your computer to do the jobs you want it to do.

The following table lists representative systems with 80386SX and 80386 CPUs.

Table 3.3
80386SX and 80386 Systems

CPU	Computer	Bits*	Speed
80386SX	IBM PS/2 Model 55SX	16	16 MHz
80386SX	AST 386SX-20 Premium	16	20 MHz
80386	Northgate Slim Line 386/20	32	20 MHz
80386	Dell System 325D	32	25 MHz
80386	COMPAQ DeskPro 386/33L	32	33 MHz

*CPU has a 16-bit or 32-bit data path.

80486

The 80486 is the current top-of-the-line CPU in the Intel family. The 80486 has several features that give it a performance advantage over the 80386. One advantage is special circuitry to do floating-point arithmetic, a feature that makes the 80486 ideal for running software such as CAD programs. If you have an 80386 computer, you need to purchase a special coprocessor chip, the 80387, and insert the chip into a socket on the system board to achieve the kind of performance you get standard with an 80486. Even if you add the 80387 coprocessor to an 80386 computer, the 80486 still does floating-point calculations faster because all the circuits reside on the same chip.

Another feature of the 80486 is special circuitry, *cache RAM*, that helps process instructions faster. Cache RAM provides a way for the CPU to anticipate the next instruction and minimizes the time needed to process the instruction. This feature helps programs run faster on an 80486 than they run on an 80386.

A computer with an 80486 CPU has a premium price tag. Manufacturers tend to load an 80486 computer with high-performance components. The price, therefore, often is much higher than the price of an 80386 computer.

One factor to watch for when considering an 80486 computer is whether it is an upgraded 80386 computer. Some manufacturers, including IBM, lift the 80386 CPU out of its socket on the system board and replace the 80386 CPU with a circuit board that has an 80486 CPU. Other manufacturers design their computers to be upgradable. These computers do not have the CPU on the system board. Instead, the CPU is on a board that fits into a connector on the system board. The board may contain an 80286, 80386SX, 80386, or 80486 CPU. Don't expect a computer upgraded to an 80486 to deliver the same kind of performance as one designed specifically to take advantage of the features of the 80486 CPU. If your main concern is running your applications as fast as possible, investigate the design of the system board.

Motorola CPUs

Motorola CPUs used in personal computers are the 68000, 68020, and 68030. Like the Intel CPUs, each new Motorola CPU improves on the older version's speed, capability to handle information, and special features.

The Motorola 68000 is a CPU with a 16-bit data path that runs at a minimum speed of about 8 MHz. This CPU is used in the Macintosh Classic, Commodore Amiga 500 and 2000, and Atari Mega and ST. The Macintosh portable uses a 16 MHz version of the 68000.

The 68020 is a CPU with a 32-bit data path that runs at a speed of about 16 MHz. One important feature of this CPU is cache RAM built into the chip (similar to the Intel 80486). The Macintosh LC and Amiga 2500 use this CPU. Some older Macs, such as the Macintosh II, also use this CPU. The Motorola 68020 can be considered to be competitive with the Intel 80386, although the latter is somewhat more powerful.

The 68030 has a 32-bit data path and a current maximum speed of 40 MHz. The 68030 also has built-in cache RAM and is designed to process data and program instructions much faster than the 68020 or 68000. The 68030 also has a built-in memory management unit. This feature enables programmers to more easily implement multitasking—run more than one program at a time. The Macintosh SE/30 and Amiga 3000/16 use a 16 MHz version of the 68030 CPU; the Macintosh IIsi uses a 20 MHz version; the Macintosh IIci and Amiga 3000/25 use a 25 MHz version; and the Macintosh IIfx uses the 40 MHz version. The Motorola 68030 is somewhat more powerful than the Intel 80386.

Because Motorola designs new CPUs to be compatible with older versions, software that runs on the Macintosh Classic (the low end of the Apple line) also runs on the Macintosh IIfx (the high end of the Apple line). The Commodore Amiga computers follow the same practice—software that runs on the Amiga 500 also runs on the Amiga 3000/25.

Choosing among models in a product line is a price versus performance decision. If you use desktop publishing software on the Macintosh, you are likely to be dissatisfied with the performance and features of a 68000-based computer such as the Macintosh Classic. If you are using word processing, spreadsheet, and educational software, however, you may find the Classic quite acceptable—for a monochrome system. If you want a color system, the low-end Apple model is the Macintosh LC.

The following table lists representative systems with 68000, 68020, and 68030 CPUs.

Table 3.4
68000, 68020, and 68030 Systems

CPU	Computer	Bits*	Speed
68000	Macintosh Classic	16	8 MHz
68000	Macintosh Plus	16	8 MHz
68000	Amiga 2000	16	8 MHz
68000	Atari ST	16	8 MHz
68020	Macintosh LC	32	16 MHz
68020	Macintosh II	32	16 MHz

continues

Table 3.4—*continued*

CPU	Computer	Bits*	Speed
68020	Amiga 2500	32	16 MHz
68030	Macintosh SE/30	32	16 MHz
68030	Macintosh IIsi	32	20 MHz
68030	Amiga 3000/25	32	25 MHz
68030	Macintosh IIfx	32	40 MHz

*CPU has a 16-bit or 32-bit data path.

ROM

ROM (read-only memory) permanently holds programs needed to operate the computer. For computers other than IBM compatibles, you don't need to consider ROM software. No matter how much ROM exists and no matter how well the programs operate, you have to take what the manufacturer gives you. After you purchase a computer, however, try to keep abreast of the changes made to the ROM software and have your computer dealer replace ROMs with updated versions when possible.

With IBM compatibles, you need to consider only one question: Is the ROM BIOS compatible with the IBM ROM BIOS? The *BIOS* (Basic Input/Output System) is software that handles communication between the CPU and components, such as disk drives, printers, and so on. Years ago, this question was important, but now the answer is invariably yes. Companies like Phoenix, Award, AMI, and DTK have been making IBM-compatible ROMs for many years and do a great job. You have to worry about a ROM problem only if you plan to buy an IBM compatible from a completely unknown manufacturer who uses an unknown ROM BIOS, or if you plan to buy an old IBM compatible.

Checking the ROM BIOS for compatibility is difficult because problems, such as software not running properly, don't always show up right away. Most computer manufacturers provide specifications that tell you the manufacturer of the ROM BIOS. If you don't see the information, ask about it.

RAM

RAM (random-access memory) is volatile memory. Anything stored in RAM—your latest budget figures, your sample chapter—is lost when you turn off power unless you have saved the information to disk.

Because the price of a personal computer increases with the amount of RAM, you must consider the memory requirements of the operating system, operating environment, and application software you intend to use.

You can find out this information by looking at the memory requirements listed on the software package. Generally, the more RAM you have in your computer, the better.

Two kinds of RAM exist: dynamic RAM and static RAM. Dynamic RAM is cheaper and slower than static RAM. In computers with high-performance CPUs, you should look for some static RAM (many 80486 computers have 256K of static RAM). Static RAM is used as a memory cache. A memory cache performs the human equivalent of thinking ahead. The cache holds frequently used data. If the CPU needs the data again—and it usually does—the static RAM cache can supply the data much faster than main memory. A memory cache speeds up the overall operation of the computer. Static RAM is needed to take full advantage of the speed of the 80386, 80486, and 68030 CPUs. Of all the Macintosh computers, only the top-of-the-line model has static RAM (32K).

When you purchase a computer, a certain amount of RAM is on the system board. The physical chips used as RAM on the system board of a computer are standard chips, *dual-in-line package (DIP)*, or *single-in-line memory modules (SIMM)* (see figs. 3.1 and 3.2). To increase the memory in your computer, you must know what kind of chips your computer uses.

Fig. 3.1. A standard RAM chip.

Fig. 3.2. A single-in-line memory module or SIMM.

The following sections describe RAM as it pertains to IBM and compatible, Apple Macintosh, Commodore Amiga, and Atari ST and Mega computers.

IBM and Compatible Computers

Memory in IBM and compatible computers that run under PC DOS and MS-DOS generally is classified as conventional, extended, or expanded. Conventional memory is the first 1,024 kilobytes (one megabyte) of memory and is physically made up of RAM and ROM. Computer specifications, such as "includes 640K RAM," refer to the first 640 kilobytes of conventional ,memory. This part of memory is where programs run (often referred to as the *640K DOS limit*). The remainder of conventional memory is used by programs stored in ROM, data stored in video RAM, and in other ways. Typically, this area is not fully used.

Extended memory is RAM beyond one megabyte. Extended memory can be used only by certain computers (80286 through 80486) and certain programs designed to use extended memory. A specification for 80286 through 80486 computers, such as "includes 1M RAM", means that you have 640K RAM available for use as conventional memory and 384 kilobytes of RAM available for use as extended memory. As the amount of RAM in the computer is increased, the amount of extended memory is increased.

Expanded memory is RAM that becomes part of conventional memory in the area above 640K. Large amounts of expanded memory can be made available to a program through a clever scheme that enables chunks of expanded memory to be swapped in and out of a small part of conventional memory. All IBM and compatible computers can use expanded memory, although not all programs can take advantage of expanded memory. Normally, you add expanded memory to an IBM or compatible computer by plugging a special expanded memory board into an expansion slot. These boards should adhere to LIM EMS 4.0, which is the Lotus-Intel-Microsoft Expanded Memory Specification Version 4.0.

Extended memory easily can be converted to expanded memory with an EMS emulation program. You usually are provided with this software when you purchase an IBM or compatible computer.

The amount of RAM you need depends on the requirements of your operating system and application software. For example, an IBM-compatible computer running Lotus 1-2-3 Release 2.2 needs only 640K of conventional RAM. Certain versions of 1-2-3 and many other programs also can use expanded memory. An IBM-compatible computer running MS-DOS and software such as Lotus 1-2-3 Release 3.1 needs 1M RAM minimum and more memory if you create large spreadsheets (1M equals 1000K). To run a graphical operating environment like Microsoft Windows 3.0 in *enhanced mode* on computers with 80386SX, 80386, or 80486 CPUs, you need two megabytes of RAM.

Macintosh, Amiga, and Atari Mega and ST Computers

Macintosh, Amiga, and Atari Mega and ST computers don't suffer from the DOS 640K limit (these computers don't use MS-DOS). Therefore, you don't have to worry about conventional, extended, and expanded memory on these machines. You do need a general idea of how much RAM you need in the computer. For example, a Macintosh computer running System 6.0.2 and software like QuarkXPress 3.0 requires 2M RAM.

System Unit Case

Choosing the case that covers the system unit may seem trivial, but you probably will spend a good deal of time trying to figure out what size and what style of case you prefer. Cases for IBM and compatible computers range in size from large floor standing (tower) models to small desktop models. Some cases are regular height; some are slim-line. The space a computer takes on a desk is called its *footprint*. The smallest cases are just two inches high and can fit on a regular sheet of paper. Naturally, a system unit this size leaves little room for disk drives or expansion boards. A tower unit, on the other hand, can accommodate a variety of floppy and hard disk drives, tape drives, CD ROM drives, and expansion boards. Because the unit stands on the floor, it doesn't take up any desk space.

If you decide to purchase a computer with a small footprint, look inside the system unit to see how disk drives are positioned, how many expansion slots are available, and how the slots are oriented. Computers with very small dimensions sometimes have slots that hold expansion boards horizontally rather than vertically. You may not be thinking about expanding your system right away, but most people eventually add circuit boards to their computers. If you have a limited number of slots, or the orientation of the slots forces you to squeeze the boards into a small space, your plans for expansion may be squelched. Unless you have a real need for a computer with a small system unit, a standard-size unit is better in the long run.

Keyboard and Mouse

Because the keyboard and mouse are the primary ways to enter information into a computer, you should select these components carefully.

Keyboards differ in several ways: the number of keys, the feel of the keys, and the placement of the keys. The most popular keyboard is the 101-key keyboard described in the preceding chapter. Not all computers come equipped with this model, however. Some computers, such as laptops, just don't have the room to include 101-keys. If you have a choice, select the 101-key model.

Although keyboards may look the same, the feel of keyboards varies from one manufacturer to another. Some keyboards have a mushy feel; some have a solid feel. Some click when you press the key; some are silent. Some keyboards have bumps on the F and J keys to remind your fingers where the home keys are. If you type a great deal, you should be concerned about the feel of the keyboard. The only way to know how a keyboard feels is to try it.

Remember that keyboards are replaceable items. You can buy a new keyboard from companies like Keytronics and Northgate. Some keyboards have nonstandard arrangements, especially for the Backslash, Control, and Caps Lock keys. If you work at one computer, you may get used to the unusual arrangement. If you work on two or more computers, you should have keyboards that match—especially if you are a touch typist.

A mouse sometimes comes with an IBM or compatible computer system, and sometimes a mouse is offered as an add-on option. If you plan to use a graphics operating environment such as Microsoft Windows, a paint program, or a drawing program, you need a mouse. Macintosh and Amiga computer systems come with a mouse.

A mouse may seem to be an innocuous piece of equipment, but one model can differ from another in several ways. Mice differ in the number of buttons, the feel or shape, and the technology. Macintoshes use a one-button mouse; Amigas use a two-button mouse; and IBM compatibles use a two- or three-button mouse. Choosing a two- or three-button mouse for a computer is a personal preference. The third button is not used by most programs.

Place your hand on a mouse, roll it on the desktop or a mouse pad, and push the buttons to get an idea of how well the mouse reacts to your hand movements. Test a few different models before making your decision. Don't base your decision on other factors, such as price or software included with the mouse.

Although one mouse may look and feel different from another, most use a similar technology. These *opto-mechanical* mice have a ball on the underside that rolls when you push the mouse. An alternative to this kind of mouse is an *optical mouse*, which has lights on the bottom and rolls over a special light-sensitive pad. You may want to use an optical mouse if you work at a small desk with limited space. Optical mice are not as popular as opto-mechanical mice.

Some computers, such as the Macintosh, Amiga, and Atari ST, provide a mouse and a mouse port. Other computers, such as the IBM PS/2 series, do not come with a mouse but provide a port for the mouse. Most IBM-compatible computers don't provide a mouse port. For these machines, you must use a bus or serial mouse. A bus mouse comes with a circuit board that fits into one of the system board's expansion slots. A serial mouse connects to one of the serial ports at the back of the system unit. If you have one serial port and you use it for your modem, buy a bus mouse. If you have no expansion slots but have an extra serial port, buy a serial mouse. If a serial port and an expansion slot are available, the choice is up to you.

Instead of purchasing a mouse, you can purchase a special type of keyboard that has a trackball set into it. Rolling the ball with your fingertips produces the same results as moving a mouse, with the keyboard keys acting as the mouse buttons. Another alternative to a mouse is a separate trackball, such as the one shown in figure 3.3. This device attaches to the computer the same way that the mouse does, but does not have to be moved. Instead, you roll the ball with your fingertips and press the buttons on either side.

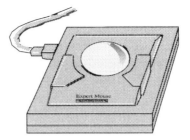

Fig. 3.3. *A trackball can be used to move around the screen—instead of a mouse.*

Monitors and Video Adapters

When you purchase a computer system, one of the first decisions you must make is whether you want a monochrome or a color monitor. If you are trying to put together a low-cost system, a monochrome monitor may meet your needs.

After you decide the kind of monitor you want, you must select a *video adapter*, a circuit board you insert into an expansion slot to provide you with video signals. Some computers have video circuits built into the system board. For these computers, you need match only the monitor to the built-in video. Some computers come with video circuits and have the monitor built-in, such as laptops, portables, and some Macintoshes.

Monochrome Monitors

For IBM-compatible computers, you need a monochrome monitor and a monochrome graphics video adapter, as described in the preceding chapter. The monitor should have the following characteristics: sharpness of characters in the center and on the edges of the display, the picture tube correctly set in the case (you can tell by checking whether the on-screen text is horizontal), a tilt and swivel base, and a nonglare screen. If you are unhappy with the computer company's monitor, consider a monochrome monitor from a third-party supplier. Another, more expensive, monochrome option for IBM compatibles is a VGA adapter and a VGA monochrome monitor.

The Apple Macintosh started out as a monochrome system with built-in video circuits and monitor. This heritage still survives in the Macintosh Classic and SE/30 computers. The built-in monitor, however, is small—only 9 inches diagonally. If you plan to do serious desktop publishing work, for example, you need a larger monitor.

Color Monitors

Monochrome monitors are fine for word processing and desktop publishing, but color monitors are far more popular for most other applications. Any application that uses graphics can benefit from a color display. These applications include spreadsheet, computer-aided design, paint and drawing programs, and so on. The current standard for IBM and compatibles running standard applications is VGA. The other color standards, CGA and EGA, offer less resolution and colors than VGA.

When IBM introduces a video standard such as VGA, other companies try to improve on the standard by manufacturing monitors and adapters with better resolution and more colors. For this reason, some video monitors and adapters are called VGA, and others are called super VGA, premium VGA, and so on. Super VGA is an industry standard for IBM-compatible computers. A super VGA monitor and adapter cost slightly more than standard VGA, but the super VGA offers better resolution (800 x 600) than VGA (640 x 480), which produces sharper images.

Video adapters use RAM to store video information. Generally, the more RAM you have on a video board, the greater the resolution and number of colors the video board can produce. For example, for a super VGA board to produce 256 colors, the board needs at least 512K. You may want to purchase this amount right away or opt for a lesser amount, such as 256K, and upgrade later.

To display VGA, you need a VGA monitor or a multiscan monitor. A multiscan monitor displays higher resolutions than a VGA monitor. A multiscan monitor can display super VGA, for example. A standard VGA monitor cannot display super VGA. If you first purchase a VGA monitor and adapter and later decide to upgrade, you need your new monitor and adapter. With a multiscan model, only a new adapter is needed.

The general qualities to look for in a color monitor are sharp characters and images throughout the display; bright, vivid colors; a nonglare screen; and controls for contrast, brightness, and horizontal and vertical size.

Before you purchase a color monitor for an Apple Macintosh IIfx, a video adapter from Apple or a competing manufacturer is needed to display color. Apple color cards are described in terms like *8-bit color* or *24-bit color*. The greater the number of bits, the greater the number of colors, and therefore, the more realistic computer images. After you choose a video adapter, you need to choose a monitor that works with the video adapter—a standard monitor or a multiscan monitor.

Some manufacturers build color video circuitry right onto the computer's system board. Examples of computers with built-in video circuitry are the IBM PS/1, the PS/2 family of computers, the Apple Macintosh LC, IIsi, and IIci computers, Commodore Amiga computers, and Atari Mega and ST computers.

If video circuitry is built into the system, you do not need a separate video adapter, but you still need a monitor. The monitor should support the built-in video, such as a VGA monitor or support many standards, such as a multiscan monitor. If you are not satisfied with the built-in video, you usually can add a video adapter of your own choice at an additional expense.

High-performance computers, such as computers that use 80386, 80486, and 68030 CPUs, often are used for high-end color graphics applications, such as color desktop publishing and computer-aided design. Large-screen color monitors and sophisticated graphics boards are available for these kinds of applications. Important considerations for high-end graphics work are the number of colors, the resolution, and the speed of an adapter and monitor combination. IBM compatibles have the 8514/A standard; Macintosh and Amiga computers have the 24-bit color standard. Graphics cards with coprocessors, such as the Texas Instruments 34010 processor, speed the display of graphics. Before you decide on an adapter and monitor for high-end graphics, make sure that they can support the software you plan to use.

Monitor Size

A 9-inch diagonal display, such as the one built into the Macintosh SE/30, is not the best display for desktop publishing, an application for which the Macintosh excels. For this work, a 15-inch, full-page or 19-inch, dual-page monochrome monitor can do a better job, because these monitors can display one or two pages of a document. Figure 3.4 contrasts the size of a standard Macintosh monochrome display and a full-page display.

Full-page monochrome monitors sell for $500 and up (video adapter included); dual-page monochrome monitors sell for about $900 and up (video adapter included). A representative list of these monochrome monitors for Apple Macintosh and IBM-compatible systems is given in the following table (prices shown are typical mail order prices):

Table 3.5
Monochrome Monitors

Monitor and Adapter	Type	Size	System	Price
Samsung	Full Page	15"	Macintosh	$ 500
Ehman	Full Page	15"	Macintosh	$ 500
Princeton Multiview	Full Page	15"	IBM compatible	$ 700
Samsung	Dual Page	19"	Macintosh	$ 900
Radius	Dual Page	19"	Macintosh	$1550

For color applications, oversize monitors come in all different sizes—16-inch, 19-inch, 20-inch, and larger. These monitors can be used for color desktop publishing applications, high-end graphics work, presentations, and so on. Keep in mind, however, that these color monitors can be expensive, especially when coupled with a sophisticated video adapter. A representative list of these monitors for Apple Macintosh and IBM and compatible systems is given in the following table (prices shown are typical mail-order prices):

Table 3.6
Color Monitors

Monitor	Adapter	Size	System	Price
Ikegami	8-bit color	19"	Macintosh	$3000
Ikegami	24-bit color	19"	Macintosh	$4000
RasterOps 24L	24-bit color	19"	Macintosh	$6000
Princeton UltraSync	(not included)	16"	IBM and compatible	$ 879
Mitsubishi HL6605	(not included)	16"	IBM and compatible	$1075
Mitsubishi HL6905	(not included)	20"	IBM and compatible	$2050
NEC 5D	(not included)	20"	IBM and compatible	$2350

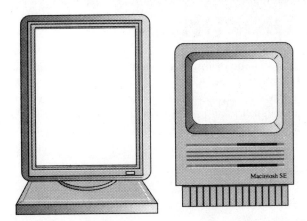

Fig. 3.4. The screen display of a full-page monitor versus a Macintosh SE/30 display.

Floppy Disk Drives

The preceding chapter describes different types of floppy drives. Personal computer floppy drives can be 5 1/4-inch or 3 1/2-inch, high-density or double-density (other kinds of floppy drives for personal computers exist but are not widely used). Apple, Commodore, and Atari computers use 3 1/2-inch floppy disk drives, as do IBM PS/1 and PS/2 computers and laptop computers. Many IBM-compatible computers use 5 1/4-inch floppy drives. A 3 1/2-inch disk cannot be placed in a 5 1/4-inch floppy disk drive.

One solution is to have drives of both sizes in each computer. Because a drive can be double density or high density, you really have four choices rather than two. Deciding what type of floppy disk drive to put into an IBM-compatible computer depends on the drives in other computers. If you have to share information or programs with an associate, you should have a drive that matches the drive in your associate's computer.

A new IBM PS/2 or PS/1 computer comes standard with a high-density 3 1/2-inch floppy disk drive. If you purchase an IBM compatible, your first choice should be a high-density 3 1/2-inch drive; a good choice for a second drive is a high-density 5 1/4-inch floppy drive. A new Macintosh computer comes standard with a 3 1/2-inch high-density floppy drive.

Hard Disk Drives

A hard drive enhances the overall performance of a computer system. Sometimes a computer manufacturer includes a hard drive as a standard feature of the computer, but usually you can specify the kind of hard disk drive you want. You need to look for several qualities in a hard drive. Among them are size, performance, and controller technology. The following sections explain these qualities.

Size

The size of a hard drive means two things: the physical size of the drive and the amount of information the disk can hold. Like floppy disks, hard drives come in 3 1/2-inch and 5 1/4-inch varieties. You install most hard drives inside the system unit, but for a little more money, you can buy an external hard drive.

A 5 1/4-inch hard drive may be half-height or full-height. Height is measured in terms of the room inside the system unit. A full-height drive occupies an entire disk drive bay in the system unit; a half-height drive occupies half as much space. If the computer has a small footprint and a low height, the computer probably accepts only 3 1/2-inch hard drives. Large system units normally accept only 5 1/4-inch hard drives. (To place a 3 1/2-inch hard drive into a large system unit, you must mount the hard drive on a 5 1/4-inch metal frame.) Small system units normally accept only 3 1/2-inch hard drives.

The storage capacity you choose for your hard drive depends on the programs you use and the amount of information you generate. You must consider the amount of space your programs use, the amount of space your information uses, and how long you want to keep your information on the hard drive.

To calculate needed space, create a chart for each program you plan to use (see table 3.7). The time period you select for answer 3 also should be used for answer 4 (days, weeks, months). Add the results for each program to determine the minimum hard drive capacity you need. If you have never used a computer before, you can ask a friend who does use one to help with the chart, or you can call the company that makes the software you plan to use.

Table 3.1
How Much Hard Disk Space Do You Need?

1. Size of the program (kilobytes): _____

2. Average size of the files you create (kilobytes): _____

3. Number of files generated each day (week, month): _____

4. Amount of time the information needs to be on the hard drive: _____

5. Multiply 2, 3, 4: _____

6. Add 1 and 5: _____

Choose a hard drive capacity that exceeds the number you calculate. Remember that you need space on your hard drive for the operating system and for some program operations (application programs often create temporary files as they work). Hard disks for personal computers range from 20M to more than 600M. If you store information such as images and voice recordings, you need more storage space.

Performance

Hard disk performance is measured in terms of access speed and transfer rate. *Access speed* refers to the amount of time needed for the hard drive to find the information you need. *Transfer rate* refers to the amount of time needed to move that information from the hard drive to RAM or vice versa.

Access Speed

The fastest hard disk drives have an average access time of about 15 ms. You should consider a hard disk drive with an access time of more than 60 ms only if you will use the drive in a low-cost IBM compatible with an 8088 or 8086 CPU. For all other personal computers, look for the fastest hard disk drive you can afford.

Transfer Rate

How fast a hard drive moves information back and forth to RAM is called the *transfer rate* of a hard drive. The transfer rate partially depends on the type of hard drive controller or interface. Macintosh, Amiga, and Atari computers use only one type of interface. IBM and compatible computers, however, use several different kinds.

When hard disk drives and controllers are advertised, the abbreviations MFM, RLL, ESDI, and SCSI are used. These give an indication of the data transfer rate to expect with the drive/controller combination. If you want in-depth information on these types, refer to one of the Que books that covers this topic, such as *Upgrading and Repairing PCs*. If you want to know how these items affect machine performance, see the table below:

Type: MFM, Modified Frequency Modulation
Interface: ST-506/412
Transfer rate: 5 million bits per second
Recommended for: 8088 through 80286 computers
Drive capacity: 20 to 60 megabytes

Type: RLL, Run Length Limited
Interface: ST-506/412
Transfer rate: 7.5 million bits per second
Recommended for: 8088 through 80386SX computers
Drive capacity: 40 to 80 megabytes

Type: IDE, Integrated Drive Electronics
Interface: ST-506/412 or other depending on the manufacturer
Transfer rate: Varies from 5 to 10 million bits per second depending on the manufacturer
Recommended for: 80286 and 80386SX computers
Drive capacity: 40 to 100 megabytes

Type: ESDI, Enhance Small-Device Interface
Interface: ESDI
Transfer rate: 10 million bits per second (capable of faster transfer rates)

Recommended for: 80386SX, 80386, and 80486 computers
Drive capacity: 100 megabytes and over

Type: SCSI, Small Computer Systems Interface
Interface: ST-506/412 or other depending on the manufacturer
Transfer rate: 10 million bits per second (capable of faster transfer rates)
Recommended for: 80386SX, 80386, and 80486 computers
Drive capacity: 100 megabytes and over

Hard Cards

A hard card is a circuit board with a hard drive attached to the board. A hard card can be inserted into an expansion slot on IBM-compatible computers. Hard cards are a convenient way of adding a hard drive to a personal computer, but hard cards often are priced higher than conventional drives and offer no performance advantages. Hard cards are sometimes useful for moving information from one computer to another, but any movement of the drive entails opening the system units of both computers, removing the drive from one computer, and inserting the drive into the other—not an elegant solution for moving data between two systems.

Removable Hard Disks

Some hard disk drives offer the same kind of convenience as a floppy disk drive—you can remove the disk from the drive. Naturally, individual disks are much more expensive than their floppy cousins. This kind of hard disk drive is not widely used, and unless you have a specific reason for choosing one, you are better off with the standard type.

Slots and Buses

Personal computers, unlike most other electronic products, are not limited to performing one kind of task. Instead, a PC can do many different kinds of tasks depending on the software and hardware that is added to the PC. To make sure that the personal computer you buy can do what you want it to do now and in the future, an important aspect to investigate is the computer's expandability. Expandability depends on two factors: the number of expansion slots in the computer and the type of bus in the computer.

Expansion slots reside on the computer's system board. To expand a computer's capabilities, you insert an electronic board into an expansion slot. Generally, the smaller the computer, the lower the number of expansion slots. When you shop for a computer, determine how many of its expansion slots are needed to provide the functionality you want. Some computers use expansion slots for serial ports, parallel ports, video, and other functions. Other computers include these functions on the system board. A personal computer with only three expansion slots may be acceptable if many important functions are already built into the motherboard.

You can get an idea of the number of expansion slots you need by considering some of the popular boards that can be inserted into these slots. Some expansion boards you may consider are FAX, MIDI, modem, sound, joystick, scanner, memory, and high-performance graphics. Make a list of the applications that appeal to you and compare your list with the number of expansion slots in the PC you are considering.

To help you with the list, the following table includes some typical scenarios.

Desktop publisher
Expansion 1: Full-page monitor
Expansion 2: Scanner
Expansion 3: Modem
Expansion 4: Fax
Expansion 5: Memory

Small-business user
Expansion 1: Modem
Expansion 2: Fax
Expansion 3: Memory
Expansion 4: Bar Code Wand

Home User
Expansion 1: Sound board
Expansion 2: Joystick
Expansion 3: Modem
Expansion 4: MIDI (for music)

A bus is the electronic roadway that connects the components of a computer system. Various bus designs are available for personal computers. The design of the bus affects the design of the expansion slots, which affects the expandability of the computer.

When you purchase a computer, you should inquire about the type of bus the computer uses. Table 3.8 lists bus type versus computer type for representative systems, expansion cards that can be used with them, and other information.

Many PC-compatible computers with 80386 and 80486 CPUs have proprietary buses. A manufacturer designs a proprietary bus to give its computers features not found in most of its competitors. For example, the Hewlett-Packard Vectra 486 PC has a bus especially designed to improve the performance of graphics. Even though a computer may have a proprietary bus, it often coexists with a standard bus, such as ISA or EISA. Proprietary buses have one major drawback. If a manufacturer decides to stop supporting the bus, you gain no further benefits from having the bus in your PC. If the benefits associated with a proprietary bus are encouraging you to purchase a certain computer model, keep in mind that you may become completely dependent on the manufacturer for new products and upgrades that support that bus.

Table 3.2
Computer Buses

Bus name	Computers	Bus width	Expansion boards
ISA Industry Standard Architecture	8088-80486 IBM AT compatibles	16 bits	ISA
EISA Extended Industry Standard Architecture	80386, 80486	32 bits	ISA, EISA
MCA Micro Channel Architecture	IBM PS/2 model 50 and higher	16 or 32 bits	MCA
NuBus	Macintosh II computer line	NuBus	

Serial and Parallel Ports

Serial and parallel ports are the main avenues to the outside world for a personal computer. To attach a device to your computer, you need to attach that device to a connector on the computer. Some devices come with their own proprietary connectors; other devices can be attached to the serial or parallel ports of the computer.

The serial port can be connected to many different kinds of devices, including a modem, a mouse, a printer, and a plotter. The parallel port is used chiefly for printers. Some computers have built-in serial and parallel ports, and other computers don't. If a computer doesn't have any ports, or if you need more ports than are built into the computer, you must purchase a serial port or parallel port expansion board. Generic boards, called *multi i/o boards* (multiple input/output), normally contain two serial ports, a parallel port, and other features. Macintosh computers use serial ports exclusively.

If you are purchasing an IBM-compatible computer, make sure that it has a parallel port for printing, a serial port for a modem, and a second serial port or a mouse port for a mouse.

Printers

The most popular kinds of printers are laser printers, dot-matrix printers, and inkjet printers. Printers usually print in black, but color models are available for those with big budgets. The decision to buy a printer usually is based on output quality, the number of fonts or type styles available, speed, price, and the need for color.

The printer you purchase depends on the applications you use. For example, if you need to print thousands of numbers from a spreadsheet everyday, you want a dot-matrix printer that prints very fast in the draft (computer print) mode. If you are typing letters for a small business, a dot-matrix printer with letter-quality print or a low-cost laser printer would be the choice. If you are publishing a newsletter, a laser printer with a variety of fonts would suit your purposes best. To learn more about printers and the factors that should go into a purchasing decision, see Chapter 6.

Other Equipment

After you have decided on a personal computer system, you still need to think about many other pieces of equipment. The following sections discuss some of the purchases you are most likely to make.

Modems

A *modem* is a device for sending information from one computer to another over phone lines. You can use a modem to share programs and data with other computer users. With a modem, you can upload (send) information to or download (receive) information from another computer. You also can chat, which means that you can type at your keyboard, and the words are transmitted to the person on the other end of the phone line. That person, in turn, can respond to you.

Other popular uses for modems are connecting to bulletin board systems (BBSs), on-line services such as CompuServe and Prodigy, electronic mail services such as MCI Mail, electronic databases such as Dialog, and electronic stock market services such as the Dow-Jones News/Retrieval service.

Like most other computer products, speed is a major issue with modems. You pay for the telephone call you make with a modem just as you do for a voice call. If you are downloading a large spreadsheet from a distant location during business hours, you want to transfer the information as quickly as possible. The speed of a modem is defined by its *baud rate*, the number of bits per second that the modem can send or receive. A 2400-baud modem, for example, is faster than a 1200-baud modem. The only modems you need to consider are 2400-baud and 9600-baud models.

A 2400-baud modem gives you reasonable speed at a reasonable price. If this speed is not fast enough for you, the next fastest models operate at 9600 baud. To increase the speed of transfers even more, some modems compress the information before sending it. These modems have features like built-in data compression and error correction. Compressing data before sending it makes it seem as though the modem is sending information as fast as 19,200 baud. To achieve this kind of throughput, the sending modem and receiving modem must adhere to the same communications standard. Compressed data expands again after it is received at the other end of the connection. Error correction ensures that the information sent is the same as the information received. Features like high speed, data compression, and error correction make a modem more costly, but the hardware can pay for itself if you telecommunicate often.

A fast modem does not always save money. If you connect to an on-line service and spend time exploring the available features, you usually are charged for the time you are connected to the service, regardless of how fast information is sent back and forth.

External modems connect to the serial port. Internal modems connect to an expansion slot on the system board. The modem you choose may depend on what is available in your system: the port or the slot. A laptop computer, which is meant to be small and easy to carry around, should always use an internal modem.

To operate a modem, most people use communications software. To ensure compatibility between the modem and the software, the wise choice is to purchase a modem that uses the Hayes AT command set, because Hayes is the company that has set the standards for personal computer modem communications.

Manufacturers sometimes put more than one communication device on a board. You find boards that can work as modems and fax machines; boards that work as modems, fax machines, and answering machines; and boards that have more than one modem. Multiple-modem boards are useful for setting up a computer as an electronic bulletin board.

Scanners

A *scanner* is a device that enables you to transform printed text or images into electronic text or images. The major uses for a scanner are desktop publishing, optical character recognition (OCR), and faxing. If you are creating a newsletter and want to insert a picture into the body of the copy, you can scan in the picture and then use it in the program. To avoid retyping copy, you can scan in an image of a page of text and then let OCR software read and transform the image into a document that can be used on a word processor.

To send text or images to another location, you can use a scanner to produce an image of the page. This image then can be transmitted to any fax machine.

You can choose from several types of scanners, depending on what type of material you want to scan. A flatbed scanner scans documents, periodicals, and books. An overhead scanner scans these items and 3-D objects. A sheet-feed scanner scans single sheets of paper. To scan a stack of pages, some scanners have a sheet-feeding mechanism built into the scanner or available as an option. A hand scanner is an inexpensive way to scan material such as small images or columns of text. Figure 3.5 shows examples of the different kinds of scanners.

Scanners scan at different resolutions. The higher the resolution, the more dots the electronic image contains, and the sharper the image is. A low-cost scanner can produce images with a resolution of 300 dots per inch. This resolution is acceptable for all but the most demanding applications. More expensive scanners can produce images with much higher resolution. Most scanners produce black-and-white and half-tone images, but some expensive scanners can produce color images.

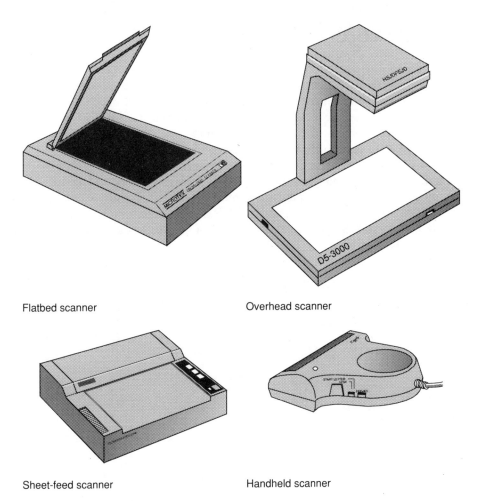

Fig. 3.5. Examples of different kinds of scanners.

Surge Protectors

Personal computers and their peripherals are connected to power lines, and some peripherals are connected to the phone lines. Power surges in these lines can destroy data and ruin equipment. This danger is especially true during a lightning storm. To protect against catastrophe, always use a surge protector. A surge protector protects the devices plugged into it (see fig. 3.6). In normal daily operation, a surge protector is a convenience, too. If you turn on everything plugged into the surge protector, you can turn everything on or off at the same time by flipping the switch on the surge protector. Make sure that the product you buy contains surge protection and is not just a multiple plug outlet. To protect the modem and other devices from surges on the telephone line, you can get surge protectors that fit into the modular wall plug (RJ-11 jack).

Fig. 3.6. A surge protector.

Furniture

Because a personal computer system has so many components, computer furniture helps aesthetically and ergonomically. The main things to look for in computer furniture are sufficient room for each component, enclosed areas for documentation and software, correct height for typing, and room to feed and receive paper traveling in and out of a printer. Although these requirements may sound simple, most computer furniture fails them.

Supplies

When you purchase a computer system for the first time, you need to consider certain supplies. First, you should buy one or more boxes of floppy disks. These disks should be compatible in size and density to the floppy disk drive in the computer. Next, you need paper. For dot-matrix printers, you need a box of fanfold paper. These boxes usually hold 2,500 sheets of paper. For laser printers, you need one or more reams of copy paper.

Other

Besides furniture, many kinds of computer accessories are available to make the hours you spend with a computer easier to endure. Everyone can benefit from a nonglare screen on the monitor, as well as a tilt-and-swivel monitor base. Good lighting, such as that provided by a high-intensity lamp, is imperative. Typists need copy holders. Floppy disk holders keep the workplace organized. If your desk doesn't stand at the correct height for typing, consider a pull-out tray for the keyboard that can be attached to the underside of the desk. These accessories help you avoid the physical strain that often accompanies long hours at the computer.

Chapter Summary

This chapter described the variety of components available for personal computers. This chapter showed the differences among CPUs and how these differences affect a purchasing decision. The chapter also explained how other components of a computer system—such as RAM, ROM, keyboard, mouse, monitor, hard drive, floppy disk, expansion slots, buses, ports, and other kinds of devices—affect performance. Most sections of this chapter provided purchasing recommendations for different degrees of performance.

In the Next Chapter

The next chapter offers guidelines for selecting a computer manufacturer. Chapter 4 explains the considerations when choosing a manufacturer—available software, compatibility, performance, price, support, upgrades, warranties, service, and so on.

4

What Type of Computer Do I Want?

IBM Corporation and Apple Computer, Inc. are well-known manufacturers of personal computers. If you have no limit on the amount of money you want to spend on a computer system, you can pick a top-of-the-line PC from one of these two companies and feel certain that you own a great system. This scenario, however, is not realistic for most people. You should consider products from a variety of manufacturers to find the computer that offers the best value for your money. In this chapter, you learn about different manufacturers. This information can help you choose the computer system that best suits your needs.

The criteria that a buyer uses to pick a personal computer manufacturer varies from person to person. You may choose a company with a high level of support, or you may select a company with the lowest prices. Also, you may want to purchase from a well-known manufacturer, although the computer costs hundreds of dollars more than a system from a comparable, but lesser known, company.

Issues of support, price, and name recognition are important, but you also may want to consider other issues. For example, you may want to consider what a personal computer does best. The following applications usually are associated with the following computers:

- Desktop Publishing—Apple Macintosh
- Business Applications—IBM and compatibles
- Multimedia—Commodore Amiga
- Music Creation—Atari ST or Mega

Just because one computer may perform a particular task very well does not mean it cannot perform other tasks as well—or better than—another computer. For example, an IBM computer may be better at multimedia than an Amiga computer, or a Macintosh computer may be stronger in a certain business application than an IBM or compatible computer. Things change fast in the microcomputer industry, and companies always are improving products and changing strategies. View the market with an open mind and choose a system that works for you.

This chapter considers computer buying factors, such as software availability, ease of use, performance, and price. Manufacturers are compared with each other in these categories but not with the aim of choosing an overall winner. The goal of this chapter is not to recommend a specific manufacturer but rather to review the pros and cons of each so that you understand the manufacturer with which you may be dealing.

Comparing Manufacturers

There are four major personal computer types: Apple Macintosh, IBM and compatibles, Commodore Amiga, and Atari Mega or ST. Each of these personal computers has its own software, operating system, user groups, magazines, and so on. You need to pick one of these computer types. The type you choose plays a major part in determining what you can do with a personal computer and how well you do it.

This section is arranged to help you choose the best personal computer manufacturer for your needs. Consider the following areas before you decide on a computer type:

- Software availability
- Ease of use
- Performance
- Price

With these four categories in mind, try to decide which ones are most important to you. You are well on the way to choosing a manufacturer that can satisfy your personal computer needs.

Software Availability

All computers mentioned in this book can run word processors, spreadsheets, databases, games, and so on. However, to run a particular software package, such as Lotus 1-2-3 Release 2.2, you need to purchase a computer that can run the software—in this case, an IBM or a compatible computer. The software package you want to run often determines the type of computer you need to buy.

Some companies do develop software that runs on more than one type of computer—for example, the spreadsheet application program Excel from Microsoft. One version of Excel runs on the Macintosh, and another version runs on IBM and compatible computers. In cases like this one, other factors affect your decision about which computer type to buy.

Ease of Use

A generally accepted fact of computing is that the average person finds a graphical user interface easier than a command interface to learn and use. A graphical user interface, GUI (pronounced gooey), has pull-down menus (see fig. 4.1) for making menu selections, windows (see fig. 4.2) for running application programs, and icons (see fig. 4.3) to represent application programs.

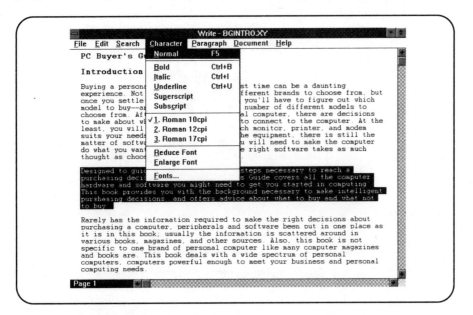

Fig. 4.1 The pull-down menus of a graphical user interface enable you to select menu items.

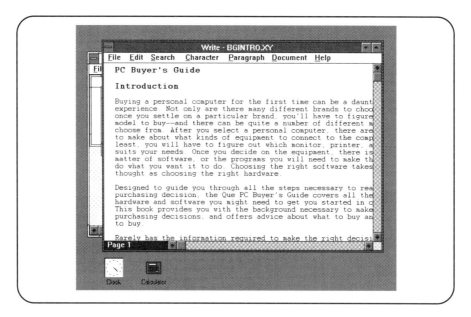

Fig. 4.2. *A graphical user interface often uses a window to run an application, such as the spreadsheet shown here.*

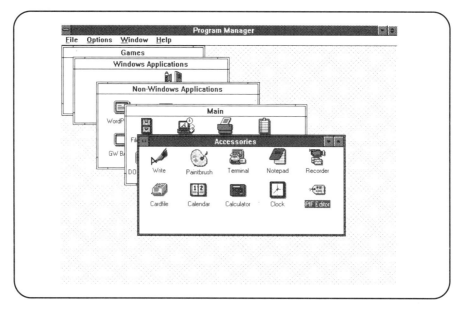

Fig. 4.3. *A graphical user interface often uses icons to represent applications.*

A graphical user interface is consistent from application to application. Therefore, you often can learn quickly how to operate several different applications. Apple Macintosh, Commodore Amiga, and Atari Mega and ST computers have graphical user interfaces. On IBM and compatible computers, you also can use a graphical user interface, such as Microsoft Windows.

Many of the most popular and more capable programs that run on IBM and compatible computers do not use a graphical user interface. The rules of operation vary tremendously from program to program. The way you operate Lotus 1-2-3, for example, has no relation to the way you work with WordPerfect. This operational difference makes transferring your skills from one program to another difficult.

If you plan to use your computer for one job, such as word processing, an IBM or compatible without a GUI is as good a choice as any of the other computers. In fact, you have a larger choice of word processors on an IBM or compatible than with any of the other computers. You can thoroughly learn the rules of operation of that program. If you plan to use several different kinds of software packages, however, consider purchasing a Macintosh or an IBM or compatible that runs under a graphical user interface, such as Windows.

Remember that the ease-of-use issue is highly subjective. Many have struggled successfully with IBM and compatible computers, learning the intricacies of its operating system, MS-DOS (or PC DOS), and the different rules of operation for all kinds of application programs. If you choose this path, you follow a well-traveled road.

Performance

Personal computer performance, as noted in Chapter 3, depends a great deal on the computer's CPU and its rated speed, which is measured in megahertz (or MHz). Performance also depends on the speed of disk drives, video adapters, RAM, coprocessors, and all the other components that make up a personal computer system. Some companies cater to high-performance needs. Others do not. Most companies offer a line of computers with varying degrees of performance.

If you are mainly interested in performance, compare the offerings of many different companies to see how much bang you can get for your buck. If you make the decision to purchase a high-performance IBM compatible, rather than an IBM PS/2 computer, you can save yourself thousands of dollars. The same holds true for components. Many companies make high-performance components for Apple Macintosh, Commodore Amiga, Atari Mega and ST, and

IBM and compatible computers. Knowing the performance of these components, relative to the performance of brand-name components, can aid you in constructing a high-performance system at a reasonable price.

Performance is not just a hardware issue, it's also a software issue. Before you purchase software, try to get an idea of how fast it works. Software that is easy to use may not always work as fast as you would like. If you are considering a word processor, for example, watch a demonstration of how fast it can do a job, such as replacing all the periods in a long body of text with exclamation points. If you need a database, find out how fast it can sort 1,000 names, 10,000 names, or any other job you expect of the software.

The performance of a computer system always should be uppermost in your mind as you try to sort out all the variables that go into making a purchase decision. A high-performance system will serve your needs better than one with lesser performance—no matter what the application may be.

Price

Until now, you read about three suggested ways to compare manufacturers—by software availability, ease of use, and performance. Of the manufacturers you consider, three make unique computers: Apple, Commodore, and Atari. The rest make computers that follow software and hardware standards established by IBM. If you use price to choose a manufacturer, compare the companies from this latter group. It doesn't make much sense to purchase an Atari computer because of its price if you really need IBM compatibility or if you want a wealth of business programs from which to choose.

You definitely can use price as a guideline to choose among manufacturers. IBM and Apple often give significant corporate discounts, but such is not the case for people who buy computers one or two at a time. Shop around for the best price, therefore, if you are in the market for a high-performance computer and the best software. Buying an IBM, however, does not always mean that you receive a superior product. IBM often sells less computer for more money. Don't be afraid to choose one of IBM's competitors if that computer offers what you want.

Remember that there are costs associated with owning a personal computer. Although personal computers are very reliable, you sometimes have to spend money on repairs and spare parts. Spare parts for IBM-compatible computers usually are less expensive than those for any other personal computer. The costs are less because you can purchase the parts from many companies. The parts usually are interchangeable no matter what manufacturer originally sold you the computer.

Price is most significant when you intend to purchase an IBM or compatible computer. Otherwise, the other factors play more of a role in your purchase decision. If you eventually decide to buy a Macintosh, an Amiga, or an Atari Mega or ST computer, your thoughts about price should focus on what you can afford in the product line, rather than what a competitor may offer.

Reviewing Manufacturers

This section covers most of the personal computer companies that have been around for a while and have established reputations. As each company is described, you will find that each one has strengths and weaknesses, and each company has unique objectives that it strives to achieve. Some firms excel at service and support; some offer money-back guarantees; and others concentrate on high performance. In the following sections, you can get a sense of what each company stands for so that you can decide if a company's computer is appropriate for you.

IBM

IBM (International Business Machines) has been a standard setter in the microcomputer industry since the introduction of the IBM PC in 1981. IBM personal computers generally cost more than those from other companies, but in return, you get innovation, quality, and relative stability, although often not the highest performance. IBM stopped selling its PC, XT, and AT computers several years ago and replaced them with the PS/2 and PS/1 computers that the company sells today.

IBM models fall into two categories: Micro Channel and non-Micro Channel computers. A good reason to purchase an IBM computer is the Micro Channel architecture. (Micro Channel is an advanced circuit architecture that makes the computer easy to upgrade and also can increase its performance.) Other good reasons to purchase an IBM are overall quality and the backing of a company that won't go out of business in the foreseeable future.

Some disadvantages of buying an IBM computer are the higher cost and lower level of performance when compared to the competition. (Some competitors offer computers that operate faster than IBM computers.) You can find more information about specific IBM models at the end of this chapter.

IBM computers are excellent general-purpose business computers. A huge number of software packages are designed to run on IBM computers. Many of which are industry standards, such as Lotus 1-2-3, WordPerfect, and dBase.

You can buy IBM computers at authorized dealers, such as ComputerLand, Entre Computer Centers, Nynex Business Centers, and Sears Business Centers. IBM's entry-level computer, the PS/1 also is sold through department stores, such as Sears Roebuck, Dayton Hudson, and Dillard. IBM warrants its computer systems for one year from the date of purchase. In terms of service, IBM expects dealers to provide trained technicians and maintain a repair facility. The dealer also can provide on-site service.

Apple Computer

Apple Computer has sold personal computers since the late 1970's. Apple's initial success, the Apple II, gave birth to a line of computers that Apple still sells today. But Apple is an innovative company, and in 1985, the company pioneered the graphical user interface for personal computers with the introduction of the Macintosh computer. Today, Apple sells several different Macintosh models, usually at what seems to be a premium price. However, when compared with similar offerings from other manufacturers that provide GUIs and networking capabilities, the actual price is quite competitive. Unlike IBM, Apple Computer has no direct competitors. No computers are billed as Macintosh compatibles. To run Macintosh software and use circuit boards designed for Macintosh computers, you must purchase an Apple Macintosh.

Because of its graphical user interface, the Macintosh is excellent for graphics applications, such as desktop publishing. Also, as a high-performance business computer, the Macintosh is a fine choice for word processing, spreadsheet, database, and almost any other application that you can imagine.

You can purchase Apple computers from computer dealers, such as Connecting Point Computer Centers, The Computer Factory, and Nynex Business Centers. Apple warrants its products for one year and offers an extended warranty program called Apple Care. Service and support is provided by Apple dealers.

IBM Compatibles

Two categories of IBM compatibles are covered in this section: computers you can buy in retail stores that sell personal computers and computers that you can buy through mail order. IBM compatibles sold in retail stores are brands such as Acer, AST, ALR, Compaq, Epson, NEC, Tandy, and so on. Stores often sell their own brand. IBM compatibles sold through mail order are Dell, Gateway, Northgate, Swan, ZEOS, and so on. Some companies that originally sold through mail order, CompuAdd for example, now also sell through retail stores.

Because separating one IBM-compatible computer manufacturer from another is a difficult assignment, the following sections offer information to help you with this task. For each company, some background information is supplied to help you understand the company's goals, financial stability, and service policies. (Any IBM compatible that uses the ISA bus is referred to here as a standard-fare computer.)

Keep in mind that most companies whose products are sold through computer retail stores expect those dealers to provide service and support. Mail-order firms, on the other hand, handle service and support themselves and often do a very good job. (In the sections that follow, mail-order companies are grouped together after companies that sell through computer retail outlets.)

Acer

Acer America (San Jose, CA) manufactures standard-fare IBM-compatible computers. Acer maintains a low profile; you probably have to call the company to find a dealer in your area.

Acer computers come with a four-month on-site warranty, which can be extended to 12 months or two years for an extra charge, and a one-year parts and labor warranty. Acer does not provide telephone support; you must depend on the dealer or a certified service center for support. If a customer brings in a computer for repair, the dealer's service is followed up with a personal call from the company. An Acer computer is a fine choice that certainly deserves careful consideration.

ALR

ALR or Advanced Logic Research (Irvine, CA) specializes in fast, high-performance PCs and sells them for less than most competing brands. You can upgrade many ALR computers, which means that you can switch from an 80386 to 80486 CPU just by swapping a board. This feature enables you to purchase a computer for less money at the start and later upgrade its performance.

If you are considering a high-performance computer from ALR, make sure that you purchase it from an authorized dealer that provides proper technical support. Computers on the cutting edge of technology tend to have more problems than older, more proven technologies. Problems occur because the company may use new untried technology, and a greater chance exists for something to go wrong. If problems occur, you need to have a reliable way to have the computer quickly repaired.

ALR is one of the few companies that offer an 80286 computer that easily can be upgraded to an 80386SX and then to an 80486 computer. If you don't want to buy a low-end 8088 model but cannot afford an 80386SX, an ALR Power Flex is a good compromise.

You can buy an ALR computer through authorized dealers, such as Entre Computer Centers. ALR warrants its products for one year, and on-site service is available. Although ALR expects you to rely on a dealer for service and support, the company does provide a technical support number and a bulletin board on which you can find technical bulletins and other service updates.

Altec

Altec Technologies Corp. (Industry, CA) is one of several companies that sell their computer systems direct to the buyer. Making 80286-, 80386- and 80486- based computers, Altec is best known for the 386/25 computer system.

Altec offers several advantages. First, Altec offers the standard one-year parts and labor warranty; the first four months of the warranty is performed on-site. After the first four-months, however, you deal directly with Altec for warranty claims. Second, Altec offers a toll-free technical support number that you can call for help with your system. Finally, Altec manufactures its own video monitor. After warranty, you only have one company to call if you need your computer or video monitor serviced.

AST

AST Research (Irvine, CA) made its fame with a circuit board called the Sixpack that provided several expansion functions for the old IBM PC and XT computers. AST parlayed its success with this board into the manufacture of high-performance IBM-compatible personal computers. AST is an innovative company, with proprietary designs, such as the Cupid Architecture, that enable you to upgrade the CPU by swapping a board. Although priced lower than competing models from IBM and Compaq, AST still demands a premium price for its computers.

You can purchase AST computers through authorized dealers, such as Connecting Point Computer Centers. For customer support, AST uses authorized dealers, a nationwide network of authorized service centers, a 24-hour bulletin board system called AST On-Line!, and a toll-free technical support line. AST offers a one-year warranty on parts and service.

AT&T

AT&T (Morristown, NJ) is well known as a communications company, but it has not played a leading role in the hardware design of personal computers. Its first models actually were produced by a different company—Olivetti. These computers had slight incompatibilities with the IBM standard; they did not sell as well as models from IBM or some other makers of IBM compatibles, such as Compaq. Now AT&T makes its own standard-fare IBM compatibles. You may want to consider one of these models if the AT&T computer is priced competitively with other brands you are considering.

You can purchase AT&T computers through authorized dealers (call AT&T for a dealer in your area). AT&T depends on authorized dealers for service and support. It also has a "We Guarantee It" product satisfaction policy.

Austin

Austin Computer Systems (Austin, TX) is a mail-order company that sells high-performance IBM-compatible desktop and portable computers at competitive prices. All of Austin's 80386 and 80486 models include Microsoft Windows 3.0 and a Microsoft Mouse.

Austin offers toll-free technical support, a one-year warranty on parts and labor, and one year of free on-site service from GE. Consider a personal computer from Austin Computer Systems for a high-performance machine at an affordable price.

Compaq

Compaq Computer (Houston, TX) is one of the leaders of the personal computer industry. The company has accomplished firsts, such as building the first IBM-compatible portable computer and building the first personal computer with an 80386 CPU. Compaq also was a driving force behind the development of the EISA bus standard. Compaq specializes in high-performance desktop and portable computers that are well-designed and solidly built. Like IBM and some other major manufacturers, Compaq sells its computers at a premium price.

Compaq computers are sold through authorized dealers, such as The Computer Factory, ComputerLand, Nynex Business Centers, and Sears Business Centers. Compaq trains and certifies authorized dealers, who offer end users (customers) support and service. Be aware, however, that Compaq often uses nonstandard parts in its personal computers. If something breaks, therefore, you may have to replace parts with expensive Compaq parts.

Consider Compaq if you want a state-of-the-art desktop or portable personal computer and can afford the premium prices.

CompuAdd

CompuAdd (Austin, TX) is a mail-order company that also sells products through its CompuAdd Superstores. CompuAdd sells standard-fare IBM compatibles and portable computers at competitive prices. CompuAdd engineers and manufactures its personal computer systems.

CompuAdd has a toll-free technical support number that covers all the products it sells. Additionally, the company has a 900 service number that provides PC information, advice, and technical help for non-CompuAdd products (free for the first minute, two dollars per minute thereafter). The company also has a program called Direct Effect that enables you to call on a fax phone and immediately receive specification sheets on any CompuAdd product. CompuAdd products are backed with a no-risk, 30-day money-back guarantee. Products also have a one-year warranty for parts and labor. If you have a problem with a CompuAdd PC, you can ship it to the company's Austin Service Center or take the computer to one of the Superstores. If any problem occurs in the first 90 days, CompuAdd will ship you a replacement part within 48 hours. If you purchase a CompuAdd 325, 333, or 425 system, you get free on-site service during the one-year warranty period through Memorex/Telex.

Consider a CompuAdd computer if you want average performance at an affordable price. If there is a Superstore in your area, you can drop in and check out the system before you make a decision.

Dell

Dell Computer (Austin, TX) sells high-performance IBM-compatible desktop and portable computers primarily through mail order but also through value-added resellers. The company competes directly with other companies, such as Compaq computer, by manufacturing similar products at significantly lower prices. Dell operates its own factory and maintains its own research and development staff.

Dell offers a 30-day, no-questions-asked money-back guarantee, a one-year limited warranty on parts and labor, and toll-free technical support. It also offers one free year of next-day on-site service through Xerox.

Consider a Dell computer for high performance at a reasonable price and for the security of knowing that on-site service is available free of charge if you need it.

DTK

DTK Computer (City of Industry, CA), a subdivision of Datatech Enterprises of Taiwan, was an early supplier of IBM-compatible motherboards and other components. In 1989, DTK started selling a complete personal computer through distributors. DTK has chosen smaller distributors to carry its product and refers you to distributors if you have problems. These smaller distributors do not necessarily sell through dealers. You will find DTK computers for sale in places like copy centers or business centers.

If you have a problem, you can call DTK directly, but you pay for the phone call. DTK also runs a 24-hour bulletin board service. For repairs, you take the DTK back to the distributor, who usually sends the problem computer to California for repair. Although the number of DTK personal computers sold is small, many other compatibles currently on the market are actually DTK computers on the inside. Consider a DTK if the price is right but do not expect much in the way of service.

Epson

Epson America (Torrance, CA) is best known for its superb line of dot-matrix printers. Epson personal computers, however, had a hard time getting off the ground. For a few years, Epson tried to create its own unique computer—totally different from IBM, Apple, and other standards. Finally, Epson gave up and started making IBM compatibles.

Today, Epson trails only IBM, Apple, and Compaq in sales. Epson computers are inexpensive, reliable, and easy to repair. Although Epson does not normally try to compete on performance, some of its high-end models use the advanced EISA bus design, which provides very high performance. Epson also manufactures a line of portable computers.

Epson computers are sold through authorized dealers, such as ComputerLand, Entre Computer Centers, and MicroAge. Epson depends on dealers for technical support and service—the company offers no telephone support. Consider an Epson computer for average performance at a low price, if you are sure that the dealer can support the product as problems arise.

Everex

Everex Systems (Torrance, CA) started out designing IBM-compatible boards and parts for other companies. Several years ago, however, the company finally decided to build its own name brand recognition. Today, Everex is best known for its high-performance STEP line of IBM-compatible computers and its new Tempo line of low- and medium-performance computers.

You can find Everex computers in computer retail stores, but the company sells its products mostly to value-added resellers (a value-added reseller sells a complete hardware and software solution to a niche market, such as attorneys and doctors).

Everex encourages end users to use dealers or resellers for technical support and service. However, it does answer calls directly. Everex has a one-year warranty on parts and labor and uses on-site service to make repairs during the warranty period.

Although finding a supplier may be difficult, consider an Everex computer for a competitively priced product that delivers high performance.

Gateway 2000

Gateway 2000 (N. Sioux City, SD) is a mail-order company that sells standard-fare IBM-compatible computers at competitive prices. The company includes a free copy of Microsoft Windows with all 386 and 486 systems.

Gateway 2000 offers a 30-day money-back guarantee, a one-year warranty on parts and labor, free on-site service from TRW, and toll-free technical support. The company also maintains a bulletin board for technical support. If you return a Gateway 2000 PC to the company for repairs, labor is free. Consider a Gateway 2000 if you want average performance at an affordable price.

Hewlett-Packard

Hewlett-Packard (Cupertino, CA) is an engineering-driven company, which means that they take pride in manufacturing high-performance personal computers. Hewlett-Packard is one of those companies that spent much effort during the 1980s trying to build computers that were technically superior but not completely compatible with the IBM standard. Like most of the other companies who used this strategy, Hewlett-Packard failed. They did, however, produce a laser printer for IBM compatibles that made them number one in that segment of the market.

Hewlett-Packard makes very reliable personal computers, just like they make reliable laser and inkjet printers. Hewlett-Packard also uses innovative design techniques to improve the performance of its personal computer systems. For this reliability and innovation, you pay a premium price. If you are interested in a personal computer from Hewlett-Packard, you should consult a dealer who can explain the high-performance features of these computers to you.

You can purchase Hewlett-Packard computers through authorized dealers, such as ComputerLand and Microage. Hewlett-Packard relies on dealers for end-user service and support. Hewlett-Packard provides full training and certification to a dealer and even travels to the dealer to service a PC if needed.

Kaypro

Kaypro (Carlsbad, CA) was a force in the PC industry in the early eighties. Recently, however, the firm suffered financial reversals and finally filed Chapter 11 in April 1990. Kaypro sells standard-fare IBM compatibles. If you have an opportunity to purchase a Kaypro computer at a good price, make sure to check on the current status of the company before you buy.

Leading Edge

Leading Edge (Westborough, MA), more of a successful marketing company than a manufacturer, successfully sold IBM compatibles in the mid-1980s. Leading Edge entered Chapter 11 early in 1989. It now has merged with Daewoo, a huge Korean company. Leading Edge sells standard-fare IBM compatibles at very competitive prices.

You can purchase Leading Edge computers at computer retail stores (call the company for a retailer in your area). Leading Edge offers a 20-month warranty on its desktop models and certifies dealers so that they can support end users. Consider Leading Edge if you are interested in average performance at a good price.

NEC

NEC Technologies (Boxborough, MA), an affiliate of Japan-based NEC, made its first major impact in the personal computer market with its line of multiscan monitors and still remains a leader in this area today. NEC also attempted to become a leader in the notebook portable market with its NEC Ultralite but was not as successful as it was with monitors. Like several other large companies, NEC at first tried to buck the IBM standard by selling personal computers that were not completely compatible with IBM models. Now NEC's desktop models are standard-fare IBM compatibles that have a reputation for reliability.

NEC computers are sold through computer dealers such as The Computer Factory. NEC service while under warranty is excellent, but out-of-warranty service is expensive. Most warranty service and repair is done through the mail directly with NEC. Consider a NEC computer if you want average performance and good reliability at a competitive price.

Northgate

Northgate Computer Systems (Eden Prairie, MN) is a large mail-order company that sells IBM-compatible computers designed for above-average performance at affordable prices. Northgate manufactures its own computers and handles its own research and development.

Northgate offers a 60-day money-back guarantee, a one-year warranty on parts and labor, free on-site service for one year through Bell-Atlantic, and 24-hour 7-day toll-free technical support. If a part fails, Northgate ships you a new one overnight at the company's expense. For an additional charge, Northgate warrants the keyboard for an additional five years.

Consider a Northgate computer if you are interested in a computer with high performance at an affordable price and if you want to take advantage of Northgate's special support deals, such as the 5-year warranty on the keyboard and a technical support hotline that is available around the clock.

Packard Bell

Packard Bell (Chatsworth, CA) made radios in the 1920s and TV sets in the 1950s. Today, its old reputation for dependability is used to sell personal computers, although this Packard Bell is actually a different company. Packard Bell sells standard-fare IBM compatibles that compete on price with similar models from other companies.

Packard Bell computers are sold through computer retailers (call the company for a retailer in your area). Packard Bell offers a one-year warranty on parts and labor and four months of free on-site service. For technical support, Packard Bell supplies a toll-free voice-automated hotline. Consider a Packard Bell if you're interested in a PC with average performance and if the model you want is competitively priced.

PC Brand

PC Brand (Chicago, IL) is a mail-order company that sells standard-fare IBM-compatible computers at competitive prices. The company offers a five-year warranty for all systems that it sells, free on-site service through TRW for its 80386SX, 80386, and 80486 systems, toll-free technical support, and a 30-day money-back guarantee. Consider a PC Brand computer for average performance at a competitive price, plus a warranty period that is five times longer than warranties from most other companies.

Swan

Swan Technologies (State College, PA), formerly called Tussey, is a mail-order company that sells standard-fare IBM-compatible computers at competitive prices. Swan offers a 30-day money-back guarantee, one year of free on-site service from TRW (an independent computer service company) for all systems except for XT models, a 12-hour toll-free help line, and a bulletin board. Replacement parts under warranty are shipped overnight without charge. Consider a Swan computer if you want average performance at a competitive price.

Tandon

A well-known and well-respected name in the computer industry, Tandon (Moorpark, CA) offers computer systems based on the 80286, 80386, 80386SX, and 80486 CPUs. Tandon's claim to fame is its disk drives. Many of the original IBM PCs were delivered with disk drives made by Tandon. Tandon has accumulated many patents on disk drive technology since its first patent in 1975.

Tandon sells computers in different sizes and for different needs. Not only do they offer desktop PCs, but they also make notebook, laptop, and tower PCs.

Tandon sells their computers in one of three ways. First, you may contact them through their 800 line to purchase direct. Second, national sales representatives are stationed throughout the country to service large customers. Finally, Tandon systems are available through value-added resellers (VAR) and value-added distributors (VAD). When purchasing a system through a VAR or VAD, you normally get a complete system, including application software. VARs and VADs normally are contacted when you have specific needs.

Tandon's warranties are much like other manufacturers—one year parts and labor. However, Tandon does offer on-site service in certain areas during the warranty period or under extended warranty contracts. If you are not in a Tandon service area, then you must return your computer to a depot repair center, where the system will be repaired within 3 to 5 days.

Tandy

Tandy (Fort Worth, TX) sells its computers through a large chain of Radio Shack stores. Tandy was one of the first players in the personal computer market, with a PC called the TRS-80. However, Tandy did not compete successfully with IBM and Apple and finally dropped the TRS-80 line. Trying to become more of a mainstream computer manufacturer, Tandy made the same mistake as many other large companies by selling computers that were not completely compatible with the IBM standard. Today, most of Tandy's desktop and portable computers are compatible with the IBM standard.

Tandy is one of the few manufacturers that sell a Micro Channel Bus computer, but its line also includes standard-fare IBM compatibles. These computers usually are priced higher than models from competing manufacturers. However, Radio Shack stores often run sales that bring its prices more in line with the competition.

Tandy is wooing the home market with its RL-1000 personal computer. This computer comes with DeskMate software, a graphical user interface specific to Tandy computers. The RL-1000 is a typical Tandy offering—a computer that costs 30 to 40 percent more than its competitors. Although many of Tandy's lower end systems are higher priced than others, the Tandy Micro Channel computer makes an excellent lower cost alternative to a comparable IBM PS/2 computer. Keep in mind, however, that your local Radio Shack store may not carry the high-end models; these computers usually are found at a Radio Shack computer center.

Tandy offers a one-year warranty on parts and labor. If a computer needs repair, it can be returned to the store, which provides on-site repair, or sent to a Tandy service center. Tandy also has a technical support line, but it is not toll free.

Texas Instrument

Shortly after IBM introduced the personal computer, Texas Instrument (TI) released a personal computer. Although TI's computer system used MS-DOS, as did IBM's offering, TI's computer was not completely compatible with the IBM PC. The incompatibilities caused TI's initial personal computer to be relatively short lived.

Now, however, TI sells laptop and notebook computers, besides larger computer systems. The laptop and notebook computers from TI are widely accepted because they are IBM compatible.

You may purchase TI's computers through established dealers. Warranty repair also is provided through the dealer. Call TI's 800 line to find the dealer in your area.

Toshiba

Toshiba set standards for laptop personal computers. Toshiba offers a wide variety of laptop and notebook computers based on the 80C88, 80286, 80386SX, and 80386 computers. Even though the laptop computers offered by Toshiba are small, they are powerful, offering systems using only disk drives through computers that have hard disk drives with a capacity of 200M.

The Toshiba computers offer a very readable screen. Using LCD, Plasma, and color technologies, Toshiba offers computers that can meet any portable need. For the features, however, you pay a premium price compared with laptop computers manufactured by other companies.

Toshiba's computers are sold through retail dealers, such as ComputerLand, Sears Business Centers, and NYNEX. Service, including Toshiba's one-year warranty, also is provided through the dealer.

Wyse

Wyse Technology (San Jose, CA) was always better known for its terminals than it was for its personal computer products. Wyse traditionally has built standard-fare IBM compatibles that are attractively designed. The company was acquired in January 1990 by Channel International, a consortium of investors from Taiwan, and today, Wyse is undergoing a period of transition. At the time of this writing, the company was preparing to announce several new products and changes in the way it supports end users.

Wyse sells its products to distributors who sell to end users or to computer dealers. Wyse dealers, however, can be difficult to locate. Consider a Wyse if you can find a dealer in your area and if you are interested in attractively designed computers with average performance.

Zenith

Zenith Data Systems (Mt. Prospect, IL) is a subsidiary of the French company, Groupe Bull. Zenith made its name in the portable computer market in the late 1980s but also sells high-performance desktop models. Zenith's desktop 80386SX and 80386 models include Microsoft Windows and the Microsoft Mouse. Because Zenith doesn't compete on price, expect to pay more for its desktop models than you would for some competing brands. Zenith portables, on the other hand, offer excellent performance at competitive prices.

Zenith sells computers through authorized dealers (call the company for a dealer in your area). Zenith provides service and support through authorized dealers and offers a toll-free number and a bulletin board for technical support. Consider a Zenith desktop or portable system if you want a high-performance, brand-name personal computer.

ZEOS

ZEOS International (St. Paul, MN) is a large mail-order company that sells high-performance IBM compatibles at affordable prices. The company maintains a research and development staff and has its own manufacturing facilities. ZEOS treatment of many of the fine details enhance the quality of its products. For example, if you order a monochrome system, it comes with a genuine Hercules adapter, not a compatible adapter card. In some of its systems, ZEOS adds a second cooling fan to improve system reliability.

ZEOS backs its computers with a no-questions-asked 30-day money-back guarantee, a one-year warranty, and a 24-hour 7-days-a-week technical support line. The company also maintains the ZEOS bulletin board. Consider ZEOS if a high-performance computer at an affordable price interests you.

The Rest

Many more companies sell IBM-compatible computers than can be mentioned in this book. Some companies sell through dealers; others sell through mail order. All these companies sell basically the same kind of computers, with little technical twists here and there. Finding distinctions among them is hard but not impossible, if you ask companies to explain what sets their computers apart from the crowd. The differences are found mainly in technical features, service, support, price, and financing methods. You also may find differences in the competence of the sales and support staffs. No matter what company you consider, you must evaluate your selection based on the criteria that are important to you.

Commodore

Commodore Business Machines (West Chester, PA) has sold personal computers since the mid 1970s. Although the company sells several distinctly different types of computers, including IBM compatibles, its most innovative and powerful computers belong to the Amiga line.

The Amiga excels at animation and video manipulation, such as subtitles, fades, and so on. The Amiga was designed to output standard television type signals for use in a special effects video studio. The Amiga product line started with the 1000 model, which is no longer produced. Today, the Amiga line includes the 500, 2000, and 3000. The Amiga 500—the low-end product—is small with just one slot typically used for memory expansion or IBM XT emulation. The 2000 and 3000 have more expandability and more power.

Amiga is a computer that lends itself well to an emerging applications category called *multimedia*. Many different types of electronic equipment can be connected to personal computers: CD ROMs, video disc players, stereo amplifiers, and speakers. With the right software, you can integrate these different pieces of equipment to give multimedia presentations that include full-motion video and stereo sound. A personal computer like the Amiga 3000 enables you to implement multimedia for a far lower cost than you can with a

Macintosh or IBM computer. Commodore develops software as well as hardware, and one of its products—AmigaVision—is an icon-based authoring system that enables you to create interactive multimedia applications.

You can purchase an Amiga at authorized Amiga dealers (call Commodore for a dealer in your area). Commodore has established a 24-hour 800-number technical support line. If the technical support line cannot solve the problem, Commodore has you ship the computer via Federal Express to its headquarters and replaces or repairs the computer within 72 hours. Consider buying an Amiga if you are a video buff or if you want to connect several electronic components to the Amiga and use it for multimedia presentations.

Atari ST or Mega

Atari (Sunnyvale, CA) is best known for its video game machines of the late 1970s and early 1980s. Atari still sells game machines and a line of personal computers. However, Atari is more successful in selling its computers outside of the US, in countries like Germany. Eighty-two percent of Atari revenue is generated outside of North America.

There seems to be just one reason to purchase an Atari ST or Mega in this country: MIDI music. MIDI stands for Musical Instrument Digital Interface. An industry standard developed in 1982, MIDI, enables you to store music played on a keyboard or play previously recorded music through the computer. Musicians use the Atari computer to store background vocals on a hard disk for use during record production and live performances. The Madonna tour has done this. Ron Riddle of the Blue Oyster Cult has converted from an IBM PC to an Atari. The Beach Boys albums are currently produced on an Atari ST. The list goes on: Tony Banks of Genesis, Matt Clifford of Rolling Stones, and more. Schools that offer training to prepare for a career as a studio technician, sound engineer, recording engineer, or road technician sell Atari computers as part of the training.

Software packages for Atari are available in all the major categories, such as desktop publishing, databases, accounting, spreadsheets, and so on. The best software uses the GEM graphical user interface. Despite the business software, however, the number of games advertised for Atari computers in the U.S. outnumber all other software categories combined.

You can buy an Atari ST or Mega through authorized dealers, which include music stores (call Atari for a dealer in your area). Consider purchasing an Atari if you are into electronic music, want an inexpensive system, and don't care about IBM and Macintosh compatibility.

Reviewing Your Choices

By now you should have an idea of the kind of computer you intend to buy. If not, this short review should help you crystallize your ideas. First you need to settle on a manufacturer. You should choose one of the following: IBM, IBM compatible, Apple, Commodore, or Atari.

If you select an IBM or compatible computer maker, you need to decide what CPU and speed you want. The following list shows the choices available (at the time of this writing) for IBM and compatible computers:

CPU	Speed
8088	4.77, 8, 10 or 12 MHz
8086	10 or 12 MHz
80286	8, 10, 12.5, 16, or 20 MHz
80386SX	16 or 20 MHz
80386	16, 20, 25, or 33 MHz
80486	25 or 33 MHz

If you choose Apple, Commodore, or Atari, you need to select the CPU and speed you want but from a different CPU family. The following list shows what is available (at the time of this writing) for Apple, Commodore, and Atari computers.

Apple Macintosh

CPU	Speed
68000	8 or 16 MHz
68020	16 MHz
68030	20, 25, or 40 MHz

Commodore Amiga

CPU	Speed
68000	8 MHz
68030	16 or 25 MHz

Atari Mega or ST

CPU	Speed
68000	8 MHz

Keep in mind that the higher the CPU number and the faster the speed, the more expensive is the computer and the better the performance.

Selecting a Video Adapter

Another important consideration is the video adapter. This circuit board generates the computer's video signals. For some computers, a video adapter is built into the system board. This is true for IBM PS/2 and PS/1 computers, Atari ST and Mega, Commordore Amiga computers, and some Macintosh computers. All portable computers also come with a built-in video adapter. If you intend to purchase an IBM-compatible computer, you need to select the type of video adapter you want. The following list shows some of the choices:

Monochrome system

Hercules monochrome graphics adapter
Hercules compatible monochrome graphics adapter
Enhanced Graphics Adapter (EGA)
Video graphics array (VGA) adapter
Super VGA adapter

Color system

Color graphics adapter (CGA)
Enhanced graphics adapter (EGA)
Video graphics array (VGA) adapter
Super VGA adapter

Notice that an EGA, VGA, or Super VGA adapter can provide a monochrome and a color display. However, the VGA and Super VGA adapters require less setup between a monochrome and color monitor than does the EGA adapter.

Your choice of video adapter can affect your choice of a monitor. Certain adapters work only with certain monitors. One exception is a multiscan monitor. These monitors often work with all the IBM video standards. If you don't choose a multiscan monitor, you have the following choices:

Video adapter	*Video monitor*
Hercules monochrome graphics	Digital monochrome monitor
Hercules compatible monochrome graphics	Digital monochrome monitor
CGA	CGA Color monitor
EGA	EGA Color monitor/digital monochrome monitor
VGA	VGA Color or monochrome monitor
Super	VGASuper VGA Color or monochrome monitor

Of the Macintosh models available at this writing, only the IIfx lacks built-in video. The IIfx requires that you select a video card to meet your needs. Even Macintoshes with built-in video do not have just one video option. Macintoshes that support multiple video modes adapt to the resolution of the monitor that you attach to the computer. The following list outlines your Apple video options.

Monochrome

512 × 384 pixel resolution
640 × 480 pixel resolution
640 × 870 pixel resolution (portrait display)
1152 × 870 pixel resolution (two-page display)

Color

512 × 384 pixel resolution
640 × 480 pixel resolution

The Macintosh Classic and SE/30, with built-in 9-inch monitors, support only the 512 × 384 monochrome video mode. The LC, IIsi, and IIci support the 512 × 384 and 640 × 480 monochrome and color modes. In addition, the IIsi and IIci can support the 640 × 870 portrait display. The portrait display enables you to view an entire page—a nice feature for desktop publishing.

Apple also offers an 8/24-bit color adapter. You can use this adapter with any of the monitors listed previously. However, you get the most benefit from this video card with a portrait or a two-page display. A 24-bit adapter contains more memory than an 8-bit adapter, which enables the computer to show a larger array of colors and greater resolution.

Apple's 8/24-bit video adapter can be used in the IIfx, IIsi, and IIci.

Of course, Apple is not the only manufacturer of video adapters. Before you select a Macintosh, determine your needs and then choose the video card that best meets your requirements.

Deciding How Much Memory

The next issue to consider is memory, or RAM. Most computers come with a sufficient amount of RAM to get you started. After you use your computer for a while, you may find that you need more RAM—for example, if you are building a large spreadsheet and your computer informs you that you are out of memory. Make sure to ask, before you buy a computer, how to add RAM in case you want to do the job yourself.

Selecting a Hard Drive

To round out your computer system, you should consider a hard disk drive. In most cases, computer manufacturers offer a choice of sizes (from 20 megabytes to over 600 megabytes). Some IBM-compatible computer manufacturers also offer a choice of hard disk drive type. The following are the choices:

MFM (modified frequency modulation)
RLL (run-length limited)
IDE (integrated device electronics)
ESDI (enhanced small device interface)
SCSI (small computer systems interface)

ESDI and SCSI drives are high-performance drives, normally used with 80386 and 80486 computer systems. IDE drives are used in many IBM-compatible systems because of their excellent performance versus their affordable cost. SCSI drives are used with all Macintosh systems.

Selecting a Manufacturer

If you are interested in an IBM or compatible computer, you need to focus your attention on a particular CPU and speed as a starting point for comparison shopping. For example, its better to compare different manufacturer's 80386SX offerings than to compare one manufacturer's 80286 to another's 80386 model. For example, an IBM PS/2 Model 55SX should be compared with an AST 386SX Premium. After you compare, you can take into account the other factors described previously: video adapter, video monitor, RAM, and disk drives.

Finally, ask about the architecture, or design, of the computer: ISA, Micro Channel, EISA, or proprietary. The architecture of a personal computer can affect its overall performance. However, advanced architectures, such as Micro Channel and EISA, significantly increase the cost of a system.

After you narrow the selection to a few models, you are ready to consider several other factors. One factor is expandability. You can increase the functionality of your system by adding new circuit boards. If a system has one or two expansion slots, expandability is limited; you may not be able to add capabilities to your system, such as a fax or scanner, for example.

Another factor to consider is the documentation that ships with a system. Some manufacturers offer sparse documentation, and others offer well-written and thorough guides to help you to become proficient with your system. Finally, many manufacturers and dealers offer special deals. One company may bundle a top-quality software package, such as Lotus 1-2-3 Release 3.1, with a system. Another company may offer a rebate of several hundred dollars. These factors can sway your final purchase decision.

Selecting a Model

When you shop for a personal computer, not only do you need to compare models from different manufacturers, you also need to compare different models in a manufacturer's line. Because IBM and Apple personal computers are two of the top brands used in business, an examination of each firm's product lines can illuminate this comparison.

IBM Models

IBM no longer sells or produces its PC, XT, and AT computers. Today, the company markets two lines of computers: the PS/2 and PS/1.

The IBM PS/2 product line is divided neatly into two categories, according to the design of the internal bus: industry standard architecture (ISA) or Micro Channel architecture. PS/2 computers with an ISA bus are the Model 25, Model 30, and Model 30-286. The Model 25 differs from the 30 in terms of size and expandability (two expansion slots versus three expansion slots); the Model 30 differs from the 30-286 in terms of CPU (8086 versus 80286). The built-in video for these computers is called MCGA (or MultiColor Graphics Array), which can be considered an enhanced version of the CGA standard.

IBM's PS/2 computers that have a Micro Channel bus are the Model 50, Model 55SX, Model 60, Model 70, Model 80, Model 90, and Model 95. These models differ in CPU and speed, as well as other features. Some PS/2s are designed to sit on a desktop, and others are floor-standing (tower) models. Table 4.1 describes the features of the various IBM models.

**Table 4.1
IBM Personal Computer Product Line**

CPU	Bus	Video	Expansion slots		Style
Low-end models					
PS/1	80286	Proprietary	VGA	3	Desktop
PS/2 Model 25	8086	ISA	MCGA	2	Desktop
PS/2 Model 30	8086	ISA	MCGA	3	Desktop
PS/2 Model 30-286	80286	ISA	MCGA	3	Desktop
PS/2 Model 50	80286	Micro Channel	VGA	3	Desktop
PS/2 Model 60	80286	Micro Channel	VGA	7	Floor-Standing
Mid-range models					
PS/2 Model 55SX	80386SX	Micro Channel	VGA	3	Desktop
PS/2 Model 70	80386	Micro Channel	VGA	3	Desktop
PS/2 Model 80	80386	Micro Channel	VGA	7	Floor-standing
High-end models					
PS/2 Model 90	80486	Micro Channel	XGA	3	Desktop
PS/2 Model 95	80486	Micro Channel	XGA	6	Floor-standing
Portable model					
PS/2 Model P70	80386	Proprietary	VGA	0	Luggable

IBM's newest Micro Channel computers (as of this writing) are two PS/2 Models: 90 and 95. These computers use a 80486 CPU and incorporate a new graphics standard from IBM, called XGA. This standard offers higher resolution and more colors and works significantly faster than IBM's older graphics standard, VGA. (XGA also is available as an option for other Micro Channel computers.) The desktop PS/2 Model 90 and the floor-standing PS/2 Model 95 are worthy of your consideration, but be advised that the suggested retail prices of these computers top $12,000 and $14,000, respectively.

You probably are aware that IBM also sells a computer targeted for the home user, called the PS/1. IBM attempted to make the PS/1 as easy as possible to use by providing a mouse and a graphical user interface that divides the screen into four quadrants. Clicking on a quadrant connects you to an on-line service such as Prodigy, loads Microsoft Works (software included with the system), starts IBM DOS, or launches any of your own software. IBM also provides a toll-free technical support line. IBM sought to take advantage of the connectability of personal computers by building a modem into the PS/1.

Besides Prodigy, PS/1 owners can connect to other on-line services, such as the PS/1 Users Club and an education and entertainment service called Promenade. Although these features seem like a boon to the novice, the computer uses several nonstandard features, such as proprietary expansion slots and a power supply housed in the monitor. In addition to these variations, the price may cause you to stop and think before you buy a PS/1. If you are seriously interested in a personal computer that gives you the most for your money, you are better off choosing another IBM or a model from a competing manufacturer.

IBM-Compatible Models

IBM-compatible computers share many features: they use the Intel (or compatible) family of CPUs—8088 through 80486; most of the desktop models use the ISA bus (any IBM compatible that uses the ISA bus is referred to here as a standard-fare computer); and some high-performance 80386 and 80486 models use the EISA or the Micro Channel bus. System units come in various styles: standard desktop, low-profile desktop, and floor-standing (often called tower) models.

When you shop for a computer, look at the model name. The name often gives a clue to the computer's performance. For example, a Compaq DeskPro 386/33 computer is a desktop computer with an 80386 CPU that runs at a speed of 33 MHz. For more information on IBM compatibles, read the preceding section that discusses different manufacturers.

Macintosh Models

If you plan to purchase an Apple Macintosh computer, you should know about the features that distinguish one Macintosh from another. Apple sells three Macintosh models that come with built-in monochrome displays: the Macintosh Classic, the Macintosh SE/30, and the Macintosh Portable. (The first two are an all-in-one design reminiscent of the original Macintosh). The remaining Macintosh models are built around a separate system unit and use a separate monitor that connects to the unit: Macintosh LC, IIsi, IIci, and IIfx.

The low end of the line is the Classic, which uses a 68000 CPU, and the high end of the line is the IIfx, which uses a very fast 68030 CPU. The LC, IIsi, and

IIci have built-in color circuits. Of all the current Macintosh models, only the IIci and IIfx have more than one expansion slot. These computers also have an advanced bus design, called NuBus. The availability of a NuBus expansion slot is an important consideration, if you plan to add more functionality to the computer. (Most add-in circuit boards are designed to work with the NuBus.)

When you consider the Macintosh line of computers, you should weigh cost against other factors, such as speed, power, and expandability. Table 4.2 indicates the features of the various Macintosh models.

Table 4.2
Apple Macintosh Product Line Features

	CPU	Bus	Video	Expansion slots	Style
Low-end models					
Macintosh Classic	68000	Proprietary	Monochrome	0	Desktop*
Macintosh LC	68020	Proprietary	8-bit color	1	Desktop
Mid-range models					
Macintosh SE/30	68030	Proprietary	Monochrome	1	Desktop*
Macintosh IIsi	68030	NuBus	8-bit color	1	Desktop
High-end models					
Macintosh IIci	68030	NuBus	8-bit color	3	Desktop
Macintosh IIfx	68030	6 NuBus slots 1 DOS slot	None	7	Desktop
Portable model					
Macintosh Portable	68000	Proprietary	Monochrome LCD	1	Luggable

Chapter Summary

This chapter reviewed the rationale for purchasing a personal computer from one particular manufacturer versus another. The chapter gave you some criteria to help you decide on a manufacturer: software availability, ease of use, compatibility, performance, and price. The chapter presented short profiles of a selection of personal computer companies. The personal computer systems and service and support policies of each company were described. Finally, the chapter included a review of what was presented in the book so far and added some specifics for the IBM and Apple product lines that you can use as a basis for comparison among manufacturers. Hopefully, this chapter gave you sufficient insight to help you decide whether you want an IBM, Apple, IBM-compatible, Commodore, or Atari computer.

In the Next Chapter

You have some ideas about the personal computer you want, and you know which company, or group of companies, you are considering. The next chapter recommends various models and prices for particular applications. Chapter 5 also describes portable computers and the differences you find among the various styles. Finally, Chapter 5 makes suggestions about purchasing a used computer.

5

What Computer Model Do I Want?

Regardless of the computer manufacturer you select, you need to choose among the different models the company offers. This chapter helps you decide which model is appropriate for running specific software applications, such as word processors, spreadsheets, databases, graphics, and electronic communications. Chapter 5 also shows you which model to choose if you want a flexible computer to run different applications.

Personal computers usually are pictured as desktop machines, but they come in all shapes and sizes. This chapter shows you how luggables, laptops, and notebook computers may fit your computing plans. This chapter also explains how to purchase a used computer. Buying a second-hand computer may save you money if you know where to find the right equipment at the right price.

Selecting a Model Based on an Application

If you are purchasing a computer to run a single application, selecting a specific model is fairly easy. The following sections give you specific recommendations based on a particular piece of software.

Before any recommendations are given, however, you should know why certain models are not recommended at all. IBM and compatible computers that use the 80286 CPU are not recommended because companies are pushing 80386SX computers, instead. The main reason for exclusion is that computers with this CPU are more expensive than computers with 8088 or 8086 CPUs but cannot run many of the newer software programs.

Computer models that come without a hard disk are not recommended, except for some laptop models. A hard disk may add $200 or more to the cost of a PC but is absolutely worth the extra expense. A hard disk adds a great deal of storage capacity to the system and significantly improves the speed of such disk operations as saving and retrieving files.

For IBM and compatible computers, color systems using CGA or EGA are not recommended, because VGA is the current standard. A VGA adapter and monitor may add $150 or more to the cost of a color system. The system is worth the money, however, because VGA produces sharp, clear text and many more colors than CGA or EGA.

The prices given are advertised prices—not suggested retail. The prices were gleaned from local newspapers and computer magazines and usually rounded to the nearest $10, $50, or $100, depending on the price of the item. Keep in mind that the cost of computer equipment varies from place to place and store to store, and the price of computer equipment usually decreases with time.

The recommendations for particular computer models, printers, and software products are merely examples of the equipment and software worth considering. The products you actually choose should be compared within the recommended class of product.

Word Processing

Word processing can be simple or sophisticated, depending on the program's features and whether you want to use them. If you want to do simple word processing—typing your work on a PC, saving it on disk, and printing it out—any computer model from any manufacturer will do. You will not notice how slowly the computer operates, unless you perform such tasks as replacing one word with another word each time it occurs in a long document.

A more sophisticated word processor may include such features as a spelling checker, an electronic thesaurus, and picture-integration capability in a document. If you require these features, you need a more expensive system.

A word processing program also needs more computing power if you want to display a variety of fonts on-screen. Less computing power is required for IBM and compatible computers that work in text mode, which does not show different fonts, than in a graphics mode, which does.

Low-End Word Processing

The following are recommended as simple word processing systems:

IBM-Compatible Computer

8088 XT computer, such as Epson Equity I+
   640K of RAM
   5 1/4-inch, 360K floppy disk drive
   Monochrome monitor
   Hercules-compatible video adapter
	$ 350

20M hard disk drive	$ 200
9-pin dot-matrix printer, such as Epson LX-810	$ 150
Word processing software, such as Professional Write 2.2	$ 165
Total cost	$ 865

This configuration uses the least expensive IBM-compatible components available and a respectable word processor. This system is appropriate for the home or for a small office, if you substitute a 24-pin dot-matrix printer, such as the Epson LQ-510, which sells for about $250.

Apple Macintosh Computer

8 MHz 68000 Macintosh Classic
   2M of RAM
   3 1/2-inch, 1.44M floppy disk drive
   Monochrome monitor with built-in video
   40M hard disk drive
	$1,400

9-pin dot-matrix printer, such as Apple ImageWriter II	$ 470
Word processing software, such as WriteNow 2.2	$ 120
Total cost	$1,990

This configuration uses the least expensive Macintosh components and a respectable word processor. This system is appropriate for the home or a small office.

High-End Word Processing

The following are recommended as sophisticated word processing systems:

IBM-Compatible Computer

16 MHz 80386SX computer, such as Epson Equity 386-SX	$1,250
1M of RAM	
3 1/2-inch, 1.44M floppy disk drive	
VGA monochrome monitor and VGA video adapter	
40M hard disk drive	
24-pin dot-matrix printer, such as Epson LQ-1050	$ 600
Word processing software, such as WordPerfect 5.1	$ 250
Total cost	$2,110

This configuration uses a more powerful IBM-compatible computer, a more durable printer, and a superior word processor. This system is appropriate for a small business that relies on word processing.

IBM Computer

16 MHz 80386SX PS/2 Model 55SX	$3,000
1M of RAM	
3 1/2-inch floppy disk drive	
VGA color monitor with built-in VGA video	
60M hard disk drive	
Laser printer, such as Hewlett-Packard LaserJet IIP	$1,000
Word processing software, such as WordPerfect 5.1	$ 250
Total cost	$4,250

This configuration uses brand-name computer and printer components and a superior word processor. This system is appropriate for small- or medium-size businesses that need crisp-looking correspondence and don't mind spending the extra money for upkeep that a laser printer demands.

Apple Macintosh Computer

16 MHz 68030 Macintosh SE/30	$3,000
2M of RAM	
3 1/2-inch, 1.44M floppy disk drive	
Monochrome monitor with built-in video	
80M hard disk drive	
Keyboard	$ 150
Laser printer, such as GCC Technologies PLP II	$ 1,400
Word processing software, such as Microsoft Word 4.0	$ 250
Total cost	$4,800

This configuration uses a more powerful computer system than the low-cost Macintosh version and uses a laser printer and a sophisticated word processor. This system is appropriate for small- or medium-size businesses that want the quality and can afford the cost.

Spreadsheets

Spreadsheets also can be simple or sophisticated, depending on the features the program offers and whether you take advantage of them. If you want to create a simple spreadsheet by entering numbers for small budgets, saving it on disk, and printing it, any computer model from any manufacturer will do. You will not notice how slowly the computer operates, unless you build larger spreadsheets with many formulas and links to other spreadsheets. A spreadsheet program with high-quality output that integrates text, graphs, and pictures requires more computing power.

Spreadsheet programs usually store all the data and formulas you enter in RAM. If you enter too many numbers and formulas, you see a message that says you are out of memory. If you intend to create large complex spreadsheets, you need a fast computer with a great deal of memory.

Low-End Spreadsheets

The following are recommended as simple spreadsheet systems:

IBM-Compatible Computer

8088 XT computer, such as Epson Equity I+
    640K of RAM
    5 1/4-inch, 360K floppy disk drive
    Monochrome monitor
    Hercules-compatible video adapter
	$350

20M hard disk drive	$200
9-pin dot-matrix printer, such as Epson LX-810	$150
Spreadsheet software, such as Quattro	$100
Total cost	$800

This configuration uses the least expensive IBM-compatible components and a basic spreadsheet program. This system is a low-budget one, appropriate for the home or a small office. You can substitute a wide-carriage printer, if necessary to print wide spreadsheets. If you discover after using Quattro for a while that you would like a more powerful product, you can purchase the more powerful Quattro Pro ($350), which runs fairly well on this system.

Apple Macintosh Computer

8 MHz 68000 Macintosh Classic
    2M of RAM
    3 1/2-inch, 1.44M floppy disk drive
    Monochrome monitor with built-in video
    40M hard disk drive
	$1,400

9-pin dot-matrix printer, such as Apple ImageWriter II	$ 470
Spreadsheet software, such as Excel 2.2	$ 250
Total cost	$2,120

This configuration uses the least expensive Macintosh components and a quality spreadsheet. This system is appropriate for the home or a small office where expenses must be kept to a minimum.

High-End Spreadsheets

The following are recommended as sophisticated spreadsheet systems:

IBM-Compatible Computer

16 MHz 80386SX computer, such as Epson Equity 386-SX
    4M of RAM
    3 1/2-inch, 1.44M floppy disk drive
    VGA color monitor and VGA video adapter
    80M hard disk drive
	$2,050

24-pin wide-carriage printer, such as Epson LQ-1050	$ 600
Spreadsheet software, such as Lotus 1-2-3 Release 3.1	$ 450
Total cost	$3,100

This configuration uses a more powerful IBM-compatible computer with additional memory to run large spreadsheets and a larger hard disk for ample storage capacity. The printer is of higher quality than the lower-cost system and has a wide carriage. The spreadsheet software uses a DOS extender, which uses all the memory in the system. The software also has advanced spreadsheet-publishing features. To take advantage of these features, substitute a laser printer, such as the Hewlett-Packard LaserJet III, for the 24-pin printer. This system is appropriate for a small business.

IBM Computer

16 MHz 80386SX PS/2 Model 55SX	$3,400
4M of RAM	
3 1/2-inch floppy disk drive	
VGA color monitor with built-in VGA video	
60M hard disk drive	
24-pin wide-carriage printer, such as Epson LQ-1050	$ 600
Spreadsheet software, such as Lotus 1-2-3 Release 3.1	$ 450
Total cost	$4,450

This configuration uses brand-name computer and printer components and a superior spreadsheet program. This system is appropriate for small- or medium-size businesses, who want quality products and can afford the cost.

Apple Macintosh Computer

20 MHz 68030 Macintosh IIsi	$4,000
5M of RAM	
3 1/2-inch, 1.44M floppy disk drive	
80M hard disk drive	
Keyboard	$ 150
Multiscanning monitor, such as the 14-inch Sony 1304 HG	$ 800
24-pin wide carriage printer, such as Epson LQ-2550	$1,000
Spreadsheet software, such as Microsoft Excel 2.2	$ 250
Total cost	$6,200

This configuration uses a color Macintosh model, which enables you to run spreadsheet software in color rather than black-and-white. The system has more memory and a larger hard disk than the low-cost system and includes a laser printer. This system is appropriate for small- or medium-size businesses that can afford the cost.

Databases

Like word processors and spreadsheets, your database needs can be modest or more demanding. For such modest needs as tracking a few thousand names for a mailing list or a few hundred items from a baseball-card collection, any low-end PC can do the job.

If you want to develop a more sophisticated database and possibly incorporate pictures into the database, you need a more powerful system with a large-capacity, fast hard disk. A database program continually searches a hard disk for database records; a hard disk with a fast access time gets the job done faster.

Low-End Databases

The following are recommended as simple database systems:

IBM-Compatible Computer

8088 XT computer, such as Epson Equity I+
  640K of RAM
  5 25-inch, 360K floppy disk drive
  Monochrome monitor and Hercules-compatible
    video adapter
	$ 350

20M hard disk drive	$ 200
9-pin dot-matrix printer, such as Epson LX-810	$ 150
Database software, such as PC-File 5.0	$ 80
Total cost	$ 780

This configuration uses the least expensive IBM-compatible components available and a respectable database. This system is appropriate for the home or a small office. You may want to substitute a 24-pin dot-matrix printer, such as the Epson LQ-510, which sells for about $250, if you plan to print wide reports.

Apple Macintosh Computer

8 MHz 68000 Macintosh Classic
  2M of RAM
  3 1/2-inch, 1.44M floppy disk drive
  Monochrome monitor with built-in video
  40M hard disk drive
	$1,400

9-pin dot-matrix printer, such as Apple ImageWriter II	$ 470
Database software, such as FileMaker Pro	$ 220
Total cost	$2,090

This configuration uses the least expensive Macintosh components and a respectable database. This system is appropriate for the home or a small office, when expenses must be kept to a minimum.

High-End Databases

The following are recommended as sophisticated database systems:

IBM-Compatible Computer

16 MHz 80386SX computer, such as Epson Equity 386-SX
   1M of RAM
   3 1/2-inch, 1.44M floppy disk drive
   VGA monochrome monitor and VGA video adapter
   80M hard disk drive
	$1,550

9-pin wide-carriage printer, such as Epson FX-1050	$ 410
Database software, such as dBase IV 1.1	$ 500
Total cost	$2,460

This configuration uses a more powerful IBM-compatible computer, a high-capacity hard disk, a wide-carriage printer, and a superior database program. This system is appropriate for a small business. If you plan to integrate pictures into the database, substitute a VGA or a multiscanning color monitor.

IBM Computer

16 MHz 80386SX PS/2 Model 55SX
   1M of RAM
   3 1/2-inch floppy disk drive
   VGA color monitor with built-in VGA video
   60M hard disk drive
	$3,000

9-pin wide-carriage printer, such as Epson FX-1050	$ 410
Database software, such as dBase IV 1.1	$ 500
Total cost	$3,910

This configuration uses brand-name computer and printer components and a superior database program. This system is appropriate for small- to medium-size businesses.

Apple Macintosh Computer

16 MHz SE/30 68030 Computer
   5M of RAM
   3 1/2-inch, 1.44M floppy disk drive
   Monochrome monitor with built-in video
   105M hard disk drive
	$3,600

Keyboard	$ 150
24-pin wide-carriage printer, such as Epson LQ-2550	$1,000
Database software, such as 4th Dimension V2.01	$ 475
Total cost	$5,625

This configuration includes the SE/30 computer (a more powerful model than the Macintosh Classic), a high-capacity hard disk, a laser printer, and a sophisticated database program. This system is appropriate for small- to medium-size businesses that can afford the cost. If you need color, you can upgrade with a color adapter board and a color monitor.

Graphics

Graphics programs, such as paint, drawing, presentation, and computer-aided design (CAD) programs, demand a great deal of computing power. For this reason, you should not purchase a low-end system to run a graphics program. To run paint and presentation programs, a mid-range computer is sufficient.

To run drawing and CAD programs, a top-of-the-line PC is the best choice, because these programs often perform complex drawing functions, such as rotation and redrawing. You may be dismayed by the cost of these high-end systems. If these prices are not within your budget, or your company's budget, you can run these programs on a less powerful computer, but you pay a penalty each time that you wait for the computer to complete a task. Additional hardware, such as a graphics coprocessor board, sometimes can expedite drawing or CAD programs, but coprocessors are expensive, too.

The following are recommended as systems for running paint and presentation software:

IBM-Compatible Computer

16 MHz 80386SX computer, such as Epson Equity 386-SX
    1M of RAM
    3 1/2-inch, 1.44M floppy disk drive
    VGA color monitor and VGA video adapter
    80M hard disk drive
	$1,750

Color inkjet printer, such as Hewlett-Packard PaintJet	$1,000
Paint software, such as PC Paintbrush IV Plus	$ 125
or	
Presentation software, such as Freelance Plus 3.01	$ 350
Total cost	$2,875/$3,100

This system gives you enough computing power and hard-disk capacity to run paint or presentation programs. This configuration is suitable for a small business, and you may save approximately $450 on this system by substituting a 24-pin dot-matrix printer with color capability. A similar system that uses an IBM 55SX computer costs approximately $1,300 more.

Apple Macintosh Computer

16 MHz LC 68020 Computer	$2,700
2M of RAM	
3 1/2-inch, 1.44M floppy disk drive	
40M hard disk drive	
12-inch RGB Display	
Color inkjet printer, such as Hewlett-Packard PaintWriter	$1,000
Paint software, such as Pixel Paint Professional	$ 400
or	
Presentation software, such as Microsoft PowerPoint	$ 250
Total cost	$3,950/$4,100

This configuration is the least expensive Macintosh color system and is suitable for a small business. You may save approximately $500 by substituting the Apple ImageWriter II printer, which has color capability.

The most complex systems for running draw and CAD software may cost more than $10,000 and sometimes more than $20,000, particularly if you use very high-resolution graphics adapters, large screen monitors, and thermal color printers. If you are considering a purchase of this kind, you should ask an experienced person to assist you. If you are interested in a more reasonably priced system, you may want to consider one of the software packages listed or a system similar to those recommended for paint and presentation software.

The following are recommended as drawing and CAD software:

IBM-Compatible Computer

Drawing software, such as Corel Draw,	$ 350
which runs under Microsoft Windows 3.0	$ 100
CAD software, such as Generic CADD 5.0	$ 250

Apple Macintosh Computer

Drawing software, such as Adobe Illustrator 88	$ 275
CAD software, such as Generic CADD level 3	$ 325

Electronic Communications

Electronic communication depends on the modem you use, not on the kind of computer. If you want to connect to an on-line service, such as CompuServe or Prodigy, you need only a low-end computer (such as those recommended for low-end word processing), communications software, and a standard modem.

The following are recommended for simple electronic communication:

2400-baud modem	$ 100
Communications software, such as CompuServe Navigator	$ 50
or	
Communications software, such as ProComm Plus 1.1	$ 70

ProComm is a more general communications program than CompuServe Navigator. A low-cost modem sometimes includes communications software.

If you are interested in high-speed communication, you need a high-speed modem and such special features as data compression and data correction. The computer you use is not of paramount concern.

The following is recommended for high-speed electronic communication:

9600-baud modem, such as Intel 9600EX MNP	$600

If you want to perform special communications tricks, such as controlling one computer with another by telephone, you can use any modem; you simply need the proper software.

The following is recommended for for telephone communication:

Remote-control software, such as PC Anywhere III	$60

Desktop Publishing

Desktop publishing software demands a high level of computing and printing power. You need a superior PC and a powerful laser printer, and this combination may be very costly. Desktop publishing products are in high demand by computer users; therefore, software companies have responded with products that work with inexpensive computers and printers. The finished product, which often is a newsletter, suffers from a lack of quality but seems to satisfy the demand in this market.

The recommendations given here reflect the diversity of the desktop publishing market. If you want professional desktop publishing, don't consider a low-end system. Apple Macintosh computers are better suited for desktop publishing than IBM and compatible computers, even when both systems run the same software. Aldus, for example, makes a version of PageMaker for the Macintosh and for IBM and compatible computers.

Low-End Desktop Publishing

An inexpensive desktop publishing system for IBM-compatible and Apple Macintosh computers can be identical to the system for word processing—with different software, of course.

The following are recommended for desktop publishing software:

IBM-Compatible Computer

Low-cost desktop Computer publishing software, such as PFS: First Publisher 3.0	$ 100

Apple Macintosh Comptuer

Low-cost desktop Computer publishing software, such as Publish-It!	$ 225

High-End Desktop Publishing

For professional desktop publishing, you need a system as powerful as the following:

Apple Macintosh Computer

16 MHz SE/30 68030 Computer
    5M of RAM
    3 1/2-inch, 1.44M floppy disk drive
    Monochrome monitor with built-in video
    105M hard disk drive
	$3,600

Keyboard	$ 150
PostScript laser printer, such as Texas Instruments microLaser with 4.5M of RAM	$2,500
Additional full-page monochrome monitor and adapter, such as the 15-inch Sigma Designs PageView	$1,050
Desktop publishing software, such as PageMaker 4.0	$ 500
Word processing software, such as Microsoft Word 4.0	$ 250
Drawing software, such as Adobe Illustrator 88	$ 275
Total cost	$8,325

High-quality desktop publishing programs usually retrieve text from a word processor and images from a drawing program. These requirements add to the cost of the total package. For professional desktop publishing, you also need a full-page display monitor and a PostScript laser printer (see Chapter 6).

An alternative for IBM and compatible computers is to use a high-end word processor, such as WordPerfect 5.1, for desktop publishing. The system configuration is the same as those listed in the word processing section, except for the printer; a laser printer is the best choice for desktop publishing.

The following is the configuration for a word processing system to be used for desktop publishing:

IBM and Compatibles

16 MHz 80386SX computer, such as Epson Equity 386-SX
    1M of RAM
    3 1/2-inch, 1.44 M floppy disk drive
    VGA monochrome monitor and VGA video adapter
40M hard disk drive
	$1,250

Word processing software, such as WordPerfect 5.1	$ 250
Laser printer, such as the Hewlett-Packard LaserJet III	$1,600
Total cost	$3,100

Education

Educational software usually is designed to work with low-end computers. For IBM and compatible computers, plan to buy a VGA color system, because most programs use color. This caveat is not true for the Macintosh; educational software works well with the monochrome Macintosh Classic.

The following are recommended as low-cost systems to run educational software:

IBM-Compatible Computer

10 MHz 8088 XT computer, such as Leading Edge D-86
    640K of RAM
    3 1/2-inch, 720K floppy disk drive
    VGA adapter
	$ 350

20M hard disk drive	$ 200
VGA monitor	$ 300
9-pin dot-matrix printer, such as Epson LX-810	$ 150
Educational software: four titles at $40 each	$ 160
Total cost	$1,160

This configuration uses an inexpensive IBM-compatible computer with a VGA color adapter and color monitor. This system is appropriate for the home and can be used for applications other than education.

Apple Macintosh Computer

8 MHz 68000 Macintosh Classic
    2M of RAM
    3 1/2-inch, 1.44M floppy disk drive
	$1,400

Monochrome monitor with built-in video
40M hard disk drive
9-pin dot-matrix printer, such as Apple ImageWriter II $ 230
Educational software: four titles at $40 each $ 160

Total cost $2,030

This configuration uses the most inexpensive Macintosh components, is appropriate for the home, and can be used for applications other than education.

Accounting

Accounting programs for businesses are often specialized databases. Although some businesses use off-the-shelf accounting packages, many design their own accounting systems with database software. Accounting programs cost from $100 to several thousand dollars, depending on the needs of the business. See the database section for information on purchasing a PC system for accounting.

Building a General-Purpose PC

Many people have a specific application in mind when they shop for a personal computer, but a PC is very flexible. If you think you may use a system for a variety of applications, consider building a general-purpose computer. The term *building* does not mean putting together a computer kit or even buying all the parts separately and putting them together yourself. In this case, building means selecting components that are useful for a variety of applications—not just one. The general-purpose configurations in the following sections are for IBM, IBM-compatible, Macintosh, and Amiga computers.

IBM General-Purpose Computer

Unless you need more power for a particular application, the best IBM model is currently the IBM PS/2 55SX. This computer is reasonably priced and appropriate for today's software and for future applications. The IBM PS/2 55SX features built-in VGA color circuitry and a high-performance hard disk drive, which are the two primary features needed for general-purpose computing. The 55SX can run Windows 3.0 and, when equipped with sufficient memory, can even run OS/2 2.0.

The following is the configuration for the general-purpose IBM model:

IBM Computer

16 MHz 80386SX PS/2 Model 55SX	$2,700
1M of RAM	
3 1/2-inch, 1.44M floppy disk drive	
Built-in VGA video	
60M hard disk drive	
VGA or Multiscan monitor	$ 500
Mouse	$ 100
Total cost	$3,910
Same system with 5M of RAM	$4,500

IBM-Compatible General-Purpose Computer

IBM-compatible computers come in many different configurations. If you are interested in purchasing one of these computers, go to a computer store or call a computer mail-order company, armed with a list of specifications. Most parts for IBM-compatible computers are interchangeable therefore, you should get exactly what you want. If the company cannot give you what you want, shop somewhere else.

The following is the configuration for the general-purpose IBM-compatible computer:

IBM-Compatible Computer

20 MHz 80386SX Computer	$1,300
2M of RAM	
3 1/2-inch, 1.44M floppy drive	
80M IDE hard disk with IDE adapter	$ 680
Super VGA Adapter	$ 300
14-inch multiscan color monitor	$ 500
Mouse	$ 100
Total cost	$2,880
Same system with 6M of RAM	$3,280

This system gives you a good blend of CPU speed, hard disk speed and capacity, and high-resolution color graphics. Whether you want to run software under MS-DOS, Windows 3.0, or OS/2 2.0, you can do it with this system.

Macintosh General-Purpose Computer

If you want to use the Macintosh as a general-purpose computer, your best bet is one of the Macintosh II computers that features color support and NuBus expandability.

The following is the configuration for the general-purpose Macintosh model:

Apple Macintosh Computer

Macintosh IIci	$5,050
5M of RAM	
3 51/2 inch, 1.44M floppy disk drive	
Built-in 8-bit color	
Mouse	
101-key keyboard	$ 150
14-inch multiscan color monitor	$ 500
105M SCSI hard disk drive	$ 830
Total cost	$6,530

Buying a Portable Computer

Buying a portable computer is much like buying a desktop model. You need to consider the CPU, memory, floppy disks, hard disks, and video display. A portable computer, however, differs from a desktop model in four significant ways.

The first difference is size. Portables can be as large as a piece of luggage or as small as a notebook. Portable computer sizes generally are categorized as luggable, laptop, and notebook. These sizes are described in more detail in the sections that follow.

A second difference is the video display. Most portables do not use the common picture tube found in video monitors. Instead, they use a flat-panel, monochrome display. Flat-panel, color displays are available but are very expensive, currently adding about $5,000 to the cost of a system.

The third difference is that many portables have an integrated keyboard. The keyboard usually is much smaller than those used with desktop computers.

One final difference is the type of power. Some portables use AC power exclusively, some use battery power exclusively, and some can use both energy sources.

You should decide first on the size of the portable you want. Then carefully examine the display. Some displays are hard to read, particularly if room lighting is not perfect. More information about displays is given in the following sections.

Try out the keyboard next. Manufacturers of portable computers make tradeoffs in keyboard size to keep the machine small. Some applications, such as WordPerfect 5.1, use function keys extensively, and some portables do not have a separate row of function keys on the keyboard. You must decide what you need in a portable keyboard.

If the size of the portable, the video display, the keyboard, and the power (AC or battery) are all satisfactory, then ask about CPU, RAM, disk drives, and other features you need.

Luggables

Portable computers that can be carried around, but not that easily, are called luggables. Luggables come in several shapes. One is the lunch box shape (see fig. 5.1). This kind of portable weighs approximately 20 pounds. The lunch box comes in two different styles, and the key difference is the display flexibility. One type enables you to tilt the display; the other enables you to move the display up and over the top of the case. See figure 5.2 for a comparison of the two types. One style is not better than the other; it's purely a matter of preference.

Fig. 5.1. A lunch-box type, luggable portable computer.

Another luggable has the shape of a laptop but is bigger and better suited for a desk than a lap. Figure 5.3 shows a size comparison between this kind of luggable and a laptop computer. These luggables usually are 14 to18 pounds, depending on features.

Fig. 5.2. The two different lunch box styles with two different video displays. The video display on the left can be raised up.

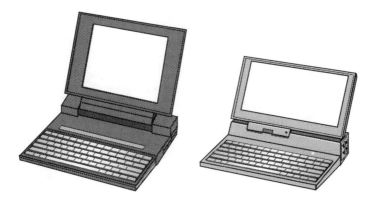

Fig. 5.3. Some luggables have the same shape as laptop portables but are significantly larger.

Luggables are useful when you want to make presentations at remote locations because they often are as powerful as desktop computers. You can prepare a presentation at the office and take it with you.

If you are considering a luggable, choose one that has a CPU as powerful as a 16 MHz 80386SX, a hard disk of 40M or larger, and a VGA-compatible display. The most readable displays on these computers are the DC plasma yellow-and-black and gas plasma reddish-orange and black displays. The choice between the two is your preference.

Unlike the smaller portables, luggables have keybards that are much like desktop models. Luggables can work from AC power or battery power, but battery power lasts only a couple of hours.

Luggables are costly, especially such brand names as Compaq and Toshiba. The Toshiba Model 3100SX, for example, costs approximately $4,000. You may purchase alternative luggables, however, from some mail-order manufacturers, who charge approximately $1,000 less.

If you are interested in a luggable Macintosh, Apple offers the Macintosh Portable. This computer has a 16 MHz 68000 CPU, a liquid crystal display, and the keyboard has an integrated trackball that replaces a mouse. This computer sells for approximately $3,200 and is the only portable that Apple sells.

Laptops

Laptop computers are small enough and light enough—appproximately 10 pounds—to sit comfortably on your lap. A laptop enables you to work while traveling, work at a remote location, or even work at home.

Many laptops are low-end IBM-compatible computers. The CPU is often a low-power 8088 or 8086. Some offer hard disk drives; some offer only floppy disk drives. The real attraction of this kind of laptop is price. The Toshiba T1000SE laptop sells for approximately $1,200. Although laptops come with more powerful processors, the only reason to buy a laptop is for the low price. Stick to a floppy drive model with an 8088 or 8086 CPU and one or two 3 1/2-inch, high-density floppy disk drives. Laptops with 80286 or 80386SX (or more powerful) CPUs are not recommended. These laptops are not bad choices, but better choices exist, as described in the following section.

Notebooks

Notebook portables essentially put the power of a computer into a package that you can carry under your arm. Usually under seven pounds, notebook computers are the wave of the future in portable computing. If you are interested in a high-powered portable computer, choose a notebook computer with a 10-inch diagonal, paper-white VGA display, an 80386SX CPU, and a 20M hard disk. At this writing, most notebooks use 80286 CPUs, but this situation should change quickly. Notebook computers with these features cost approximately $3,300 and are available from such companies as Texas Instruments, Sharp, and CompuAdd. A notebook computer, which easily fits inside a briefcase, is shown in figure 5.4.

Fig. 5.4. *A notebook computer.*

Many notebook computers lack a floppy disk drive. To use software applications, such as a word processor, you must transfer the software from a desktop computer to the notebook computer's hard disk. To make this transfer, connect the serial ports of the two computers with a cable and a software-transfer program, such as LapLink. Notebook computers come with MS-DOS and a software-transfer program built into ROM or installed on the hard disk. If you don't want to use a transfer program, look for a notebook computer with an optional external floppy disk drive, which costs about $225. Some notebook computers, such as the Compaq LTE 386s/20, do have an internal 3 1/2-inch floppy disk drive and a hard disk drive. The price of the Compaq notebook, however, is more than $6,000.

Buying a Used Computer

Some users wonder why anyone would purchase a used computer when new IBM-compatible systems, including printer and software, are available for less than $1,000. The reasons for buying a used computer include quality and price. The used computer may be a genuine IBM system for less than $1,000. Or, the used computer may be an IBM-compatible for less than $600. Price and brand name are the only reasons you should purchase a used computer. If you don't benefit in brand name or price, you are not making a sensible purchase.

Purchasing a used computer can be fraught with danger. If you purchase a very old system, the system may be ready to quit. If you purchase an oddball system, you may find yourself on a computing island, with no one to talk to about problems you may encounter.

If you are considering a used computer, do the following:

- Obtain documentation for the computer
- Obtain documentation for any boards added to the computer
- Obtain documentation for any software
- Determine the age of the computer
- Determine the approximate price.

When you are looking for a used computer, you should make sure first that it works. Then ask about the CPU, RAM, disk drives, video adapter, and video display. If you are considering an IBM or compatible computer, make sure that it has 640K of RAM. Most of the newer programs cannot run on a system with 256K of RAM. Don't buy a used computer without a hard disk drive. A hard disk is indispensable if you expect reasonable computing performance. Again, for IBM and compatible computers, don't pay a premium for a CGA or EGA adapter and monitor. These video standards are out of date. You get more for your money if the system uses a Hercules or compatible monochrome graphics adapter and a monochrome display.

Check prices with the *Computer Blue Book Price List*, published by the National Association of Computer Dealers for $15.95. This 364-page book provides a list of prices for computer products and a directory of companies in the computer industry.

Purchasing a Used IBM Computer

IBM has manufactured many computer models since the first IBM PC in 1981. Compatibility is the strongest benefit of purchasing an IBM computer. You don't have to worry about whether a circuit board or a software program will work with an IBM computer—these products are designed for IBMs. The keyboard is another benefit. An IBM keyboard probably is the best keyboard made for personal computers. Compatibility and quality are the two things you get with the IBM name.

IBM PC

You need to be very careful when purchasing a used IBM PC. This computer typically has just two floppy disk drives. You cannot install a hard disk drive unless you add a stronger power source and sometimes a new ROM. If the IBM PC has been upgraded with a hard disk and a new power supply, you may want to consider purchasing it. If you cannot ascertain whether these additions have been made, forget the computer.

IBM PC XT

An IBM PC XT may make an excellent used computer purchase for several reasons. The PC XT has none of the problems associated with the PC, and the XT can be upgraded easily to a faster computer when you feel the need for more power. All you have to do is add a circuit board, such as the Intel Inboard 386, to change the IBM PC XT to a 16 MHz 80386 computer.

IBM AT

The IBM AT computer is a slow 6 or 8 MHz 80286 computer. If you purchase it as a used computer, you may pay several hundred dollars more than for a used XT. You receive some immediate performance benefits in the short term, but you probably will want more performance in the long term. If you upgrade the AT to an 80386 computer, you have essentially the same computer as an upgraded XT, with somewhat faster hard disk performance. Consider purchasing a used AT only if a more economical XT is not available.

IBM PS/2

A used PS/2 Model 25, Model 30, or Model 30/286 is not upgraded easily. The price must be very low, therefore, before you consider purchasing one of these IBM models. A used PS/2 with an 80286 CPU, such as the Model 50, is difficult to upgrade. If you want to purchase one of these computers, the price must justify the used purchase. You will be locked into a computer with an 80286 CPU, and you will not be able to run software designed for more advanced CPUs.

If you have an opportunity to purchase a used IBM PS/2 model with an 80386SX or 80386 CPU, compare the price to a new model. If the price difference is significant, grab the used model.

Purchasing a Used IBM Compatible

Of all the computers you may consider purchasing, a used IBM compatible may give you the most trouble. Older IBM compatibles notoriously are incompatible with circuit boards and software designed for IBM computers. If you are not very careful, you may buy a computer with a proprietary design that does not accept standard add-in cards. The AT&T 6300, for example, is an older IBM compatible that cannot use VGA adapter boards or any other kind of color adapter designed for IBM computers. If you are considering a used compatible, be certain that it can accept standard circuit boards and can run software designed for IBM computers. If you cannot determine this, ask a friend to help you.

New IBM compatibles are the least expensive PCs available, and prices are dropping all the time. Check the prices of comparable new compatibles before considering a used model.

Purchasing a Used Macintosh

Apple Computer is similar to IBM in having manufactured many different models of the Macintosh computer. Apple, however, is the sole supplier of Macintosh computers—no compatibles are currently available. IBM, of course, spawned a whole industry of compatible computers. When IBM makes a drastic design change, such as switching its bus design to Micro Channel, older computer models are not adversely affected. Many other companies are still selling computers with the older ISA bus.

When Apple makes a change, however, older computer models are greatly affected. If you are considering a used Macintosh, therefore, you should check the prices and features of Apple's current Macintosh line. At this writing, the Apple Macintosh line includes:

Macintosh Classic
Macintosh SE/30
Macintosh LC
Macintosh IIsi
Macintosh IIci
Macintosh IIfx
Macintosh Portable

All new Macintosh models have a 1.44M floppy disk drive and 512K of ROM. These specifications, in effect, are the new standards for Macintosh computing. If you purchase a used model you eventually must upgrade to these standards, if you want your Macintosh to be compatible with the newest models.

Apple manufacturers know that purchasers of older Macintosh computers need a way to update their machines. The company offers a way to upgrade older models. Depending on the model, and the age of your machine, an upgrade costs $300-$700 and can be purchased through Apple dealers.

Before you purchase a used Macintosh, do two things:

1. Check the price of a comparably equipped new model.
2. Then check the cost of upgrading the used model so that it is compatible with the new model. If the cost of the used model plus the upgrade will save you some money, then the used model is worth considering.

Purchasing a Used Amiga, ST, or Mega

Like Apple, both Commodore and Atari manufacture computers that do not have compatible rivals from other companies. If you want to purchase a used Commodore Amiga or a used Atari ST or Mega computer, you should follow the advice given for Apple Macintosh computers. First check out the current line from either company. Determine how the newer models differ from the older ones. Find out how much it would cost to upgrade an older model. Compare the price of the used computer plus the upgrade to the price of a new model and make your decision.

Purchasing Some Other Kind of Used Computer

Many other brands of computers are available besides the ones discussed in this book. You may find a used Commodore 64, Apple II Plus, Coleco Adam, Timex Sinclair, or another model. Unless you have some special interest in one of these models, don't consider any of them. Although any computer has some merit as a computing device, these models generally are very slow and difficult to upgrade.

Evaluating a Used Computer

Purchasing a used computer is much like purchasing any other used commodity. To make a good purchase, you must know something about the product and its cost when it was new. You must be very observant when you examine the computer. Turn on the machine. Look at the display. Is it crisp and clear? Do you see any movement? Are there any lines on the display that don't look like they belong there? Look at the keyboard. Is it clean? Does it look like it has been well taken care of? Press every key. Does every letter or number appear on-screen? Look at the system unit. Listen to the disk drives. Ask the owner to copy files from the hard disk to the floppy disk drive. How do the disk drives sound? Are they very noisy? If yes, this is a bad sign, especially for the hard disk. Ask the owner to remove the cover of the computer. Does it remove easily? It should. Look inside. Is the system board clean, or is there dust and dirt everywhere?

If possible, bring a software program that you intend to run on the computer. Ask the owner if you may try the program. Type at the keyboard to see how it feels. If everything seems to work and the overall impression you have is that the system has been well cared for, you probably have found a good used computer.

Finding a Used Computer

After you decide to purchase a used computer, the problem is finding one. The first and probably the best place to look is the classified section of a local newspaper, where you can find individuals selling used computers. Why do they want to sell? Probably because they need the money. When a person is selling for this reason, you can easily negotiate the price down 20 percent.

Look next in the business section of the newspaper. Many newspapers have a special section dealing with computers. You usually can find the name of a computer-brokerage service in this section of the newspaper. These services buy and sell computers. If you decide to use one of these services, however, remember that you are dealing with a business person who is trying to make a profit on the deal.

Your local computer store is another place to look. These stores sometimes accept trade-ins, refurbish them, and then resell them. The store also may purchase manufacturer's close-outs. Remember that you are dealing with a business and not an individual; you may not get as great a bargain.

Larger cities have flea markets or swap meets for computers. You may find a good buy here, because you are dealing with individuals. You also may find good contacts for computer support at these events.

Computer publications are your last source for finding used computers. You occasionally may find a used computer for sale. Because these publications usually are distributed throughout the country, however, you may not find a seller in your area.

Chapter Summary

This chapter presented specific recommendations for buying a desktop personal computer for a variety of applications, such as word processing, spreadsheets, databases, graphics, electronic communication, desktop publishing, education, and accounting. For each application, a recommendation was given for a typical system for the home and for a small business from IBM, Apple, and an IBM-compatible manufacturer. Personal computer systems for general-purpose use also were suggested. The chapter covered the different types of portable computers and suggested ways to choose a specific model. Finally, the chapter explained how to find and evaluate used computers.

In the Next Chapter

Chapter 6 deals with printers. The chapter first describes types of printers: dot-matrix, inkjet, laser printers, and others. The chapter then explains which type of printer is best for the kind of documents you want to produce. Chapter 6 also discusses which applications need which kind of printer. Finally, the chapter includes specific recommendations of different printer types.

6

What Printer Do I Want?

When you work with an applications program such as a word processor, spreadsheet, database, or desktop publisher, you need to print the results of your efforts. For example, if you type a letter, you need to print and send it to someone. Without a printer, your computing power is severely limited. You should plan to buy a printer at the same time as or very soon after you buy the other components of your system.

This chapter asks questions about your printing needs and explains the kinds of printer technology and the features to look for when purchasing a printer. The chapter then tells you what kinds of jobs require which kinds of printers and which kinds of printers are best suited to particular kinds of software packages. Finally, this chapter gives you information on specific printers and recommends which ones may best suit your needs.

Printing

Before you decide what printer to connect to your personal computer, you should consider the kinds of printing you want to do. Ask yourself these questions:

- What do I want to print—text, graphics, or both?
- What quality of output do I need? (Does it matter how the characters or images look when they are printed on the page?) Compare the type quality of the text samples in figure 6.1.

- What typefaces do I need? Do I need a variety of typefaces and fonts? (The term *typeface* is defined later in the chapter.)
- Do I want to print in black-and-white or in color?
- Am I concerned with printing speed?
- How much money can I spend?

> A veteran applications analyst in start-up companies, even Ms. Lahey was unprepared for what she saw. "Never in my life have I seen such a promising start for a company still being run out of a garage," she
>
> ```
> A veteran applications
> analyst in start-up com-
> panies, even Ms. Lahey
> was unprepared for what
> she saw. "Never in my
> life have I seen such a
> promising start for a
> comapny still being run
> out of a garage," she
> ```

Fig. 6.1. The difference between Times Roman print (left) and draft print (right).

The answers can help you decide which kind of printer is best for you.

Understanding Printer Technology

The major difference among kinds of printers is the way they form characters on the page. Some form characters by striking an inked ribbon with pins; others by spraying ink on paper; others by depositing a black powder, called toner, on paper. Different manners of printing affect the print quality and the speed of a printer. To help you understand the various kinds of printers available, the sections that follow describe printer differences.

Before starting, however, a few definitions are in order. When you print a document, the characters that appear on the page have a particular design, called the *typeface*. The typeface has a name, such as Courier, Helvetica, or Times Roman. Thousands of typefaces exist, but a printer may have one, two, or several.

All typefaces contain letters, numbers, and symbols in a variety of sizes from very small (the fine print you see in advertisements) to very large print (the print used for headlines). The collection of all characters of a particular point size and weight is called a *font*. For example, in the Times Roman typeface, one of the fonts is 10-point Times Roman.

When you purchase a printer, you should investigate the number of typefaces and fonts the printer provides.

Dot-Matrix Printers

Dot-matrix printers produce alphanumeric characters and graphic images by striking an inked ribbon with tiny metal rods called pins. The pins are located in a print head which moves back and forth to create one line of text or graphics (see fig. 6.2). Dot-matrix printers usually use 9 or 24 pins to produce a series of dots on the page. Combinations of these dots make up the alphanumeric characters or graphic images.

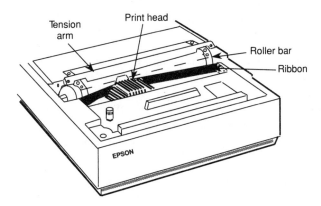

Fig. 6.2. A dot-matrix printer.

Nine-pin printers are less expensive, but they generally produce lower quality type than 24-pin printers, which produce somewhat better type quality. Both 9-pin and 24-pin printers vary in speed. Generally, the less expensive the printer, the slower the printer. (However, features of the printer also contribute to the price.)

Dot-Matrix Print Quality

All dot-matrix printers can produce draft characters like the ones shown in figure 6.1. Draft characters are formed with a minimum number of dots, so the printer can produce these characters quickly. Most dot-matrix printers can produce letter-quality or near-letter-quality characters. Letter-quality characters look like they have been produced on a good typewriter; whereas near-letter quality is somewhere between draft and letter-quality type.

A high-quality dot-matrix printer may be able to produce letter-quality print in a variety of fonts and typefaces. Sometimes, this feature is standard for a printer. For example, the Epson LQ 1010 printer (a 24-pin printer) has three typefaces—Draft, Roman and Sans Serif. Mixing and matching these typefaces with different characteristics, makes for different fonts. For example, you may print a bold Roman character or an italicized sans serif character.

Some dot-matrix printers support additional font cartridges, enabling the printer to print in more than just those default fonts. For example, the Epson LQ 1010 supports a font cartridge that contains multiple fonts. One particular cartridge contains the typefaces Courier, Prestige, Script, OCR-B, OCR-A, Orator, and Orator-S.

Generally, dot-matrix printers create 12-point characters. Some dot-matrix printers can create double-high characters, equivalent to 24 points. However, dot-matrix characters are measured in characters-per-inch (CPI), like typewriters.

The normal mode for a dot-matrix printer is 10 CPI, called *Pica*. Most printers, however, may print characters at different CPI settings. Other's CPI settings are 12 CPI (Elite), 15 CPI (condensed), and 17 CPI (Elite-condensed). Dot-matrix printers also may print larger characters, called *elongated*. These CPI ratings may be 8 CPI, 6 CPI, and 5 CPI. No matter how wide the character is printed, from a wide 5 CPI to a narrow 17 CPI, the character is the same height—12 points.

The reason for the CPI rating is because the printer uses nonproportional characters. Each character takes the same amount of space. The space allocated for the letter l is the same as the space allocated for the letter m. Some printers support proportional characters. Each character only takes as much space on the line as the character requires. Proportional characters cannot be measured in CPI, because the number of proportional l's in one inch varies from the number of proportional m's.

Nearly all dot-matrix printers can print graphics. Some dot-matrix printers may even print quite high-resolution graphics. Generally, 24-pin printers print better resolution graphics than 9-pin printers do.

Although graphics printed by a 24-pin printer may be of high resolution, they also may be less than desirable. Generally, graphics printed by a dot-matrix printer look as though they are put together with stripes. The print head may have to make many passes over a piece of paper to print the graphic. Each pass makes a stripe on the page.

These stripes are most noticeable when you print a great deal of black on the paper. If you print only lines, such as with a chart or graph, the stripes may be hardly noticeable.

Dot-Matrix Printer Features

Dot-matrix printers are inexpensive, reliable, easy to use, and can produce characters of reasonable quality; however, these printers also are noisy and relatively slow.

You may choose a dot-matrix printer for several reasons. If you cannot afford another kind of printer, you can buy a 24-pin dot-matrix printer that provides a type quality good enough for business correspondence. A dot-matrix printer also is inexpensive to operate. In most cases, you only need to change the ribbon—a minor expense. Another reason to choose a dot-matrix printer is to take advantage of a particular feature, such as the capability to print on multipart forms. If you need a printer for this kind of work, you can find 9-pin dot-matrix printers that feed forms from the bottom of the printer (keeping the forms straight) and that enable you to tear off the form exactly where you want (avoiding waste).

Many dot-matrix printers have a control panel that enables you to switch easily between print modes, such as normal and condensed or near-letter-quality print. If the printer lacks a control panel, you have to rely on your application program to change modes. You can find out how easy using the printer's mode controls is by visiting a store that sells dot-matrix printers and testing a few different models. Look for buttons on the front panel. Try to switch from draft to letter-quality print and from normal to small-sized print. If the printer does not have buttons to make these changes, or if the procedure is confusing, you should ask for a demonstration of these features.

Another feature of dot-matrix printers is paper parking. With some printers, you can insert single sheets of paper or envelopes into the printer while you have normal tractor-feed paper in the machine. This feature usually is one of the best paper-handling features a printer can offer.

If you regularly print on letterhead, be sure to ask whether you can purchase a cut-sheet feeder for the printer you are considering. With a cut-sheet feeder, you load 100 or more sheets of paper into a tray. Then the paper-feed mechanism feeds the paper into the printer. You can purchase cut-sheet feeders that feed the first page (letterhead), subsequent pages, and envelopes.

Another important paper-handling feature is a tractor-feed mechanism. This mechanism keeps form-feed paper straight when you are printing long documents or labels. To print labels, make sure that the tractor-feed mechanism can be adjusted to accommodate them.

If you intend to use a dot-matrix printer for heavy-duty work, do not make the mistake of buying an inexpensive model. You can burn out the unit right away.

Instead, try to match the capability of the printer to your workload. Printers have ratings that indicate how many pages they can produce in a given time span—for example, 16,000 pages per month. If you intend to do much printing, purchase a printer that can handle the workload.

A final consideration is color. If you want to print in color, you probably will spend more for the printer. Be sure that your printer is compatible with a popular color printing standard, such as Epson. If not, you may find that your applications programs, such as paint programs, do not support the printer.

Dot-Matrix Printer Manufacturers

Because IBM selected Epson as the manufacturer of the original IBM Matrix printer, Epson has set the standard for dot-matrix printers. Most dot-matrix printers that you purchase include Epson or IBM emulation. Besides the normal mode that the printer operates in, it also may act as an Epson or IBM printer.

Nearly all software manufacturers make sure that their software supports an Epson or IBM printer. Unless you are absolutely sure that a software program that you will use supports a specific printer, make sure that the dot-matrix printer you purchase has an Epson or IBM emulation mode.

Inkjet and Thermal Transfer Printers

Inkjet and thermal transfer printers differ from standard dot-matrix printers in the way they form characters on the page. An inkjet printer has a mechanism that squirts dots onto the page to form characters. A thermal printer uses heat to transfer dots from the ribbon to the page. Both kinds are quiet and have very good type quality. These printers cannot be used for applications such as printing on multiple part forms, however, because inkjet and thermal transfer technologies do not use an impact method to create characters.

Inkjet printers offer high-quality printing at prices that are much more affordable than laser printers. Because not many inkjet or thermal transfer models exist, however, you may not be able to get the forms-handling capability, ruggedness, typefaces, fonts, and software compatibility that you want. You may want to consider a different kind of printer.

You can run into a problem with an inkjet printer when printing graphics. Because an inkjet printer sprays ink onto the page, large black areas of a graphic are wet with ink as the page comes out of the printer, and the page may curl or wrinkle as it dries.

Inkjet and Thermal Printer Fonts

Inkjet printers offer a variety of fonts, usually all of high quality. A printer such as the Hewlett-Packard DeskJet 500 also accepts optional font cartridges to expand the selection of fonts.

The standard fonts that inkjet and thermal-transfer printers produce are quite similar to those produced by dot-matrix printers. You can select among nonproportional characters of generally the same point size. Because of the high-resolution of some of the inkjet printers, however, high-quality nonproportional fonts also may be printed. Some inkjet printers print fonts that are nearly as good quality as those printed by a laser printer.

Inkjet and Thermal Printer Features

A selling point of some inkjet printers is portability. Models like the BJ-10e Bubble Jet from Canon and the Diconix 150 Plus from Kodak weigh less than five pounds and easily can be carried in a briefcase. These printers are ideal for anyone who uses an IBM or compatible laptop or notebook computer and needs a portable printer.

Inkjet and thermal printers can print in color, but color printing is an expensive option. For example, the color Hewlett-Packard PaintJet has a suggested list price of $1,395; whereas the price of a black-and-white DeskJet 500 is $729.

Inkjet and Thermal Printer Manufacturers

You do not have many inkjet or thermal printer models from which to choose. The most popular inkjet printers for IBM and compatible computers are the Hewlett-Packard DeskJet and the Canon Bubble Jet; a popular thermal transfer printer is the IBM Quietwriter. For Macintosh computers, Hewlett-Packard makes an inkjet printer called the DeskWriter. Hewlett-Packard sets the standards for inkjet printers. If you buy another model, make sure that your software supports that printer.

Daisywheel Printers

Daisywheel printers use a simple printing technology. A wheel of characters rotates, and a hammer mechanism pushes one piece of the wheel against the ribbon to form a character on the page (see fig. 6.3). These printers print with the same high quality as expensive typewriters.

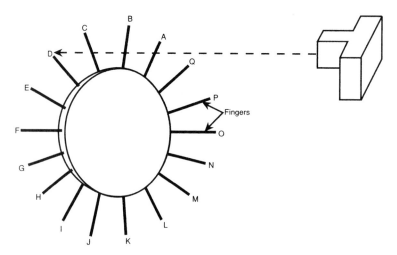

Fig. 6.3. The print wheel from a daisywheel printer.

Years ago, a daisywheel printer was the only kind of printer that could produce the sharp, clear characters necessary for business correspondence. Now, daisywheel printers are the dinosaurs of the personal computer age. Too slow to compete with lasers and unable to print graphics, these printers fell into disfavor several years ago. Most stores do not carry daisywheel printers anymore, but you sometimes can find them in close-out catalogs.

Laser Printers

Laser printers form characters in a fairly complex way. A laser beam is pointed at a rotating hexagonal mirror. The light is reflected off the mirror onto a rotating cylinder, called a drum. This reflection creates an electronic image on the drum. The image on the drum attracts a fine black powder, which adheres to the drum. When paper passes under the drum, the toner is attracted to the paper, forming the image. Finally, the image is fused to the paper by a combination of heat and pressure.

Laser Print Quality

Laser printers are a great improvement over dot-matrix, inkjet, and thermal-transfer printers. They are relatively quiet and produce better-looking text and graphics. Some laser printers also have a large selection of typefaces and fonts.

Many laser printers can scale fonts, which means that they can produce fonts of virtually any size. Best of all, lasers are fast. Most models print a standard page of text in less than 10 seconds. Laser printers look similar on the outside, but they do have many distinguishing features.

Laser Printer Language

A major difference among laser printers is the page description language built into the printer. The two prominent languages used in laser printers are Hewlett-Packard's Printer Control Language (PCL) and Adobe PostScript. Most laser printers use one language or the other or a language compatible with PCL or PostScript. Adobe PostScript is the more powerful language. With PostScript, you can print numerous typefaces, scale the typefaces to almost any size, and add special effects. Hewlett-Packard's PCL is much more limited.

The new Hewlett-Packard LaserJet III, however, expands the capabilities of PCL with an improved version of the language called PCL 5. PCL 5 can do some of the things PostScript can do, such as scale fonts and add special effects to type. A printout from a LaserJet III (see fig. 6.4) shows how the printer can add special effects to type. Normally, you would need a laser printer with the PostScript language to produce this kind of special effects. Because Hewlett-Packard sets the standards for PCL laser printers, you can expect many other printers to use this improved version of PCL in the future.

Fig. 6.4. The Hewlett-Packard LaserJet III printer can add special effects to type, a characteristic usually reserved for PostScript printers.

A PostScript printer is the best choice for desktop publishing, because many desktop publishing programs have better support for PostScript printers than for PCL printers. A PostScript laser printer is the kind to use if you want to be creative with type. With a PostScript printer, each typeface is available in hundreds of sizes. To create newsletters with big headlines or advertising copy with fancy graphics, use a PostScript laser printer.

The most expensive, top-of-the-line PostScript printers are sold by Apple. The Apple LaserWriters not only work with Macintosh computers but also can be connected to IBM and compatible computers. You should compare any PostScript printer you are considering to the latest model of the Apple LaserWriter.

Not all applications programs work with PostScript printers. If you use a particular applications program, be sure that the program supports PostScript before you purchase such a printer.

For standard business applications, however, a PCL laser printer does the job just as well as a PostScript printer. If cost is an issue, note that some PostScript laser printers cost two to three times the amount of a PCL printer. Currently, the Hewlett-Packard Series III laser printer is the best PCL printer to buy because it contains the latest version of the language.

If you want PostScript capability but cannot afford a PostScript printer, you have some alternatives. You can add PostScript to many PCL printers by installing a circuit board inside the printer or by plugging in a cartridge. If this option appeals to you, make sure that the PCL printer you are considering can be expanded by one of these methods. Another alternative is to buy a software program that enables your printer to work like a PostScript printer. A software solution also can give other types of printers PostScript compatibility. Each of these alternatives differ in performance and cost, with the add-in card offering the best performance at the highest cost.

Some laser printers, designed to work with Apple Macintosh computers, use the QuickDraw program built into the Apple Macintosh ROM rather than a page description language such as PostScript. QuickDraw printers are aimed at individuals who own Macintosh computers but do not need the power or cannot afford the cost of a PostScript laser printer. Keep in mind that QuickDraw laser printers are designed for Macintosh computers; whereas PCL printers are designed for use with IBM and compatible computers.

Laser Printer Features

Some features that distinguish one laser printer from another are double-sided printing, resolution enhancement technology, paper handling, and ease of use. Double-sided printing enables you to print on both sides of the page at one time. This feature is useful if you are doing a job such as printing manuals from the laser printer.

Resolution enhancement technology is a way to produce sharper images. This feature is important if you want to lessen the effect of the jaggies that occur with some curved characters. Jaggies are a stair-step effect that occurs when a printer tries to create curved lines with dots. If you look at characters or graphics closely, you can see that curved characters, such as the letter "S", are not smooth but jagged. Whether you need to worry about this effect depends on the typeface and image quality you desire. The best way to evaluate resolution enhancement technology is to look closely at the output produced by various laser printers.

With regard to paper handling, keep in mind that each letter you print usually needs an envelope. A laser printer should have a way to feed one envelope or a stack of envelopes into the printer. This feature may be standard or optional.

Choosing a laser printer with a front panel that is easy to understand and use helps you get what you want from the printer and helps you identify problems. Be wary of purchasing a printer that forces you to learn cryptic codes for normal operations.

Sometimes a laser printer is not what it seems. Some printers that look like laser printers have inherent technology differences. A laser printer can be more broadly classified as a page printer. Other kinds of page printers are liquid-crystal shutter (LCS) printers and light emitting diode (LED) array printers. These printers look like and act like laser printers but do not use a laser beam as part of their operation. The differences between the print outputs of LCS and LED printers and laser printers are very slight. Sometimes, you can tell the difference by printing a straight line across the width of the paper. A laser printer bends the line ever so slightly at the edges. This curvature is usually not a problem unless your application demands perfectly straight lines. You may be equally pleased with the outputs of the laser, LCS, and LED printers.

Laser Printer Manufacturers

The internal parts of a laser printer, the printer engine, can differ from printer to printer. The engines are made by companies such as Canon, IBM, Kyocera Unison, Ricoh, Sharp, and TEC. Laser printers from two different companies may use the same printer engine or different printer engines. Knowing which engine a laser printer uses is important, because the toner cartridge and other parts that may need to be replaced fairly often differ from engine to engine. If you are thinking of buying a laser printer, make sure that you find out how to replace the toner and parts that wear out, such as the OPC (optical photo coupler). Also make sure that these items are readily available.

The two most popular brands of laser printers are the Hewlett-Packard LaserJet models and the Apple LaserWriter models. Stores that carry laser printer supplies almost certainly carry replacement cartridges for these and compatible printers.

Considering Printer Features

Besides differences in printing technology, printers usually differ in the kinds of features they offer. These features can relate to print quality, ports, memory, resolution, speed, paper size, and operating costs. In the following sections, these features are considered.

Print Quality

All printers have one or more resident (built-in) fonts and typefaces. Do not purchase a printer unless you can see a print sample that includes all the resident fonts. If you plan to use the printer for business correspondence, make sure to inspect the quality of the font. Manufacturers of dot-matrix printers often describe their products as having a near-letter-quality or letter-quality font. In essence, this description means that the dot-matrix printer's font looks nearly or exactly like that of a good typewriter. If you believe the manufacturer's claims without question, you may be sorely disappointed when you print a letter or a report. Look at the sample of near-letter-quality and letter-quality type from different dot-matrix printer manufacturers, as shown in figures 6.5 and 6.6.

```
I went to the woods because I         I went to the woods because I
wished to live deliberately,          wished to live deliberately,
to front only the essential           to front only the essential
facts of life. - H. D. Thoreau        facts of life. - H. D. Thoreau
```

Fig. 6.5. A sample of near-letter-quality print from two different dot-matrix printer manufacturers.

```
I went to the woods because I         I went to the woods because I
wished to live deliberately,          wished to live deliberately,
to front only the essential           to front only the essential
facts of life. - H. D. Thoreau        facts of life. - H. D. Thoreau
```

Fig. 6.6. A sample of letter-quality print from two different dot-matrix printer manufacturers.

If you do not like the printer's standard fonts, ask whether you can purchase optional font cartridges for the printer. A font cartridge gives you additional fonts and typefaces, a useful option if you are interested in spicing up the look of business correspondence and reports. For laser printers, be careful to check the kind of cartridges the printer accepts. The Hewlett-Packard Series II printers are a standard, and many third-party companies make font cartridges for these printers. If you purchase a printer that uses a different kind of cartridge, you have to depend on the manufacturer to provide the fonts you want. This concern does not apply to dot-matrix printers because no one font cartridge is standard.

If a printer does not accept font cartridges, inquire whether the manufacturer offers downloadable fonts. (Downloadable fonts, which are supplied on a disk, are fonts that the computer loads into the printer's memory). Make sure to ask for sample printouts so that you can check the quality and variety of the fonts.

If you use downloadable fonts, you must have sufficient memory in the printer to hold the fonts that you will use, plus the page that you are printing. Be sure to check with the manufacturer for recommended memory requirements for downloading fonts.

An alternative to font cartridges for laser and dot-matrix printers are programs that offer scaleable fonts. Scaleable fonts give you any character size for a particular typeface. Programs such as Publisher's Powerpak from Atech Software add scaleable fonts to programs such as WordPerfect and Microsoft Word and work with most dot-matrix and PCL laser printers. If you use Microsoft Windows 3.0 with an IBM or compatible computer, programs such as Adobe Type Manager, Powerpak for Windows, and FaceLift from Bitstream add scaleable screen and printer fonts for any Windows application. These programs often slow printers considerably, so you may want to witness a demonstration before deciding to purchase.

Ports

You can connect a printer to a computer in several ways. Most printers used with IBM and compatible computers have a Centronics parallel port. To connect the printer to the computer you need a parallel port on the computer. A parallel port may be built into or added to the computer by inserting a card into an expansion slot.

Printers intended for use with Macintosh computers have serial (also called RS-232C or RS-422), AppleTalk, or SCSI ports. All Macintosh computers have these ports built in.

Make sure that the personal computer you own or are buying and the printer you are considering have the same ports. Otherwise, the personal computer cannot send data to the printer.

Some laser printers have two serial ports, an AppleTalk port and a parallel port. Each of the four ports can be connected to a different personal computer. Laser printers with automatic port selection scan all the ports, select the first port that has a print job, and hold the other jobs until the first computer's print job is finished. If more than one computer shares the printer, look for this port selection feature when purchasing a laser printer.

Memory

Memory, or RAM, is not only an element of a personal computer system but also an important element of a printer. RAM is most important for laser printers, but you should consider it when you evaluate other types of printers. For example, a dot-matrix printer can use memory as a print buffer (information sent to the printer goes into RAM first and then is printed). If the printer has enough RAM to accept all the information you want to print, waiting time is eliminated. You can continue working on your computer while your printer is printing. If two dot-matrix models are otherwise similar in features and price, choose the printer with the most RAM.

Laser printer memory is used to store image data, fonts, and special printer programs. To print a page, the laser printer must have enough memory to store all the information about the page. A laser printer cannot print part of a page, receive more information, and then print the rest of the page. If a laser printer runs out of RAM, the printer prints half the page, ejects the paper, and then prints the other half of the page on another sheet of paper. The more white space on the page, the smaller the amount of memory required.

RAM also is used to store printer programs sent from the personal computer to the printer. These programs can be run again and again. For example, the program may draw a company's letterhead on the page. Rather than sending the letterhead from the computer to the printer for every page, a program containing the letterhead is sent to the printer once.

How much RAM do you need? Before answering this question, consider one more issue. Hewlett-Packard LaserJet printers or laser printers that emulate them (PCL printers) fill memory on a first come, first served basis. The last font or graphic entered into RAM can be deleted. After this font or graphic is deleted, the next-to-the-last font or graphic can be deleted, and so on. A font that is not being used cannot be deleted without deleting everything stored after it. This process is time-consuming and often inconvenient.

PostScript printers, however, can manage their own fonts and delete fonts from anywhere in memory. In fact, some PostScript printers have hard disks where unused copies of fonts can be stored. This hassle-free feature of PostScript does come with a penalty, however; more RAM is required.

For Hewlett-Packard or compatible PCl printers, you need a minimum of one megabyte RAM, but two megabytes are recommended. For PostScript printers, you need a minimum of two megabytes RAM, but three megabytes are recommended.

The standard amount of memory that a printer has varies with the manufacturer. For example, the standard Hewlett-Packard LaserJet III printer has one megabyte RAM; whereas the standard Epson EPL-6000 has one-half megabyte (512 kilobytes) of memory. If you choose the minimum amount of memory for an HP LaserJet or compatible printer, you may spend much time juggling fonts. If you purchase a PostScript printer with the minimum amount of RAM, the printer does not operate at maximum speed. The more RAM a PostScript printer has, the faster the printer prints (up to its rated page-per-minute speed).

Adding RAM to a laser printer is not a prepurchase option only. You may add RAM at any time. Generally, adding RAM is as easy as adding a card to your printer. For example, the Hewlett-Packard LaserJet III contains a slot on the side of the printer where a memory-expansion board slides into the printer.

Whatever amount of RAM you decide to purchase for a laser printer, make sure to shop around for the best prices. Typical prices of RAM for a Hewlett-Packard laser printer are $175 for one megabyte, $225 for two megabytes, and $350 for four megabytes. If you buy RAM from the printer manufacturer, you may find that you spend twice as much for the same amount of RAM.

Resolution

Resolution is a measurement of the sharpness of the printed image. The higher the resolution, the better the quality of alphanumeric characters and graphics. The resolution of a dot-matrix or laser printer is measured in dots per inch (dpi). Dot-matrix printers usually have different horizontal and vertical resolutions, such as 360 dpi (H) or 180 dpi (V). Laser printers normally have a resolution of 300 dpi vertically and horizontally. The resolution enhancement technology used in the Hewlett-Packard III series of printers varies the dot size so that smaller dots can be placed in areas where the normal-sized dots do not fit. This feature can sharpen the appearance of letters even though the resolution of the printer, 300 dpi, is the same as many other laser printers.

When considering a dot-matrix printer, ask about the resolution—especially if you are worried about type and graphics quality. Compare printouts from different printers to see how variations in resolution affect the print quality. As for laser printers, models with resolutions higher than 300 dpi often cost considerably more than models with 300 dpi resolution. Unless you need increased resolution, stick with 300 dpi.

Speed

With dot-matrix printers, speed is sometimes more important than print quality. To create a large mailing list and print out thousands of labels, you need a fast printer. Speed ratings for dot-matrix printers are in characters per second (cps). A printer normally has a rating for draft mode and letter-quality mode. Draft print can be generated much faster than letter-quality print: for dot-matrix printers the speed of draft print may be 200 cps; whereas letter-quality speed may be 50 cps.

To get a realistic assessment of a printer's speed, do not rely on a manufacturer's claims. You should witness a printing demonstration of the kind of material you intend to print. Examples of print jobs that require speed rather than fine appearance are mailing labels, checks, financial statements, and database reports.

For laser printers, speed ratings are in pages per minute (ppm). Several factors determine the speed of a laser printer. Some laser-printer engines are rated at 8 ppm and higher, but others have ratings as low as 4 ppm. Memory is another factor. Remember that this speed reflects print time for a page with characters only—not graphics. As mentioned earlier, the more memory a PostScript printer has, the faster the printer can process data. Yet another factor is the laser printer's CPU (such as the Motorola 68000 or 68020). Some CPUs are faster than others, and the speed of the printer is affected by the speed of its CPU.

Other elements also can affect print speed. The port controls how quickly data can be transmitted to a printer. The software application and CPU of the personal computer control how quickly data can be prepared for the printer. Each of these elements can slow the printing process. If you intend to print pages that are complex combinations of text and graphics, make sure to test the speed of this printing process. A printer rated at 8 ppm may produce only one page every 15 minutes.

Paper Size

Dot-matrix printers come in two standard sizes: narrow carriage and wide carriage. The narrow-carriage printer accepts standard 8 1/2-by-11-inch paper. The wide-carriage printer accepts 14-inch-wide paper.

You may find that the narrow carriage printer is adequate for most printing. Although you may print as many as 80 characters per line using the normal font size on the narrow-carriage printer, you may condense the characters so that you can print up to 144 characters (using 17 CPI).

If you print financial reports, you may find the wide-carriage printer more useful. Handling 14-inch paper, you may print from 140 10 CPI characters to as many as 238 17 CPI characters. Using the condensed mode on wide paper enables you to print much information on one page.

Inkjet printers generally use only 8 1/2-inch-wide paper. However, you may use legal size paper (14-inches long). Some ink printers enable you to rotate the printed output. Using *landscape* mode makes the printer act as though it is printing on 14-inch-wide paper. Landscape mode works on letter- or legal-size paper.

Laser printers use letter- and legal-size paper. Laser printers also offer landscape and the default portrait modes (portrait mode being normal, or vertical, printing). The number of characters that you may print on a page varies by the size and type style of the characters being printed.

Because paper for a laser printer is loaded into a tray placed in the printer, you may purchase additional trays for your paper. Paper trays come in the standard letter size and legal size. If you use legal-size paper, purchasing the additional tray is much more convenient.

Operating Costs

The cost of a printer includes more than just the purchase price. You need to consider the following additional items that affect the cost of your printer:

- Paper
- Consumables: toner, ribbons, and ink
- Repair of parts: drums, print heads, and so on

Prices of these items vary depending on your source of supply. Make sure to price these items, especially the cost of repairs, if you are undecided about which kind of printer to buy.

Laser printers have much in common with copy machines. Like a copy machine, a laser printer uses a black powder called toner for printing, rather than a ribbon or ink. Because laser printers use toner, they can be costly to operate. Laser printers have a larger electricity draw than do other printers. Operating a laser printer may cost two to three time more than operating a dot-matrix or Inkjet printer. Other parts of the machine, such as the drum, wear out and can be costly to replace. Keep these points in mind when deciding which kind of printer to buy.

You probably will find that dot-matrix printers are much less expensive to operate than inkjet or laser printers.

Determining Your Required Output

When purchasing a printer, you should have a clear idea of the kinds of documents you want to print. For example, desktop publishing is meant to be done with a laser printer—you can do only a crude job with a dot-matrix printer. You can print banners and very wide spreadsheets, however, only on tractor-feed dot-matrix printers. This section makes recommendations based on the output you require.

Printing Internal Reports

Internal reports are not designed to look impressive. Rather, they communicate information clearly and efficiently. Many times, internal reports are printed on tractor-feed paper that is not torn apart. In fact, the fanfold paper helps keep the pages in order. Usually, printing speed is more important than type quality, so a fast dot-matrix printer with a tractor-feed mechanism is the most effective solution. For readability purposes, select a 24-pin dot-matrix printer rather than a 9-pin printer.

Printing Letters, Resumes, and Papers

Business and professional documents such as letters, resumes, and lengthy papers usually are printed in a standard pica font, such as Courier. This kind of font is smart-looking but not too fancy. Some 24-pin printers produce the quality required for these documents. You may want to print on continuous-form paper that tears apart or on single sheets fed into the printer with a sheet-feeding mechanism.

If the print quality of a 24-pin dot-matrix printer is not sufficient, thermal transfer, inkjet, and laser printers are other possible solutions.

Printing Mailing Labels

Mailing labels rarely require high-quality print output, so you can use the cheapest 9-pin dot-matrix printer you can find. Printing long mailing lists, however, can reduce a printer's life span because the printer has to work harder; the motor stays hotter; and jamming often occurs. To print long mailing lists, you need a rugged 9-pin printer that can handle the work. The more work a printer can handle, the more the printer costs.

Make sure that the printer has a tractor-feed mechanism that can be adjusted to fit the width of the mailing labels. If not, you can purchase fanfold sheets of mailing labels with one or more labels across the width of the sheet.

If you want a laser printer for other purposes but also would like to feed sheets of mailing labels, make sure to purchase sheets that can stand the considerable heat generated inside the printer. If you frequently find yourself printing mailing labels, purchase a 9-pin dot-matrix printer just for this purpose. This way, you can leave the fanfold sheets of labels in the printer and always be ready to print.

You may select to print using 3-up labels rather than 1-up (3 labels across). To do this, you generally have to purchase a wide-carriage printer.

Printing Banners

Banners generally are used for signs or for special events, such as parties. Special software and a dot-matrix printer are required to create banners.

Banners are pages of fanfold paper that have not been torn apart, with letters printed sideways along the continuous sheets. For example, one sentence can be 12-feet long. Because banners are printed in graphics mode (one line of dots at a time), the kind of dot-matrix printer you use does not matter. Nine-pin and 24-pin models work equally well. Just make sure that the banner program supports the printer you are considering.

Printing Wide Spreadsheets

You can print wide spreadsheets in several ways. One way is with a wide-carriage dot-matrix printer and 11-by-14-inch fanfold paper. With this configuration, you can print wide spreadsheets in draft mode or letter-quality print. Very wide spreadsheets can be printed sideways. To print this way, the spreadsheet program you use must include this feature, or you must purchase special software for sideways printing. Examine the print quality of this method before making a decision.

If the required font is built in or on a plug-in cartridge, laser printers can print in landscape mode as well as portrait mode.

Printing Forms

Single-part forms can be printed on any kind of printer. You can send preprinted forms through a printer and print only the data (company name, amounts, and so on), or you can print the entire form on the printer. If a form is complicated, with many tiny characters and shaded areas, you need a laser printer to print the entire form. For simpler forms, dot-matrix and inkjet printers are sufficient. If the application you use does not enable you to print forms, special software is available for this task.

Printing continuous forms such as checks or purchase orders requires a dot-matrix or other printer with a tractor-feed mechanism. If you have many such forms to print in the course of a day, buy a printer that can handle the work.

To print on multipart forms, you need a dot-matrix printer because only dot-matrix printers form characters by impact. If you print on expensive preprinted multipart forms, make sure that the dot-matrix printer you choose can feed these forms properly. If a printer does not have the proper paper-handling features, you can waste many forms.

Look for a printer that feeds forms from the bottom of the printer rather than rolling them around the printer's platen. A blank form curled around the platen while the printer is stopped remains curled after you print the form. Check whether you can cut the form at the perforation without advancing the form past the printer's paper bail. If you advance a form to remove it, you may not be able to print on the next blank form.

Printing Newsletters, Brochures, and Other High-Quality Documents

Newsletters, brochures, and other documents that demand high print quality should be done on a laser printer. To use large fonts for headlines and to create special typographical effects, you need a PostScript laser printer or a PCL laser printer with a PostScript add-in board. If your needs are less demanding, you can use a PCL laser printer (if you have an IBM or compatible) or a QuickDraw laser printer (if you have a Macintosh).

You can print these kinds of documents with a dot-matrix printer, but print quality suffers. Although some dot-matrix printers print at 360 dots per inch, the output does not look as nice as 300-dpi laser-printer output. The dot-matrix dots are thick, overlapping, and uneven.

If you find the initial cost of a laser printer too high, an inkjet printer may be an acceptable compromise.

Determining the Right Printer for Your Applications

Different personal computer applications use printers in different ways. To decide what kind of printer you need, consider the printer requirements of your software packages. The following sections break down applications by group and examine the typical printer requirements.

Spreadsheet Applications

Spreadsheet programs are composed almost entirely of columns of numbers and, in most cases, have simple printer requirements. If the columns are printed in a proportional font (such as Times Roman), the numbers do not line up. Poor alignment makes the document hard to read. The best font for printing a spreadsheet, therefore, is a simple fixed-spaced font (such as Courier) or dot-matrix draft print. Fonts specially designed for spreadsheets also are available. With these condensed fonts, you can print many more numbers on a page than you can with standard-size fonts.

Usually, the print quality of a spreadsheet is not an issue. A good printout makes the rows and columns of numbers easy to read. Printing speed is not usually important, except for large spreadsheets or when multiple copies are needed. A 9- or 24-pin wide-carriage printer is best for basic spreadsheet printing.

Many spreadsheet programs now offer a feature called spreadsheet publishing. This feature enables you to combine numbers and text in a variety of fonts, graphs, and images. A laser printer is best for black-and-white spreadsheet publishing. To print in color, consider a color inkjet or a color PostScript laser printer. Be advised, however, that a color thermal printer costs many thousands of dollars more than a color inkjet printer.

Database Applications

Database applications also have simple printing requirements. A wide-carriage 9-pin dot-matrix printer is sufficient for most database printing. Speed, however, is usually a concern: printing one sales invoice may not require great speed, but printing a large number of records does. The time required to print a large mailing list varies noticeably with even small differences in printer speed.

To link your database application to a program that creates forms, you need a laser printer for best results. Laser printers also are best to print statistics from a database and publish them in a newsletter.

To add *pizzazz* to your database reports, you may need more than your database application. You may have to move the information from your database to a spreadsheet (with spreadsheet publishing features), a word processor, a graphics program, or a desktop publishing program.

Word Processing Applications

Word processors work with all types of printers. If you want a printed page to look like it came from a typewriter, almost any printer is adequate. For school reports and some business correspondence, a 9-pin dot-matrix printer with near-letter-quality print is sufficient. For business letters and some business reports, 24-pin dot-matrix, inkjet, thermal transfer, and PCL laser printers are best.

Today, some word processing programs have desktop publishing features that enable you to use a variety of fonts and to incorporate images into a word processing document. To use your word processor in this way, a PCL or PostScript laser printer is recommended.

To print with proportional rather than monospace fonts, your printer must support the font you want to use. Most printers support proportional fonts, but some do a better job of this than others. Check the printer's output before making a purchase. Keep in mind that many word processors for IBM and compatible computers do not support proportional fonts on-screen. Through special preview modes, the word processor approximates the correct spacing between letters. Ultimately, however, the spacing depends on the font the printer uses. If you intend to print with proportional fonts and want your screen display to match your printer output, look for WYSIWYG (what-you-see-is-what-you-get) word processors for IBM and compatible computers. Macintosh, Amiga, ST, and Mega word processors show monospace and proportional fonts on-screen.

Desktop Publishing Applications

To print a variety of fonts and graphics, you probably need a desktop publishing package. Speed and print quality are critical issues. Most desktop publishing software needs a laser printer—preferably a PostScript printer. For such applications, PostScript printers offer the most flexibility and are the easiest to use. See the section on fonts for details about why you should consider a PostScript printer for desktop publishing.

Accounting Applications

Accounting is another application with simple printing requirements. Accounting reports normally are intended for internal use, so print quality is not an issue. A 9-pin dot-matrix printer should be sufficient to handle most accounting needs.

When printing yearly information, a wide page may be required. You then may consider a wide-carriage printer. If you intend to print long reports, look for a printer with speed and a tractor-feed mechanism.

Graphics and Drawing Applications

Popular graphics and drawing programs support all kinds of printers. For reliable, consistent, high-quality graphics printing, however, you should use a laser printer. Make sure that the laser printer you are considering has enough memory to print the kind of graphics you want to print. One to two megabytes of memory should be sufficient for most applications.

For less stringent graphics printing, a dot-matrix or inkjet printer is sufficient. Check the resolution of the printer before purchasing and look at some sample printouts.

To print color graphics, choose a dot-matrix printer with color capability. Also make sure that your graphics or drawing program supports the printer and that four-color ribbons are easy to get. For better quality color printouts, consider an inkjet printer. For the best quality, the printer to choose is a color thermal printer, but this kind of printer is much more expensive than the others.

Educational Applications

Many educational programs do not have a printing option, and most of those applications that do offer printing support only 9 pin dot matrix printers. If you are interested in using a particular educational program with a 24-pin or laser printer, make sure that the software works with the printer.

Determining the Printer You Need

Deciding on a specific brand and model of printer can be a daunting task if you are not sure about the kind of printer you want and the features you need. The preceding sections should help you narrow your choices based on the kinds of printers available, printer features, required output, and the kinds of applications used. The following sections give you information about the manufacturers and price ranges of printers in specific categories.

9-Pin Dot-Matrix Printers

If you buy a low-end Apple Macintosh computer, such as the Macintosh Classic, and want to connect the computer to a dot-matrix printer, a logical choice is the ImageWriter II. This 9-pin dot-matrix printer prints in black or in color and sells for around $450. A lower cost alternative is the Seikosha SP1000, which sells for about $225.

For IBM and compatible computers, you have a large selection of 9-pin dot-matrix printers. Epson, once the recognized leader in this category, now has stiff competition. If you want an inexpensive 9-pin printer, the Epson LX810, Panasonic KX-P1180, and Star Micronics NX-1000 Multifont II are all good choices that sell for less than $200. If you want more features than these models have, more sophisticated 9-pin printers (which can cost several hundred dollars more) are available from these and other companies.

24-Pin Dot-Matrix Printers

The leading low-cost 24-pin dot-matrix printers are the Epson LQ-510 and Panasonic KX-P1124, either of which you can purchase for less than $300. If these models do not satisfy your need for speed, paper handling, ruggedness, and other features, you can choose among other models in these company's lines as well as among fine 24-pin printers from companies such as IBM, Okidata, Toshiba, and NEC. Keep in mind that many reputable companies manufacture 24-pin dot-matrix printers. If a printer has the features you are looking for at the right price, and the print quality is top-notch, you are likely to be happy with your purchase.

Inkjet Printers

If you want an inkjet printer, you have only a few models from which to choose. For IBM and compatible computers, the Hewlett-Packard DeskJet 500 and Canon BJ-130 are the popular models. These two printers cost approximately $800 to $1,100. The Hewlett-Packard DeskWriter for Macintosh computers costs approximately $1,000.

The Canon BJ-10e and Kodak Diconix 150 Plus are portable inkjet printers for IBM and compatible computers. The Diconix 150M Plus is a portable inkjet printer for the Macintosh. These printers range in price from about $400 to $600.

Laser Printers

Hewlett-Packard created the standards for laser printing for IBM and compatible computers. HP still sets the standards with its newest model, the LaserJet Series III, which retails for approximately $2,400. This model features variable-sized dots and scaleable fonts. The most inexpensive laser printer from Hewlett-Packard is the Series II, which retails for around $1,500.

Laser printers for IBM and compatible computers also are available from many other companies. Almost all of these models are PCL printers, which means that they are compatible with Hewlett-Packard LaserJet Series II printers. You may want to wait to buy this kind of printer until newer models appear with LaserJet Series III compatibility.

PostScript Laser Printers

The trend-setting PostScript laser printer is the Apple LaserWriter II NTX. Advertised prices are approximately $4,500 for this model. Many competitors are out there, however, ranging from true Adobe PostScript laser printers (such as the Texas Instruments MicroLaser 35) to compatible PostScript printers, to printers with add-in PostScript boards. Prices for these printers are in the $2,000 to $3,000 price range. The best choice among these models depends on the features you want and the price you are willing to pay.

QuickDraw Page Printers

For Macintosh users that do not need or cannot afford the features that a PostScript laser printer has to offer, a lower cost alternative is a QuickDraw page printer. The Apple Personal LaserWriter SC and GCC PLP IIS are two good choices in this category. Each of these printers sells for less than $2,000.

Color Printers

Color printers are available with prices from $350 to more than $10,000, depending on the technology. Dot-matrix color printers are the least expensive. Almost all dot-matrix printer manufacturers have color models.

The most popular inkjet models are the Hewlett-Packard PaintJet for IBM and compatible computers and the PaintWriter for Macintosh computers. Retail prices for these printers are about $1,400.

Thermal color printers have great output but cost more than the rest. Two good choices are the Tektronix Phaser PX and the QMS ColorScript 100. Color thermal printers range from about $5,000 to $15,000.

Chapter Summary

This chapter described the types of printers available for your computer system: dot-matrix, inkjet, thermal, and laser printers. The chapter also described features that may affect your choice of a particular kind of printer. The chapter went on to describe how your required output—internal reports, letters, papers, banners, wide spreadsheets, forms, newsletters, or brochures—affects the kind of printer you should consider. The chapter then showed you which kind of printers are best for applications such as spreadsheets, databases, word processors, desktop publishing, accounting, graphics, drawing, and education. Finally, the chapter recommended specific printer models in each printer category.

In the Next Chapter

The next chapter explains how to purchase a computer. Chapter 7 describes the different places you can shop for a system: retail stores, mail order, and so on. The chapter also explains the kind of questions you should ask: questions about support, training, warranties, and other important buying issues. The chapter encourages you to do research before making a purchase and tells you where to find information. Finally, the chapter gives advice on evaluating a computer vendor.

7

How Do I Purchase a Computer System?

You probably have an idea about the kind of personal computer system and printer you want. This chapter gives you advice about places to purchase a computer, such as computer stores, electronics stores, department stores, or mail-order companies. The chapter lists the questions you should ask concerning support, training, warranties, and package deals. This chapter also discusses what kind of research to do and how to find the best computer vendor to serve you. Finally, the chapter gives you tips to ensure that you purchase all the parts you need.

Where Do I Purchase a Computer?

You purchase a computer in a store or through the mail as you would any other piece of electronic equipment. Some stores specialize in computers and associated products such as printers and software. Electronics stores sell computers and other kinds of electronic products, including calculators, cameras, stereos, and VCRs. Other stores sell computers and many other kinds of merchandise. If you plan to purchase equipment through mail-order suppliers, you will find many computer companies from which to choose.

The kind of computer you want to buy determines the kind of store you should patronize. If you want a brand name computer, such as IBM, Compaq, Macintosh, Amiga, or Atari ST, check the telephone book or the business section of your local newspaper for authorized dealers. ComputerLand, the Computer Factory, Nynex Business Centers, MicroAge, and Sears Business Systems Centers are authorized sellers of IBM and Compaq computers. ComputerLand, Nynex Business Centers, Connecting Point, and Businessland sell Macintosh computers. These stores, however, rarely carry Amiga or Atari ST computers. These computers can be found in smaller independent computer-specialty stores or in stores that sell computers for a special application, such as music.

Some stores sell only one brand of computer. Radio Shack, which sells the Tandy line of computers, has business computer centers in addition to its consumer electronics stores. CompuAdd sells its line of IBM-compatible computers through CompuAdd Superstores and through mail order.

If you plan to purchase an IBM-compatible computer or a portable, you can shop in computer stores, consumer electronics stores, or through mail order. Look in a telephone book or newspaper for stores that sell the compatible you are seeking.

Computer Stores

If you intend to purchase a brand name computer, such as IBM, Compaq, or Apple, an authorized dealer (ComputerLand, Nynex, and so on) often is the only place you can shop. These stores traditionally charge premium prices for the products they carry. They also offer benefits, such as leasing and financing plans, training, and on-site service contracts. (If you purchase an on-site service contract, a repair person comes to your place of business to diagnose and repair problems that occur with your system.)

If you buy an IBM, Apple, or other computer in a computer store, you are not forced to purchase an all-IBM or all-Apple system. You can purchase monitors and printers made by other manufacturers that work perfectly well with IBM and Apple computers.

Computer stores often set up systems in the store. You can sit down at the system, try the keyboard, closely examine the monitor, and look at the print quality of pages printed by a printer. If you have little experience, this can help you get a feel for what the system offers.

Salespeople in computer-specialty stores do not necessarily have more computer expertise than salespeople in other kinds of stores. Depending on the size of the store and how it is run, you may deal with a salesperson who has little knowledge of PCs. On the other hand, you may deal directly with the store owner, who knows his products inside and out. The only way to determine the quality of store personnel is to ask such questions as "What is the speed of this computer?" If the salesperson responds with, "Fifty miles per hour. Ha. I'm just kidding. Believe me, it's very fast," you know that the degree of technical expertise is very low.

Superstores

Superstores, such as Soft Warehouse and CompuAdd, sell desktop and portable computers, monitors, printers, software, and other computer-related items in stores modeled on warehouse-sized consumer electronics stores. These stores usually offer discounted prices on a wide selection of hardware and software. If you are looking for a place to do comparison shopping, a superstore may be the place for you. Although name brand products, such as IBM and Apple, currently are not sold in superstores, other well-known brands, such as AST and Epson, often are available. (CompuAdd superstores carry only CompuAdd desktop and portable computers and components such as monitors, video adapters, and printers from a variety of well-known manufacturers.)

Electronics Stores

If you plan to purchase an IBM-compatible computer, such as Epson, NEC, AST, Leading Edge, Packard Bell, Vendex, ALR, Panasonic, or Everex, you should shop at your local electronics retailer. These stores also carry portables made by such companies as Toshiba, Mitsubishi, Zenith, and Sharp. You often find the best deals in large electronics stores, because these stores sell all kinds of electronics at very low prices. Some electronics retailers, however, advertise low prices and then persuade you to buy more expensive items. This selling technique is known as *bait and switch*; don't fall for it. If you are being pressured to buy a more expensive system than you want, try another store.

Consumer electronics stores often advertise complete systems, but don't let that stop you from buying the kinds of components you want. Ask about every component. If the component is not satisfactory, have them switch the component for one that is satisfactory. For example, if the store packages a system with a VGA adapter, and you want a super VGA adapter, making the switch is easy enough (of course, a better component adds to the cost of the system.)

Consumer electronics stores often bundle software with the computers they sell. Ask about this. You may get a free copy of MS-DOS, Windows, Microsoft Works, or other software.

Electronics stores usually have a service center you can turn to if you have problems with your PC. Get as many details as you can about the services the store provides. This information will help you avoid unpleasant surprises if you need to use the service center.

Ask about repair policies. Are repairs done at the store, or is the equipment sent back to the manufacturer? How long do you have to wait for a typical repair? Do you have to pay for shipping costs if the product is sent back to the manufacturer? Do you have to deliver the equipment to the store, or do you deal directly with the manufacturer? If the store's repair facility does not meet your expectations, you should consider purchasing your equipment elsewhere.

Department Stores

If a department stores sells a computer, it usually is a low-performance IBM-compatible model sold at a premium price. These stores are unlikely to have a service center on the premises. Unless you have a particular reason for buying a computer at a department store, you should make your purchase at a computer store, superstore, or electronics store.

The IBM PS/1 computer is being sold in department stores, such as Sears, which has a good reputation for supporting the products it sells. If you are considering buying a PS/1 in a department store, ask specifically about the store's computer support policy.

Mail Order

Like many other products, you can get the best prices on personal computers by buying through mail order. If you need some help putting together a computer system, however, mail order probably is not for you. If you know someone who will put together your system and doesn't mind dealing with any hassles that may arise, then you should take advantage of lower mail-order prices.

Depending on the mail-order company you deal with, you can order an advertised system, or one that you specify component-by-component. Many mail-order companies include a statement in their advertisements saying that they provide custom configurations.

To successfully purchase a computer from a mail-order company, first check with the Better Business Bureau or a consumer protection agency in the company's area. Many mail-order firms experience problems, even if they are well known. The Better Business Bureau can tell you whether any problems have developed in that company.

Next check whether the system you want is in stock. If your choice is unavailable, ask when the system will be sent to you. Pay by credit card and find out when you will be charged. Charges should be applied only after a product is actually shipped; check the charge date on your bill. Ask about a mail-order company's return policy. Some companies offer extended warranties and money-back guarantees with no questions asked. Ask what shipping charges you will be expected to pay. Some companies charge a restocking fee if you return a product. Find out what this fee is and decide if are willing to pay it.

Paying by credit card offers you some measure of protection against problems that may occur with a mail-order company. Check with your credit card issuer to find out the procedure for filing a claim if you ever have to.

Don't worry that you will be left to fend for yourself if you have problems with your system. Mail-order companies have some of the best support people in the personal computer industry. Find out whether the company offers toll-free technical support and what the hours are. Some companies offer 24-hour, 365-days-a-year telephone support, and others confine support to normal business hours. If you depend on the company for repairs, ask about repair policies. Some companies offer on-site service; others will replace defective parts through the mail. Ask about replacement policies and the average repair turn-around time.

When you purchase through mail order, you choose the method of payment and the method of shipment. Does the company accept credit cards? Does the company accept the kind of credit card you have? Is there a surcharge for using a credit card? Can you order products COD? Does the company ship through Federal Express, UPS, or both? Does the company ship overnight? How much will shipping cost?

Some mail-order companies will issue you their own credit cards, if you qualify. If you use this service, find out what interest rate the company charges. Some mail-order companies also will lease you a computer, if you meet certain qualifications.

The Direct Marketing Association suggests that if you have a problem with a mail-order company to deal first with the seller. If you cannot resolve the problem, you can write to: Mail Order Action Line, c/o DMA, 6 E. 43rd St., New York, NY 10017.

How Do I Find a Vendor?

If you plan to buy from a computer store, and you know what brand you want, you can find vendors for that product in several ways. The yellow pages and local newspapers are the first places to look. Computer stores advertise in the business, computer, or science sections of the paper. Electronics stores usually advertise on certain days of the week; ask your newspaper representative. Retail stores and regional chains that sell one brand of computer usually advertise in catalogs and fliers that are sent through the mail or included with Sunday newspapers.

To purchase a computer through mail order, look for company advertising in computer magazines. Certain magazines cover certain computers: *PC Magazine* and *PC World* cover IBMs and compatibles; *MacUser* and *Macworld* cover Macintosh computers; *Amiga World* covers Amiga computers; and *ST* covers Atari ST computers. Some magazines are directed at people who buy through mail order: *Computer Shopper*, *Computer Monthly*, and *PC Sources*. *BYTE* magazine covers all kinds of computer topics.

What Questions Should I Ask?

When you consider computer warranties and on-site service, remember that personal computers and other components, such as printers, monitors, video adapters, and hard disks, are reliable and may not require servicing for several years. When you purchase a computer with a one-year warranty, you are protecting yourself against defects in materials or workmanship, which usually appear right away. When you turn on a PC for the first time, for example, the video adapter or another component may die an hour or a day later. The warranty protects you against defect. If a component malfunctions, call the store where you made the purchase and ask them to replace the defective part. If you want protection against any possible problem, you should look for products with money-back guarantees. A typical 30-day money-back guarantee enables you to return equipment if you are dissatisfied.

If you are concerned about warranties and on-site service, ask the following questions before you make a purchase; the answers you should receive appear in parentheses.

Questions to ask about warranties:

- Where do I take the system for repair? Do I have to take it back to the store or mail it back to the manufacturer?

- What happens after the warranty expires? Can I extend the warranty?
- Do warranties cover the entire system, or just specific parts? (The entire system is warranted, not specific parts.)
- When does the warranty start: from the date manufactured, date shipped to distributor, date sold in the store, or date delivered to me? (Date delivered to you)
- Are the warranties you advertise yours, the manufacturer's, or some third-party service organization's? (Manufacturer's or manufacturer's plus ours)
- Who tracks the warranty: the store, the distributor, or the manufacturer? (The store)
- What does the warranty cover? (Everything, including software)
- What is the money-back period? (30 days)
- What is the period for immediate replacement from store inventory? If a product fails right away, do I get a new product, or is the defective product repaired? (Replacement within the first 90 days)
- What is the guaranteed turn-around time for damaged parts sent in for repair?
- Are repairs done at the dealer's site, or is equipment shipped back to the manufacturer? (Dealer)
- If a damaged component will be replaced, does it have to be received by the dealer or the manufacturer before a new component is sent? (No)
- Who pays for shipment of the damaged part? (Dealer)
- Who pays for shipment of the good replacement part? (Dealer)
- How quickly are parts shipped?
- What is the labor charge for out-of-warranty service?

Questions to ask about on-site (user's site) service:

- What level of training or certification do you require of the technicians you employ? (Technical training supplied by the manufacturer is best.)
- What is the response time for on-site service?

Ask these questions about warranties and on-site service to discover what level of service you are purchasing. A portion of the initial purchase price of a computer goes for service. If you are getting a good deal—the printer is on sale, for example—ask whether you get the same level of service.

Who Does Setup and Training?

When the computer arrives, you will have to set it up. Connecting the components together is not difficult. It is comparable to putting a stereo system together or hooking up a VCR. Some people prefer to do the setup themselves; others may request a friend's help or hire someone to set up the system to make certain it works.

A computer system includes hardware and software. You cannot begin to work with the system until you load the operating system and applications software. A dealer or mail-order supplier can configure a system to load the operating system and present you with a selection of applications to choose from. If no one does this for you, you have to do it yourself, which takes time and effort. You need time to read the manuals for the operating system and the applications software. To get started right away, make sure that the dealer or mail-order supplier takes care of this task for you.

If you want training, personal computer classes are offered through computer stores, training companies, colleges, high schools, and user groups. You can find these training opportunities in fliers, newspaper ads, or by asking the salesperson where you purchase the computer. The least expensive options are adult education classes given in high schools and community colleges.

If you learn well on your own, look in your favorite bookstore for a large selection of books on any personal computing subject. You also can find video tapes that explain PC hardware and teach you to use popular software programs. For system repair information, try *Upgrading and Repairing PCs* written by Scott Mueller and published by Que Corporation.

How Do I Make the Big Purchase?

After you have done your research by reading this book, looking at ads in newspapers, scanning computer magazines, talking to friends, and visiting computer stores, you should have a clear vision of what you want to purchase. Before you leave for the store or make that phone order, complete a checklist, such as the one shown in table 7.1.

This list gives you a method for comparing prices. You want a quote on everything. If the salesperson baits you with a $200 printer but requires that you purchase an $80 cable with it, you are smarter to buy a printer and cable for $250 elsewhere. The list includes the small items not discussed in this chapter.

Table 7.1
PC Buyer's Checklist

Number/description	Cost*

PERSONAL COMPUTER

Model _____ $ _____
CPU _____
Speed (MHz) _____
RAM _____
Cache RAM _____
Floppy disk drive size _____
Floppy drive capacity _____
Hard disk size _____ $ _____
Hard disk capacity _____
Hard disk/controller _____
Video adapter _____ $ _____
Case style _____
Keyboard _____ $ _____
Mouse _____ $ _____
Power cord _____
Serial port _____
Parallel port _____
Other _____

MONITOR

Model _____
Type _____
Cable _____
Tilt and swivel base _____
Power Cord _____

PRINTER

Model _____ $ _____
Type _____
Cable _____
Power Cord _____

MODEM

Model _____ $ _____
Type _____
Modem power cord _____
Modem phone wire _____
Cable _____ $ _____

continues

Table 7.1–*continued*

Warranty _____	
Extended Warranty _____	$
SOFTWARE	
Operating system disks _____	$
Diagnostic disks _____	
System setup disks _____	
Utility disks _____	
Video adapter disks _____	
Application 1 _____	$
Application 2 _____	$
Application 3 _____	$
SUPPLIES	
Floppy disks _____	$
Paper _____	$
Mailing Labels _____	$
MISCELLANEOUS	
Mouse Pad _____	$
Power strip/ surge protector _____	$
Keyboard cover _____	$

Total $_____

*Certain parts of the system may be included in a total system price.

Make copies of the checklist and compare several different personal computer systems. Using the checklist also ensures that you purchase all the parts and pieces you need to begin computing.

After you complete the checklist, follow these steps to purchase your computer:

1. Call the Better Business Bureau. Ask whether there are any outstanding complaints on the store or company.

2. Write down the name of the store, its address and phone number, and the name of the salesperson you deal with; this information may be on the invoice. Ask for four copies of the refund policy and warranty. Inquire about service by using the questions given in this chapter.

3. Pay for your microcomputer and accessories with a credit card, if possible. After you receive your equipment and make sure that the system is working properly, you can pay the entire bill to avoid significant interest charges. If what you receive, however, isn't what you actually ordered, or if the product is defective, you can contest the charge to your credit card company. Most credit card companies will refuse to make payment on a bill if you provide written documentation of a legitimate grievance you have with the charged product. Many credit card companies also will negotiate a resolution with the company that has sold you the item in question. Also, take advantage of any credit card promotions, such as those that double the length of a warranty.

4. When you get your new computer home or to your office, put it together immediately and try it out. Examine everything closely. Try all the components, such as floppy disk drives, to make sure that they are working. Format a floppy disk. Check that the capacity of the disk matches the type of disk drive you ordered (for example, a 1.44M floppy drive formats floppy disks with 1.44 MB of capacity). Look for an indication that the amount of RAM in the computer is the amount you ordered (for example, IBM and compatible computers display on-screen the amount of RAM in the system when you start up the system). Check the space on the hard disk (if you don't know how to do this, check your operating system manual). Make sure that the capacity you have is the capacity you ordered. Check the monitor. Does it provide the color and resolution you expected? Look for anything odd on the screen, such as random lines that could be the result of a faulty adapter. Check that all software programs work as expected.

If you think anything is wrong with any hardware or software component, call the dealer or mail-order company back right away to discuss the problem.

Chapter Summary

This chapter explained where to purchase a computer system: computer stores, superstores, consumer electronics stores, department stores, or through mail order.

After suggesting where to buy, the chapter explained how to find a personal computer from a particular vendor. This chapter then provided questions to ask about warranties and on-site service. Finally, the chapter furnished a checklist for making the *big purchase*.

In the Next Chapter

The next chapter defines various kinds of software and explains what tasks can be done with them: writing memos, creating budgets, compiling mailing lists, and so on. The chapter then explains differences among some of the more popular programs on the market. Finally, the chapter explains what features are important and provides specific software recommendations.

8

What Software Do I Need?

No matter what type of personal computer system you purchase, to get the most benefit from the computer, you must have the proper software. This chapter helps you decide which type of software will benefit you. Reading this information should help you categorize software—not only by what the software will accomplish but also to what degree the software will accomplish the task. In this chapter, you find help to choose the applicable environment for your software. You also see how to determine whether you need more than one software package to accomplish a task.

This chapter also shows the differences among software products within the same category and tells you what to expect from many software products, from the low end to the high end. The chapter covers features of the different products and helps you decide which ones are important for you. Finally, the chapter specifically recommends some software products.

Analyzing Your Needs

Probably the most difficult part of purchasing a computer is deciding on the right software. Many different software programs are available. Some programs may perform the same tasks, and other programs perform slightly different tasks. Programs often are created to perform at different levels. For example, although two word processors enable you to write memos equally well, only one may offer the capability to mail-merge letters.

Setting Your Software Goals

Goals are important in accomplishing anything. If you own a business, you probably prepare a yearly business plan. The business plan sets goals for the year. Knowing the goals helps you determine how best to attain them and what path you must take to attain them. Before even looking for software, write down a list of goals for your software.

Your list may be simple. For example, you may want software only for writing, or you may want software only for manipulating figures. Likely, however, you want to automate several tasks—getting the most out of your investment in a computer.

When initially setting the goals for your software use, don't try to be too specific. For example, a set of goals may be:

- To write documents
- To write reports
- To create budgets
- To manage customer names and addresses
- To manage expenses
- To create a customer newsletter

Look over the written goals. Words that you use in these goals can tip you off as to what category of software you may need. The major categories of software are word processors for writing; spreadsheets for financial planning; databases for managing information; financial or accounting packages for managing your money accounts; desktop publishing for creating newsletters, fliers, menus, and so on; communications programs for transmitting information over phone lines; graphics or drawing programs for creating pictures; music programs for creating electronic music; education programs; and entertainment applications.

Notice that the first two goals contain the word *write*. For these goals, you need a word processor. The second goal, however, also contains the word *report*. Because a report often contains values and computations, you may need a word processor that performs calculations or a spreadsheet.

The third goal contains a financial word—*budget*. You probably need a spreadsheet or an accounting program.

The fourth and fifth goals contains the word *manage*. When you manage information, database software comes to mind. The fifth goal, however, also contains a financial word, *expenses*. Spreadsheet or accounting software, therefore, may be needed to complete this goal.

Finally, the sixth goal mentions a *newsletter*. A desktop publishing program often is used to create a newsletter; however, some word processors have certain desktop publishing capabilities. To accomplish your list of goals, you have determined that you may need software in the following categories:

- Word processing
- Spreadsheet
- Accounting
- Database
- Desktop publishing

Now that you have the categories, you need to refine your goals. Determine how powerful you need software to be. Determine, also, if some of your tasks may overlap and can be serviced by one software program, rather than separate programs.

Setting Software Requirements

Refining your initial, broad goals helps you to adjust your software requirements. Refining your goals means expanding them to include each step necessary to acquire your overall goal. For example, in the goals list, "to write documents" can be expanded into writing memos and one- or two-page letters.

Encompassed in the goal "to write reports," you may need to include text, values with calculations, and graphs. A spreadsheet with graphing capabilities is necessary to fulfill this goal.

Breaking down the goal "to create budgets," you need to keep monthly budgets, as well as a yearly budget. You want to compare actual expenses for the month to your budgeted values. You also want to change values in your budget to see how that affects your overall income—for one month and for the year. Values from the budget will be used to create the reports mentioned previously. A spreadsheet adds more value here, because you may create the formulas necessary to create the budget, and by changing numbers, you can have the program perform quick recalculations that show you the effect on the month and year. Because you already have determined that a spreadsheet with graphing capabilities is necessary for report creation, you can avoid purchasing a spreadsheet program and an accounting program.

The next goal, "to manage customer names and addresses," is for simple mailing-list management. You need to print form letters to your customers. Many word processors enable you to manage names and addresses. You may type the names and addresses and then use them to print mailing labels or form letters. In some cases, word processors even enable you to sort your names and addresses so that you may arrange them by name or even zip code.

Suppose that to meet the goal, "to manage customer names and addresses," you needed to store other data about the customers. In this case a database program is needed. Using a database program, you easily can store much information. You can use the database program to search for information and to sort the information that you have. Some word processors even use the information from a database for mail-merging.

"To manage expenses," your fifth goal, you need to total expenses monthly so that you can be reimbursed. This means that you keep a record of each expense, including the date of the expense, a description, and the amount. Although this may sound like a job for a database, you also may attain this goal using a spreadsheet program. Many spreadsheet programs have some database capabilities, and because you need a spreadsheet for your other goals, you can use the spreadsheet to its fullest capabilities.

Your final goal is "to create a customer newsletter." In this newsletter, you want to print multiple columns, including graphics. A desktop publishing program can give you many nice features. You may create text with a word processor and graphics with a drawing program and then use the desktop publisher to read the text and pictures and place them on each page where you need them. Some more advanced word processors, however, perform near-desktop publishing functions. You may type and edit the text in the word processor, use columns, and even read in pictures. Because you will be purchasing a word processor anyway, you may select a word processor that enables you to create the newsletter. For the graphics that you need to include, purchase a graphics drawing program or predrawn pictures for inclusion in the newsletters.

Selecting the type of software that you need is relatively easy. Setting your goals for software helps you to determine what software is necessary. When setting the preceding goals, you determined that you need a word processor that does more than enable you to write memos and letters and to check the spelling. The word processor you select also must be able to mail-merge, print text in columns, and insert drawings.

You need a spreadsheet for calculating numbers. The spreadsheet also must have limited database capabilities. You must be able to create and save graphs with the spreadsheet.

Finally, you need some type of drawing program, or you may decide to purchase predrawn pictures. (Be sure that the drawing program can load the predrawn figures you select.)

Now you must select the brand of software to purchase. Later in this chapter, "Selecting Applications Software" presents a discussion of different brands of software, including the features and benefits they offer.

Before you start selecting the software program to use, you must know what operating system that you are using. You also must determine if you need to operate the programs at the same time; for example, to print a report from the spreadsheet while you are designing your newsletter.

Choosing a Software Environment

An important choice that you must make is what operating system and operating environment (also called *user interface*) you prefer to use to run your software. An operating system is a level of software between an application program and the computer. The operating system provides services to you and the application program—such as the storing and recalling of information from a disk drive. Besides providing services, an operating system provides a way for you to interact. The interaction that you have with the operating system is through the operating environment. Some operating systems enable you to place a different operating environment between you and the operating system.

Your choice of an operating system and environment may be ruled by the computer that you own. For example, the most-used operating system for the Macintosh computer is the System, and its operating environment is the Finder. Most likely, if you purchase a Macintosh, you will purchase software that works with System and Finder.

In the IBM and compatible realm, the most-used operating system is DOS. However, within DOS you have multiple operating environments that you may select from, although only two operating environments are common.

When selecting an operating system and an environment, consider whether you need to run all software at the same time, or if you will be running only one program at a time. Does your operating system and environment need to multitask or perform single tasks? The next few sections explore this issue, as it pertains to selecting software.

Single-Task Operating Systems and Environments

In a single-tasking operating system and environment, you run one software program at a time. For example, you use your word processor to write and print a letter. Then you exit the word processor, start your spreadsheet program, and perform calculations. When you finish with the spreadsheet program, you exit and start the next program. In most cases, this mode of operation is adequate.

A single-task operating system and environment generally does not require an overly powerful computer. You also are not required to have a large amount of RAM in the computer. As you run one program, the entire computer's processing speed is dedicated to that program. IBM and Macintosh computers both have single-task operating systems and environments.

Text-Based DOS

With IBM and compatible computers, MS-DOS is a single-task operating system and environment. Many programs run under MS-DOS. You generally can find a software program to fit your goals, no matter what type of software you need. Actually, the single-task, text-based program is the most popular type of program for IBM and compatible computers.

The MS-DOS operating environment is considered *text-based*. Characters appearing on-screen look much like the characters created by a typewriter. The characters displayed on-screen are nonproportional—each character takes the same amount of space on-screen. Nonproportional characters are contrasted with proportional characters, used in most graphics-based operating environments. The letters in this book are proportional; the letters f and t take much less space than m or M.

With the use of laser printers and the desire to print quality documents (using proportional fonts), many text-based, single-task programs use a graphics mode. Generally, you may switch between the text and graphics modes. Using the graphics mode gives you the what-you-see-is-what-you-get (WYSIWYG) feel. What you see on-screen is very similar to how the printed product looks. WordPerfect 5.1 and Lotus 1-2-3 are fine examples of powerful, single-task, text-based software programs that offer a WYSIWYG mode.

One disadvantage of a single-task operating system and environment like MS-DOS is sharing information between programs. For example, if you write a document using your word processor and need to include calculations that you performed in your worksheet, you must jump back and forth between starting your spreadsheet and word processor. For example, start the spreadsheet, perform the calculations, and save the calculations that you need in a format that your word processor can read. Quit the spreadsheet and start the word processor. Write the document with the word processor and read in the information that you created with the spreadsheet. Save and print the document. If you use different calculations in the document, you must quit the word processor, restart the spreadsheet, and start the whole process again.

If you are using only one software program or have to share data between programs in a limited way, MS-DOS may meet your needs. If you need to switch between programs and share data, however, you may want to look more at a multiple-task environment.

System and Finder

The single-task operating system for the Macintosh, System, and its graphical operating environment, Finder, is the most-used operating system and environment on the Macintosh. Most programs that meet your goals, whether simple or powerful, work with the System and Finder.

Finder is a graphical operating environment, also called a Graphical User Interface or GUI. Programs written for a GUI normally are uniform; the main features of programs look similar, and many of the operations of one program are similar to the operations of another.

When using System and Finder, however, you still are working with a single-task environment. You still must close one program before starting another. Because of Finder's design, however, transferring information from one program to another is easier. You may copy information from one program and easily paste the information into another program after you close the first program and start the second.

A decision to use the Macintosh's single-task environment should be based on a need to use one or two software programs only. If you find that you are leaving one program and entering another program frequently, you may decide on a multiple-task environment.

Multiple-Task Environments

Multiple-task environments enable you to have more than one application program active at a time. For example, you may open your word processor and spreadsheet at the same time. You do not have to close any documents or quit any programs when you switch from one application to another. Normally, a provision has been made through the multitask environment to easily transfer data from one program to another.

Some multiple-task environments for the IBM enable programs to *multitask*, to perform operations at the same time. While a large spreadsheet is calculating, and a database program is performing a search, you may write a letter. The computer divides its time among all applications.

Several multitasking environments are available for the IBM computer. Only two of these environments, however, are widely used. These environments are

Microsoft Windows and Quarterdeck DESQview. The other environments are used in a limited way or have not been as accepted yet. Less used environments for the IBM are GEM by Digital Research, Deskmate by Tandy and Ensemble (formerly GEOWorks) from Berkeley Software.

The Macintosh computer has only one multitasking environment, Multifinder. This environment is supplied with System and easily can replace Finder.

Microsoft Windows

Microsoft Windows is the most popular graphical user interface for IBM-compatible computers. The latest version at the time this book went to press, Version 3.0, makes an IBM compatible look like an Apple Macintosh computer.

Windows enables you to start and switch among multiple DOS applications. If you are using a computer with an 80386SX, 80386, or 80486 microprocessor and an adequate amount of memory, you may multitask DOS applications. If you do not need to multitask DOS applications, however, you still may open more than one program and switch among the programs. You also easily may transfer information on-screen from one program to another.

Programs are written to take specific advantage of Windows. Because Windows is an operating environment, programs written for Windows look uniform, like programs written for the Macintosh. Programs written for Windows also can multitask, and because Windows is managing the programs, they are much more efficient at multitasking than DOS programs operating within Windows.

If you need multitasking and like a WYSIWYG approach to programs, consider using Windows and Windows-specific applications. Remember, if one of the applications that meets your goals is not a Windows application, but all the others are, do not rule out Windows. You still may run the non-Windows application within Windows.

To adequately use Windows, you must have a more powerful computer than if you are running a single-task environment. Purchase a mouse to use Windows more efficiently, as most menu and dialog box choices in Windows easily can be made with a mouse. You also should purchase a computer with an 80386SX, 80386, or 80486 CPU. The computer that you purchase should have a high-quality screen, such as VGA. Your computer also should have at least 2M of RAM. If you plan to multitask multiple DOS applications under Windows, purchase at least 4M of RAM.

Recommendations for Windows products are made later in this chapter under the specific applications areas. Windows 3.0 comes with a simple word processor, drawing program, communications program, and file manager. These programs lack many features, but if you have light requirements in any of these areas, you may not have to purchase a separate program.

DESQview

DESQview is similar to Windows 3.0 in some ways but is different in other ways. DESQview enables you to start multiple programs, to switch among programs, and to multitask DOS programs. DESQview does not require that you have an 80386SX or greater microprocessor. You may multitask many DOS applications even on a less powerful computer. Using at least an 80386SX computer, however, makes multitasking more efficient, due to the design of the microprocessor.

DESQview, however, is text-based, rather than graphical. DESQview really was designed to multitask standard DOS applications, although a few DESQview-specific applications are available.

If standard DOS applications meet your needs and you need to open multiple programs or multitask, DESQview is a fine environment to select. Because DESQview is text-based, rather than graphical, the environment multitasks DOS applications quicker. Graphically updating the screen, such as Windows must do, takes quite a bit of the computer's time—degrading the performance of standard DOS applications. DESQview also enables you to copy information from program to program.

Just because DESQview is text-based, however, does not mean that it will not run graphical programs. DESQview manages graphical programs, such as drawing or CAD programs, as easily as it manages text-based DOS programs. DESQview even enables you to run Windows applications at the same time you are running DOS applications.

If you plan to use DESQview and need multitasking capabilities, you must have a large amount of memory in your computer. The amount of memory required depends on the requirements of the individual programs that you multitask, plus the memory required for DOS and DESQview. If you need only to switch among applications, however, not as much memory is required. Like Windows, hard disk space is used to store an application that you switch away from. When you switch back to an application, it moves from the hard disk back into memory.

Other IBM-Compatible Operating Environments

Several other graphical user interfaces are available for IBM-compatible computers. These interfaces are not as popular as Windows and DESQview, however.

GEM, a GUI, is available for IBM-compatible computers and is used much more widely on Atari ST and Mega computers. Applications are written specifically to take advantage of its graphical environment, even though DOS programs may be started from GEM. GEM, however, does not multitask applications.

DeskMate, a GUI offered with some Tandy desktop and portable computers, has over 100 software applications written for it, including Lotus 1-2-3 (a scaled-down version) and Symantec's popular Q&A. DeskMate comes with a simple word processor, spreadsheet, file manager, calendar, drawing program, alarm, calculator, spell checker, and phone list. Tandy even supplies a low-end network called DeskMate Workgroup. You also may start DOS applications using DeskMate and switch among these applications.

GEOWorks (Ensemble) is another fine operating environment. Programs may be written specifically to take advantage of the GUI offered by GEOs. Applications written specifically for GEOWorks multitask. GEOWorks also comes with a word processor, appointment program, communications programs, and several other utilities. Although these applications are not extremely advanced, you may be able to use them for limited work.

GEOWorks enables you to start several DOS applications. Although you may switch from one DOS application to another, DOS applications cannot be multitasked as they can with Windows or DESQview.

Multifinder

Provided with the Macintosh, Multifinder is a widely used operating environment. Because it is based on Finder, most standard Macintosh applications can be used with Multifinder. Although Multifinder does not multitask Macintosh applications, this environment enables you to open multiple applications and switch among them. Also, you easily can transfer information from one program to another by copying and pasting.

Using Multifinder requires that you have a larger amount of memory. Each application that you open with Multifinder occupies memory. The amount of memory required depends on how many applications you will open at one time.

Multitasking Operating Systems

Neither DOS for IBM and compatible computers, nor System for the Macintosh is a multitasking operating system. These operating systems, although adequate for most computer users, run one application at a time. If your goals for programs are high, you may consider purchasing a multitasking operating system. Doing so, however, requires that you buy programs specifically designed for the operating system that you choose.

A multitasking operating system is much different from an operating environment that multitasks. The operating system is designed with multitasking in mind. A multitasking operating environment actually sits on top of a single-task operating system. The operating system designed to multitask, therefore, is much more efficient than the multitasking environment. High-powered applications are written for multitasking operating systems.

IBM and compatible computers have two well-known multitasking operating systems: UNIX and OS/2. UNIX is an operating system designed for larger computers and because of its wide use, has been adapted to personal computers. Because of its complexity, however, UNIX is not discussed in this text.

OS/2

You probably have heard about OS/2, a new operating system for IBM-compatible computers. Although you may not be considering OS/2, you should have some understanding of where this operating system fits into the overall IBM computing picture. DOS was designed as a character-oriented operating system that runs one program at a time. Windows 3.0 adds a graphical user interface and the capability to run more than one program at a time. OS/2 was designed as a multitasking operating system with a graphical user interface called the Presentation Manager (PM). The look and feel of PM is similar to Windows.

Several programs written for DOS and Windows also are offered for OS/2. Although the programs may look similar, they do not operate in the same way.

Windows multitasks in the following way: Program 1 gets a certain amount of processing time; program 2 gets a certain amount of processing time; and program 3 gets a certain amount of processing time. Even if one of the programs is not processing, it still is given processing time. While each program is processing, the other programs are dormant. Because Windows keeps providing each program with processing time, however, you get the effect of multitasking.

OS/2 works differently. Rather than the entire program getting a piece of the pie, one program is broken into processes that are given computer time. If a program is setting idle, it does not need computer time. Only those processes that actually need computer time are given time. Multitasking, therefore, happens much more efficiently.

Processes under OS/2 can communicate with each other; one program can pass results to another program. Even if you are using only one program, that program may multitask. Several processes within one program may go on at the same time.

Although OS/2 programs offer better overall performance than DOS or Windows programs, OS/2 demands a more powerful computer. You must have at least an 80286 computer for OS/2 and an 80386 computer for later versions. A large amount of memory is required for OS/2—at least 2M to 4M of RAM, besides the memory required for each program you plan to use. OS/2 requires hard disk space as well. At least 10M is required for the operating system. OS/2 is not for everyone. If your goals demand much processing power, OS/2 may be a consideration. Most users who need multitasking capabilities, however, find DOS and Windows quite acceptable.

Macintosh System 7

System 7 is an operating system that many Macintosh users have been waiting for for a long time. Offering many features, System 7 is the Macintosh's multitasking operating system.

One of the key features of System 7 is that the system enables processes to communicate with one another. Not only does one program pass information to itself, but it can interact with other programs—a key feature with true multitasking.

If you decide that you need the capabilities of System 7, you first should find out if the software program you are looking at takes advantage of System 7. Some programs operate under System 7 but do not take advantage of the features. Some programs take advantage of only some of the features. Other programs may be written to take advantage of all of System 7's features. Before accepting a program for use with System 7, verify the program's compatibility level.

Considering Training and Support

No matter what software program you choose to meet your goals, you have to learn how to use it. This process can be quite an undertaking if you need more than one software program to meet your goals.

As equally important as the power of your program and the capability for a program to meet your goals, is the program's ease of use and the support provided by the manufacturer.

Foremost for an easy-to-use program is the interface, the commands that you select to operate the program. This fact is what makes a GUI popular. Programs designed for a GUI generally are uniform. Menus on different programs operate the same. Similar commands are found on similar menus within similar programs. Menus are selected easily and remain on-screen while you are using them. Probably most important, programs for most GUIs have extensive on-line help.

Just because a program is text-based, however, does not mean that it is hard to use. Many text-based programs operate similar to GUI programs. Menus are similar and remain on-screen when selected. Commands are found on similar menus. Extensive on-line help is available when you need help with a command or procedure.

Two types of support are available for programs. One is the help that the program offers you. Ask yourself, "Is the program easy to use? Does the software company offer telephone support if I need help using the program? Are additional materials available for the program, such as books, newsletters, or articles in trade magazines? Do local user's groups offer help using the program?" Positive answers to these questions can give you confidence that the software program is a good selection.

The other type of support is with upgrades to the program. A well-supported program is upgraded periodically. New features may be added to the program. Existing features may be increased or made easier to use. Knowing that a program is upgraded periodically gives you confidence that you selected a fine program.

Determining Your Hardware Configuration

Obviously, software not designed for your computer does not run on your computer. Macintosh software, for example, cannot run on IBM or Amiga computers. Software designed to run on your computer brand, however, may not run on your particular computer system if your system does not meet the software's minimum requirements.

Almost all software programs carry a label listing the system requirements. The system requirements tell you the minimum requirements your system needs to run the program. You usually can upgrade your computer to meet the requirements of the software. The following system requirements apply to Lotus 1-2-3 Release 2.2:

- IBM PC and Lotus-certified compatibles
- DOS Version 2.0 or above
- Minimum of 320K bytes of system RAM required
- 512K bytes recommended
- Hard disk and 512K bytes of system RAM required for Allways

The IBM PC mentioned in the requirements is the original IBM model with the 8088 CPU. This requirement, therefore, can be met by any IBM-compatible system. (Don't worry about Lotus certification. The term is a holdover from the days when some IBM compatibles were not very compatible.) The requirements specify that you must have at least 320K to operate the program. However, remember that amount is the *minimum*. Generally, the more memory that you have available, the better. Notice that Lotus recommends 512K of memory. Notice, too, that a hard disk is required if you use the Allways program that accompanies Lotus 1-2-3.

Contrast the requirements of Lotus Release 2.2 with the requirements of Lotus 1-2-3 Release 3.1:

- IBM PC AT and Lotus-certified compatibles, including most IBM PS/2 and Compaq models
- Hard disk with 5M available
- EGA, VGA, high-resolution CGA, or Hercules graphics adapter for WYSIWYG display
- DOS 3.0 or higher
- 1M of available system RAM

Notice that Lotus 1-2-3 Release 3.1 requires at least an IBM PC AT, which is a personal computer with an 80286 CPU. This version of Lotus 1-2-3 does not run on an IBM compatible with an 8088 or 8086 CPU, but this version runs fine on an 80286, 80386, 80386SX, or 80486 IBM compatible.

Also notice that the minimum DOS requirement is different. At least DOS Version 3.0 is required, rather than DOS Version 2.0. (As of this writing, DOS Version 4.01 is the latest version). Also specified is the type of video adapter, the minimum amount of RAM, and that you must have a hard disk. Although the minimum memory specification is 1M, you are better off purchasing more memory.

Programs for other computers usually suggest similar requirements. For example, a program may require a specific version of the operating system, or a certain amount of memory may be required. Generally, however, programs for non-IBM-compatible computers have less confusing requirements, because fewer operating systems are available. The diversity between the microprocessors also is not so great.

If you know which software programs you need, you can select a personal computer by meeting the hardware requirements of those programs. Remember that the minimum requirements generally are conservative. Although the program operates with the minimum specifications, you may find the program faster and more capable of meeting your needs with greater specifications.

Selecting Applications Software

You cannot do much with a personal computer until you purchase applications. The following sections help you select a the right software package for the type of personal computer you are considering (or own) and the kind of work you want to do.

Word Processors

A word processor enables you to type and manipulate text on-screen until every word, sentence, and paragraph is just right—then you can print the document. Word processors can be used for any kind of writing task, such as letters, memos, reports, articles, stories, books, and so on.

The basic differences among word processors are in ease of use, speed of operation, advanced features, and support programs (such as a spelling checker). A low-end program may be easy to learn and use but may lack speed. A high-end program may be fast and have advanced features, but be difficult to learn. Typically, low-end word processors support basic functions, such as moving blocks of text. Low-end word processors generally lack advanced functions such as the automatic generation of a table of contents.

Some word processors show you a true picture of your document as you work, and some don't. If you expect to see different typefaces, type styles, type sizes, and graphic elements, you need a WYSIWYG word processor. Word processors for IBM-compatible computers usually display characters on-screen in a monospaced font, the standard characters displayed on the IBM-compatible computer. Some word processors display a monospaced font but also offer a preview mode that shows how a document looks on paper.

Word processors can be characterized by the user interface. The majority of programs for IBM-compatible computers rely on function keys and control-key combinations to initiate commands. Many new versions of word processors, however, are using pull-down menus that do not require much memorization. WordPerfect and Microsoft Word for DOS, popular high-end word processors, recently have added pull-down menus to supplement their normal user interfaces. Some word processors are designed to run under Windows 3.0 and use the graphical user interface of Windows. Of course, word processors for the Macintosh and Amiga use the computer's standard graphical user interface.

Advanced functions of word processors include styles, document management, indexing, footnoting, multiple column layouts, the capability to generate a table of contents, and the integration of graphics. *Styles*, a new concept to word processors, enables you to record text formatting on a paragraph basis. The next time a paragraph needs to be in the same style, the prerecorded style can be applied to the paragraph. This feature increases productivity when creating documents that share similar styles.

Some word processors can display more than one document on-screen at a time. If you often move or copy text from one document to another, this *document management* feature may be a high priority.

Indexing generates an index from your documents. Footnotes and table of contents are useful features for advanced documents, such as documentation or legal documents. Multiple columns enables you to type down one column, return to the top, and begin typing down another, and so on; this feature is useful if you create simple newsletters. (If this feature is important, make sure that you find out the number of columns the program supports.) Graphics integration means that you can incorporate a graph or a picture into your text—another important feature for creating newsletters or business reports.

Some support programs to look for in a word processor are a spelling checker, thesaurus, outliner, and grammar checker. When comparing spelling checkers and thesauri, look for the total number of words included and the capability to add proper names and business-specific words to the group.

Low-end word processors are good for budget conscious people or for home systems when you want to work on the content of a document, save the document, and bring it into the office for completion. Low-end products are good for portable or laptop computers, because memory and hard disk requirements usually are low.

Make sure that the low-end word processor you buy can save files in ASCII format. *ASCII*, which stands for American Standard Code for Information Interchange, is a plain text file that contains no special formatting commands. If text is typed in a low-end product and saved in ASCII format, the text can be imported into a high-end word processor that can format the document with greater sophistication.

When considering a word processor, ask yourself the following:

- Is the user interface proprietary or does the program run under Windows 3.0? (Only for IBM-compatible computers.)

- Is the program easy to use?

- Is the program fast? (This question can be answered only if you compare one word processor with another.)
- Is the program a WYSIWYG word processor?
- If the program is not a WYSIWYG word processor, does it have a preview mode?
- Does the program have style sheets?
- Can I work on more than one document at a time?
- Does the program have an indexing feature?
- Does the program support footnotes?
- Can I create multiple columns?
- Can the program generate a table of contents?
- Can I integrate graphics?
- Does the program have an integrated spelling checker? How many words are included?
- Does the program have an integrated thesaurus? How many words are included?
- Does the program have an integrated outliner?
- Does the program have an integrated grammar checker?
- Does the program have a mail-merge feature?
- Can I create an ASCII file?

All of these questions should be answered after you have defined your goals for software and have determined that you need a word processor.

To answer questions like these, you can call the company and ask a customer service representative. You also can read the description of features on the software package, request a flier about the product from the company, and read reviews of word processors in computer magazines.

Table 8.1 gives specific recommendations for word processors based on a specific computer type, CPU, operating system, user interface, operating mode (WYSIWYG or monospaced), suggested retail price, and typical mail-order price.

**Table 8.1
Word Processors**

Product					
WordPerfect 5.1	Word for Windows	Professional Write 2.2	LetterPerfect 1.0	Microsoft Word 4.0	WriteNow 2.2
Company					
WordPerfect Corp.	Microsoft Corp.	Software Publishing Co.	WordPerfect Corp.	Microsoft Corp.	T/Maker Co.
PC					
IBM or compatible	IBM or compatible	IBM or compatible	IBM or compatible	Macintosh	Macintosh
CPU					
8088 or greater	80386SX or greater	8088 or greater	8088 or greater	68000 or greater	68000 or greater
Operating system					
PC-DOS/MS-DOS 4.01	PC-DOS/MS-DOS 4.01	PC-DOS/MS-DOS 4.01	PC-DOS/MS-DOS 4.01	System 6.0.6	System 6.0.6
User interface					
Function keys/ pull-down menus	Windows 3.0	Pull-down menus	Function keys/ pull-down menus	Macintosh	Macintosh
Operating mode					
Monospaced font with preview mode	WYSIWYG	Monospaced font	Monospaced font with preview mode	WYSIWYG	WYSIWYG
Sugg. retail price					
$495	$495	$249	$229	$395	$199
Mail-order price					
$275	$340	$190	$145	$255	$125

All of these products offer a good blend of features for the price. However, you may consider many other word processors. Any you do consider should be measured against the features and prices of the products listed in the table.

Spreadsheet Programs

A spreadsheet program is the electronic equivalent of the sheets of paper in an accountant's analysis pad. Spreadsheets enable you to enter numeric data into the computer in rows and columns of cells. You can create formulas that add, subtract, multiply, divide, or perform almost any other mathematical operation on the data. If you change a cell's number or formula, all cells that depend on the changed cell update their values. For example, if you change the amount of money a business pays for rent, the total amount for expenses changes automatically, and the net profit changes. This flexibility makes spreadsheet software a valuable tool for planning and forecasting. Spreadsheets are ideal for number-oriented tasks such as creating budgets, expense reports, and sales projections.

For spreadsheets that run on IBM-compatible computers, a big difference is the user interface. A program such as Lotus 1-2-3 uses a horizontal menu bar to select spreadsheet features. Other programs, such as Quattro Pro, use pull-down menus. Microsoft Excel uses the graphical user interface of the Macintosh, Windows 3.0, or OS/2. As with word processors, Macintosh, Windows 3.0, and OS/2 interfaces are easier to learn than the proprietary interfaces of other products.

Some spreadsheet programs can display more than one spreadsheet at a time. With a product such as Lotus 1-2-3 Release 2.2, only one spreadsheet can be shown on-screen. To see another spreadsheet, you must close the current spreadsheet and then open the one you want to see. Quattro Pro 2.0, however, can open many spreadsheets at the same time. When more than one spreadsheet is on-screen, you easily can link parts of different spreadsheets together.

A related spreadsheet feature is the capability to work in three dimensions. This feature enables you to perform mathematical operations on several spreadsheets at the same time and then save the related spreadsheets together in one file. Three-dimensional spreadsheets, for example, can create a summary budget from the individual budgets of several different departments. Lotus 1-2-3 Release 3.1 has multiple spreadsheet and 3-D capabilities.

Spreadsheet publishing features enable you to dress up a spreadsheet with a variety of typefaces and boxes and dress up graphs with words, symbols, and pictures. Lotus 1-2-3 Release 2.2 uses a separate add-in program called Allways to provide this feature. Quattro Pro, Microsoft Excel, and Wingz have this feature built into the program.

Some spreadsheets do not work with IBM-compatible computers that use an 8088 or 8086 CPU. See the table for personal computer recommendations.

Although many low-end spreadsheets were available a few years ago, most have disappeared from dealers' shelves or are difficult to find. One low-end spreadsheet still available for IBM compatibles is Borland's Quattro, the forerunner of Quattro Pro. Another source for low-end spreadsheets are integrated programs, discussed later in this chapter.

Ask yourself the following questions when considering a spreadsheet program:

- What is the user interface? Is it proprietary (only for IBM-compatible PCs) or does the interface follow the standards set by Windows 3.0 or the Macintosh?

- Can the program display more than one spreadsheet on-screen at a time?

- Can related spreadsheets be saved together in the same file (3-D capability)?

- Does the spreadsheet have publishing features?
- What kind of graph types does the program have? Can the program produce 2- and 3-dimensional pie graphs, line graphs, bar graphs, and so on? Can I manipulate the graph—rotate the axis, move and edit legends, add descriptive words, symbols, and pictures?

To answer questions like these and other questions you may have, you can call the company and ask a customer service representative, ask a salesperson in a computer retail outlet, read the description of features on the software package, request a flier about the product from the company, and read reviews of spreadsheets in computer magazines.

Table 8.2 gives specific recommendations for spreadsheets based on a specific computer type, CPU, operating system, user interface, suggested retail price, and typical mail-order price.

Table 8.2
Spreadsheets

Product					
1-2-3 Release 2.2	1-2-3 Release 3.1	Microsoft Excel 2.1	Microsoft Excel 2.2	Quattro Pro 2.0	Wingz 1.1
Company					
Lotus Corp.	Lotus Corp.	Microsoft Corp.	Microsoft Corp.	Borland	Informix
PC					
IBM or compatible	IBM or compatible	IBM or compatible	Macintosh	IBM or compatible	Macintosh
CPU					
8088 or greater	80286 or greater	80386SX or greater	68000 or greater	8088 or greater	68000 or greater
Operating System					
PC-DOS/MS-DOS	PC-DOS/MS-DOS 4.01	PC-DOS/MS-DOS 4.01	System 6.0.6	PC-DOS/MS-DOS 4.01	System 6.0.6
User interface					
Menu bar	Menu bar	Windows 3.0	Macintosh	Pull-down menus	Macintosh
Sugg. retail price					
$495	$595	$495	$395	$495	$395
Mail-order price					
$360	$440	$329	$245	$350	$255

All of these products offer a good blend of features for the price. You may consider other spreadsheets, however. Any you do consider should be measured against the features and prices of the products listed in the table.

Database Programs

Database programs create a structured grouping of related information, such as you may write on index cards. Two types of database programs are available: flat-file databases and relational databases.

Flat-file databases are the simplest and least expensive database programs. With these programs, all information about a particular item (person, product, or whatever) is contained in one record. A *record* is similar to an index card of information. A set of records makes up a database *file*.

Relational database programs are more complicated than flat-file databases, but relational databases also enable you to link information stored in more than one file. Suppose that you have a database of client information that includes names, addresses, phone numbers, and other data. Another file stores the sales calls and purchases of clients. With a relational database, you can link the files to access a list of phone numbers of clients who have not received a sales call in the last week. To find out whether a database program is a flat-file database or a relational database, look at the packaging information or call the company.

Databases can be used to create mailing lists, to track inventory, to store information about personnel, and to store and retrieve almost any other kind of information.

Databases differ in other ways besides how they handle files. Like other kinds of software for IBM-compatible computers, the user interface of databases differs from product to product. A product like dBASE IV 1.1 has two built-in user interfaces: pull-down menus and a command-line interface. (You type commands to perform operations.) Paradox 3.5 uses a horizontal menu bar.

An important feature to look for in a database program is its compatibility with other database programs, spreadsheets, and word processors. Transferring database information to other software programs is called *mail-merge*. You may have data in dBASE IV, for example, that you need to show in a WordPerfect document. In this case, you need a convenient method for pulling the names from dBASE and using them in a WordPerfect letter.

Many powerful database programs include a programming language to enable you to design and create your own applications. If programming is not something you are considering, make sure that the database program can handle your needs without you having to program. The more advanced database programs enable you to design custom data-entry screens, create custom reports, and create mailing labels with a report generator.

Flat-file databases provide good functionality at a low cost. Flat-file databases usually enable you to create a template for a database record. The information you enter into each record then can be used for generating reports and mailing labels and for other database functions. Most spreadsheets and integrated programs include database features that rival those of stand-alone flat-file databases.

If you plan to incorporate pictures into a database, such as employee photos for a personnel file, make sure that the database software can accommodate pictures. Macintosh and Windows 3.0 database programs are more likely to provide this feature than DOS databases.

Ask yourself the following questions when considering a database program:

- What is the user interface? Is the program proprietary (only for IBM-compatible PCs) or does it follow the standards set by Windows 3.0 or the Macintosh?
- Is the program a relational database or a flat-file database?
- Can I create the type of application I want without having to resort to programming?
- Can the information in the database easily be used by other applications such as a word processor or spreadsheet?
- Can the database store pictures?
- Does the database enable the creation of labels and data-entry forms?

To answer questions like these and other questions you may have, you can call the company and ask a customer service representative, ask a salesperson in a computer retail outlet, read the description of features on the software package, request a flier about the product from the company, and read reviews of database software in computer magazines.

Table 8.3 gives specific recommendations for databases based on a specific computer type, CPU, operating system, user interface, level of sophistication, suggested retail price, and typical mail-order price.

All of these products offer a good blend of features for the price. However, you may want to consider other databases. Any you do consider should be measured against the features and prices of the products listed in the table.

Table 8.3
Databases

Product	dBASE IV 1.1	Paradox 3.5	FoxPro 1.02	SuperBase 4 for
Company	Ashton-Tate	Borland	Fox Software	Precision Software
PC	IBM or compatible	IBM or compatible	IBM or compatible	IBM or compatible
CPU	8088 or greater	8088 or greater	8808 or greater	8038SX or greater
Operating system	PC-DOS/MS-DOS 4.01	PC-DOS/MS-DOS 4.01	PC-DOS/MS-DOS 4.01	PC-DOS/MS-DOS 4.01
User interface	Pull-down menus command-line	Menu bar	Pull-down menus	Windows 3.0
Relational/ flat-file database	Relational	Relational	Relational	Relational
Sugg. retail price	$795	$725	$795	$699
Mail-order price	$525	$580	$500	$469

continues

Table 8.3—*continued*

Product	PC-File 5.0	4th Dimension 2.1	FoxBASE II/ Mac 2.01	Microsoft File 2.0
Company	ButtonWare	Acius, Inc.	Fox Software	Microsoft Corp
PC	IBM or compatible	Macintosh	Macintosh	Macintosh
CPU	8088 or greater	68000 or greater	68000 or greater	68000 or greater
Operating system	PC-DOS/MS-DOS 4.01	System 6.0.6	System 6.0.6	System 6.0.6
User interface	Menus/function keys	Macintosh	Macintosh	Macintosh
Relational/ flat-file database	Flat-file	Relational	Relational	Flat-file
Sugg. retail price	$135	$795	$495	$195
Mail-order price	$100	$500	$300	$135

Financial Programs

Financial programs for PCs generally are divided into three categories: high-end accounting packages, low-end accounting packages, and personal finance software. Because high-end accounting software can cost several thousand dollars, perform a personal, hands-on evaluation with data that reflects your business. Low-end accounting packages and personal finance software, however, can cost less than $100.

Low-End Accounting Software

Low-end accounting software usually consists of a set of accounting modules, including a general ledger, accounts receivable, accounts payable, inventory control, billing, purchasing, budgeting, auditing, and others. This software helps small businesses prepare financial reports, invoices, 1099s, and other business-related statements.

For IBM-compatible computers, low-end accounting programs differ in the user interface used by the program. Programs such as DacEasy Accounting and Pacioli 2000 use pull-down menus, but Peachtree Complete III uses pop-up windows and function keys. The programs also differ in the number and types of modules they offer. For example, DacEasy accounting includes 11 modules; Pacioli 2000 includes 8 modules; and Peachtree Complete III has 9 modules. M.Y.O.B. for the Macintosh has 7 modules.

To move information from your accounting files to your spreadsheet, make sure that the program can export files to the spreadsheet you will be using.

Ask yourself the following questions when considering a low-end accounting program:

- What is the user interface? Is the program proprietary (only for IBM-compatible PCs), or does the program follow the standards set by Windows 3.0 or the Macintosh?
- How many modules does the program have?
- Does the program have the modules that I need?
- Can the program create the reports that I need?
- What kind of personal computer do I need to run the software?
- Can the company supply checks and forms that work with the software?

To answer questions like these and other questions you may have, you can call the company and ask a customer service representative, ask a salesperson in a computer retail outlet, read the description of features on the software package, request a flier about the product from the company, and read ads for the software in computer magazines.

Table 8.4 gives specific recommendations for low-end accounting software based on a specific computer type, CPU, operating system, user interface, suggested retail price, and typical mail-order price.

Table 8.4
Low-End Accounting Software

Product				
DacEasy Accounting 4.1	Peachtree Complete III	Pacioli 2000	M.Y.O.B. 2.0	Business Sense
Company				
DacEasy, Inc.	Peachtree Software	M-USA Business Systems	Teleware	Inman Software
PC				
IBM or compatible	IBM or compatible	IBM or compatible	Macintosh	Macintosh
CPU				
8088 or greater	8088 or greater	8088 or greater	68000 or greater	68000 or greater
Operating system				
PC-DOS/MS-DOS 4.01	PC-DOS/MS-DOS 4.01	PC-DOS/MS-DOS 4.01	System 6.0.6	System 6.0.6
User interface				
Pull-down menus	Pop-up windows/ function keys	Pull-down menus	Macintosh	Macintosh
Sugg. retail price				
$150	$199	$50	$295	$199
Mail-order price				
$90	$150	$50	$155	$159

All of these products offer a good blend of features for the price. However, you may consider other low-end accounting packages. Any you consider should be measured against the features and prices of the products listed in the table.

Personal Finance Software

Personal finance software helps you with such financial matters as balancing a checkbook, itemizing expenses, analyzing and planning expenditures, tracking investments, and planning for retirement. Some personal finance programs are even powerful enough to double as a small-business accounting program.

A good checkbook program enables you to set up accounts and current balances for checking, credit cards, IRS funds, and money market funds. You then can set up budget categories. The best programs come with categories that you can add and subtract. You describe categories as income, expense, asset, or liability. You can design monthly budgets for checking or charge accounts. By establishing income and expense categories, you can play forecasting games. The program should generate constant income and expenses for several months. Some programs enable you to create charts showing, for example, expenses compared to budgets.

Some programs perform *double-entry bookkeeping*, in which expense transactions are listed in your expense category, tax records, monthly budget, and so on. Double-entry bookkeeping requires extra work from you, however. You need to set goals for what you want the package to do and use its features accordingly. You still have to set up accounts and categories. If you want a year-end record of all tax-deductible expenditures, you must describe and mark each tax-deductible expense category in accordance with Schedule C, and so on. You must know enough about your tax situation to know how much is deductible.

None of these programs teaches you how to perform accounting. The misconception about many software products is that they think for you. Actually, programs are tools that structure your data to help you do the thinking. If you set up your accounting system correctly, a personal finance program tracks, categorizes, and catches your budget when it slips out of line.

Ask yourself the following questions when considering a personal finance program:

- What is the user interface? Is the program proprietary (only for IBM-compatible PCs) or does it follow the standards set by Windows 3.0 or the Macintosh?
- Does the program have a checkbook register?
- Can the program print checks?
- Does the program track investments?
- Does the program keep track of charge accounts?
- Does the program do single- or double-entry bookkeeping?
- Is the software compatible with tax programs such as Turbo Tax?

- What kinds of printers does the program support?
- Can the company supply checks that work with the software?
- Does the program support electronic banking?

All of these questions may not necessarily apply to your situation. For those that do, you can find answers by calling the company and asking a customer service representative, asking a salesperson in a computer retail outlet, reading the description of features on the software package, requesting a flier about the product from the company, and reading ads for the software in computer magazines.

Table 8.5 gives specific recommendations for personal finance software based on a specific computer type, CPU, operating system, user interface, suggested retail price, and typical mail-order price.

Table 8.5
Personal Finance Software

Product			
Quicken 4.0	Managing Your Money 7.0	Quicken 1.5	Managing Your Money 3.0
Company			
Intuit	Meca Ventures	Intuit	Meca Ventures
PC			
IBM or compatible	IBM or compatible	Macintosh	Macintosh
CPU			
8088 or greater	8088 or greater	68000 or greater	68000 or greater
Operating system			
PC-DOS/MS-DOS 4.01	PC-DOS/MS-DOS 4.01	System 6.0.6	System 6.0.6
User interface			
Function keys	Function keys	Macintosh	Macintosh
Sugg. retail price			
$60	$220	$60	$220
Mail-order price			
$50	$145	$45	$145

All of these products offer a good blend of features for the price. However, you may consider other personal finance packages. Any you do consider should be measured against the features and prices of the products listed in the table.

Desktop Publishing Packages

Desktop publishing software tackles page layout, producing attractive pages for newsletters, brochures, fliers, magazines, newspapers, manuals, and books. High-end and low-end desktop publishing software exists, and some word processors can double as desktop publishing programs.

Desktop publishing programs combine text created in a word processor, graphics created in a drawing program, and tables and graphs created in a business program. You should check whether the desktop publishing program you are considering supports your other software.

A desktop publishing program enables you to manipulate text, graphics, and tables until you create the effect that you want. Generally, the layout tools of high-end programs offer more flexibility and control than tools of low-end programs.

If you create complex or long documents, consider a high-end program. When comparing high-end programs, note that some are better suited for certain tasks. QuarkXpress offers sophisticated features, such as color separation. PageMaker excels at short documents, such as brochures and newsletters. Ventura Publisher may be a better choice for documents long enough to need a table of contents, figure numbers, and an index.

Low-end desktop publishing programs are best suited for one-page newsletters and fliers. If you go beyond a page, you may have problems when stories that start on page one are continued on other pages of the newsletter, especially if you have to make changes to the text. Low-end programs usually force you to compromise on typographical features such as kerning, leading, and the way text wraps around graphic images. (*Kerning* is the capability to vary the spacing between individual letters. *Leading* is the capability to vary the spacing between lines. If these term are unfamiliar, you may want to brush up on the basics of typography, especially if you intend to publish a business newsletter.)

If your typographical needs aren't too stringent, and you don't mind using tools not specifically designed for the task, you may want to use a high-end word processor, such as WordPerfect 5.1, Ami Professional 1.2, or Word For Windows 1.1. These programs include many features found in low-end desktop publishing programs.

The quality of output depends on your printer. If you intend to use a laser printer or a PostScript laser printer, make sure that the program you choose can take advantage of the printer. Some low-end desktop publishing programs, for example, do not support PostScript printers.

Ask yourself the following questions when considering a desktop publishing program:

- What is the user interface? Is the program proprietary (only for IBM-compatible PCs) or does it follow the standards set by Windows 3.0 or the Macintosh?

- Do I want to create short publications such as newsletters and fliers or longer ones such as magazines, newspapers, manuals, and textbooks?

- Does the desktop publishing program support my word processor, drawing program, and spreadsheet program?

- Does the program offer control of kerning and leading?

- Will the program wrap type around graphic images?

- Does the program allow for easy changes when stories jump from page to page?

- Does the program provide advanced technical features such as color separations?

- What kind of personal computer do I need to run the software?

- What kinds of printers does the program support? Does the program support a PostScript printer?

- How difficult is the program to learn and use?

To answer questions like these and other questions you may have, you can call the company and ask a customer service representative, ask a salesperson in a computer retail outlet, read the description of features on the software package, request a flier about the product from the company, and read reviews of desktop publishing software in computer magazines.

Table 8.6 gives specific recommendations for desktop publishing programs based on a specific computer type, CPU, operating system, user interface, type of task, suggested retail price, and typical mail-order price.

**Table 8.6
Desktop Publishing Software**

Product				
PageMaker 4.0	QuarkXpress 3.0	FrameMaker 2.1	Springboard Publisher II 2.0	Aldus PageMaker 3.01
Company				
Aldus	Quark	Frame Technology	Springboard Software	Aldus
PC				
Macintosh	Macintosh	Macintosh	Macintosh	IBM or compatible
CPU				
68020 or greater	68020 or greater	68020 or greater	68000 or greater	80386SX or greater
Operating system				
System 6.0.6	System 6.0.6	System 6.0.6	System 6.0.6	PC-DOS/MS-DOS 4.01
User interface				
Macintosh	Macintosh	Macintosh	Macintosh	Windows 3.0
Type of tasks				
Newsletters, magazines, newspapers	Newsletters, magazines, newspapers	Manuals, textbooks	Newsletters, fliers	Newsletters, magazines, newspapers
Sugg. retail price				
$795	$795	$995	$200	$795
Mail-order price				
$525	$540	N/A	$120	$510

continues

All of these products offer a good blend of features for the price. However, you may consider other desktop publishing packages. Any you do consider should be measured against the features and prices of the products listed in the table.

Communications Software

Communications software generally is used to connect two computers together by modem over telephone lines. The computers do not have to be the same type—Macintoshes can talk to IBM compatibles. You can connect to an on-line service, such as Prodigy, or an electronic mail service, such as MCI mail. Communications software links the computers so that you can send or receive files created with a word processor, spreadsheet, or other software. Connected to an on-line service, you can browse, exchange messages with other members of the service, download (receive) programs, shop electronically, and use many other services. Connected to an electronic mail service, you can send electronic mail to or receive it from any other member of the service.

Table 8.6—*continued*

Product			
Ventura Publisher for Windows 3.0	Interleaf Publisher 3.0	Express Publisher 1.0	PFS: First Publisher 3.0
Company			
Ventura Software	Interleaf	Power Up Software	Software Publishing Co.
PC			
IBM or compatible	IBM or compatible	IBM or compatible	IBM or compatible
CPU			
80386SX or greater	80386SX or greater	8088 or greater	8088 or greater
Operating system			
PC-DOS/MS-DOS 4.01	PC-DOS/MS-DOS 4.01	PC-DOS/MS-DOS 4.01	PC-DOS/MS-DOS 4.01
User interface			
Windows 3.0	Proprietary	Proprietary	Proprietary
Type of tasks			
Newsletters, magazines, newspapers	Manuals, textbooks	Newsletters, fliers	Newsletters, fliers
Sugg. retail price			
$795	$995	$150	$129
Mail-order price			
$580	N/A	$90	$99

Communications software can be classified as standard, remote control, or on-line service oriented. Standard communications programs offer similar kinds of features. They differ, however, in the extent to which certain features are supported. For example, all programs support communications protocols, such as Xmodem. (The purpose of a protocol is to send files quickly and without errors.) Some programs support a whole range of protocols, and others support just a few. Xmodem is sufficient for most file transfers, but if you need another protocol, you should check whether the program provides it.

Another feature most programs include is some way to automate communications, usually with a proprietary programming language. If you are interested in this aspect of communications, make sure to check how difficult learning and using the language is.

Remote control programs enable you to control another computer over the phone lines. Programs such as pcAnywhere III enable you to control your office PC from your PC at home. You need the same program at both ends of the line, and some companies require you to buy two copies of the software! Some standard communications programs also include remote features, but many provide limited control.

Some communications programs are designed to be used for on-line services such as CompuServe. These programs help you navigate through the various parts of the service. Standard communications programs can connect to an on-line service, but they contain no special navigation aids.

Communications software often is provided with the purchase of a modem. If you use Windows 3.0, remember that this environment includes a program called Terminal with limited communications features.

Ask yourself the following questions when considering communications software:

- What is the user interface? Is the program proprietary (only for IBM-compatible PCs) or does it follow the standards set by Windows 3.0 or the Macintosh?

- Does the program use the Xmodem protocol? What other protocols does it have?

- How difficult is the program to automate communications?

- Does the program offer remote control capability? Are two copies of the program required?

- Does the program help me navigate through an on-line service such as CompuServe?

- What kind of personal computer do I need to run the software?

- How difficult is the program to learn and use?

To answer questions like these and other questions you may have, you can call the company and ask a customer service representative, ask a salesperson in a computer retail outlet, read the description of features on the software package, request a flier about the product from the company, and read reviews of communications software in computer magazines.

Table 8.7 gives specific recommendations for communications software based on a specific computer type, CPU, operating system, user interface, type of task, suggested retail price, and typical mail-order price.

All of these products offer a good blend of features for the price. However, you may consider other communications packages. Any you do consider should be measured against the features and prices of the products listed in the table.

Integrated Programs

An integrated program provides multiple applications. Typical applications for integrated packages include word processing, spreadsheet, database management, graphics, and communications. With integrated software, you can write memos, create budgets, send electronic mail, maintain a list of client names, and so on. You do not have to learn a new program or user interface for each module.

Table 8.7
Communications Software

Product			
PROCOMM PLUS 1.1	SmartCom III 1.2	pcAnywhere III	Microphone II 3.0
Company			
Datastorm Technologies	Hayes Microcomputer Products	Dynamic Microcomputer Assoc.	Software Ventures
PC			
IBM or compatible	IBM or compatible	IBM or compatible	Macintosh
CPU			
8088 or greater	8088 or greater	8088 or greater	68000 or greater
Operating system			
PC-DOS/MS-DOS 4.01	PC-DOS/MS-DOS 4.01	PC-DOS/MS-DOS 4.01	System 6.0.6
User interface			
Alt-key/menu bar	Pull-down menus	Proprietary	Macintosh
Type of task			
Standard communications	Standard communications	Remote communications	Standard communications
Sugg. retail price			
$99	$249	$145	$295
Mail-order price			
$65	$160	$70	$225

continues

Table 8.7—*continued*

Product		
White Knight 11.6	CarbonCopy Mac	CompuServe Navigator 3.0
Company		
Freesoft	Microcom	CompuServe
Microcomputer Products	Microcomputer Assocs.	
PC		
Macintosh	Macintosh	Macintosh
CPU		
68000 or greater	68000 or greater	68000 or greater
Operating system		
System 6.0.6	System 6.0.6	System 6.0.6
User interface		
Macintosh	Macintosh	Macintosh
Type of task		
Standard communications	Remote communications	On-line navigation aid
Sugg. retail price		
$139	$199	$99.95
Mail-order price		
$95	$160	$60

Another advantage to the integrated approach is that you easily can copy a table or graph created in the spreadsheet, for example, to a document in the word processor. If data changes, both portions are updated automatically.

The popularity of high-end integrated software has declined in recent years. One reason is that stand-alone products are better at file transfers than they used to be. The features of stand-alone products also have improved. Many people prefer the power of a high-end stand-alone product, such as WordPerfect, to the overall functionality of a high-end integrated program, such as Lotus Symphony.

Low-end integrated programs are still popular. These programs offer as many as eight functions and usually sell through mail order for less than $100. If your computing needs are fairly basic, consider purchasing a low-end IBM compatible or Macintosh and low-end integrated software.

Ask yourself the following questions when considering integrated software:

- What is the user interface? Is the program proprietary (only for IBM-compatible PCs) or does it follow the standards set by Windows 3.0 or the Macintosh?

- How many modules does the program have?
- Do any of the individual modules rival the power of a stand-alone program?
- Does the word processor have a spelling checker?
- Does the communications module enable me to automate communications?
- What kind of personal computer do I need to run the software?
- How difficult is the program to learn and use?

To answer questions like these and other questions you may have, you can call the company and ask a customer service representative, ask a salesperson in a computer retail outlet, read the description of features on the software package, request a flier about the product from the company, and read reviews of integrated software in computer magazines.

Table 8.8 gives specific recommendations for integrated software based on a specific computer type, CPU, operating system, user interface, suggested retail price, and typical mail-order price.

Table 8.8
Integrated Software

Product				
Symphony 2.2	Microsoft Works 2.0	PFS: First Choice 3.1	Better Working—Eight-in-One	Microsoft Works 2.0
Company				
Lotus Corp.	Microsoft Corp.	Software Publishing Co.	Spinnaker Software	Microsoft Corp.
PC				
IBM or compatible	IBM or compatible	IBM or compatible	IBM or compatible	Macintosh
CPU				
8088 or greater	8088 or greater	8088 or greater	8088 or greater	68000 or greater
Operating system				
PC-DOS/MS-DOS 4.01	PC-DOS/MS-DOS 4.01	PC-DOS/MS-DOS 4.01	PC-DOS/MS-DOS 4.01	System 6.0.6
User interface				
Menu bar	Pull-down menus	Pull-down menus	Pull-down menus	Macintosh
Sugg. retail price				
$695	$150	$150	$60	$295
Mail-order price				
$540	$110	$110	$45	$190

All of these products offer a good blend of features for the price. However, you may consider other integrated packages. Any you do consider should be measured against the features and prices of the products listed in the table.

Paint and Drawing Programs

Paint and drawing programs for personal computers enable you to create and manipulate images. With a paint program, you create images as you would with painting tools such as pencils, pens, brushes, and paint. Paint programs can simulate paintings done with water colors, oil paints, or acrylic paints. Paint programs create a bit-mapped image. The drawback of images created with paint programs is that the images degrade if you try to enlarge them.

With a drawing program, you create images as you would using illustration tools such as technical pens, French curves, and transfer screens. These vector images stretch as you enlarge them, maintaining their resolutions and ratios at any size.

Paint programs differ with the user interface, the number of colors available, the resolution of the image, and the painting tools available. A big difference among these programs is the file format the program uses. The most popular file format for IBM-compatible computers is the PCX format found in programs such as PC PaintBrush IV Plus. For Macintosh computers, the MacPaint format is the most popular. Amiga computers have a standard format, IFF, that all Amiga paint programs can read.

Some of the differences among drawing programs are the user interface, the drawing tools available, and color support. As with paint programs, a big difference among drawing programs is the file format the program uses. The most popular file format is CGM, found in programs such as Corel Draw! and Adobe Illustrator.

With a paint or drawing program, you should find out what kind of output devices the program supports. For IBM compatibles, does the program support VGA adapters and color monitors? For Macintosh computers, does the program support 24-bit color adapters? For any computer, does the program support the kind of printer you have?

Most drawing programs and some paint programs are targeted for graphics arts professionals. Paint programs often are bundled or included with the purchase of a mouse or a graphical user interface such as Windows 3.0.

Ask yourself the following questions when considering paint and drawing software:

- What is the user interface? Is the program proprietary (only for IBM-compatible PCs) or does it follow the standards set by Windows 3.0 or the Macintosh?

- What kinds of painting or drawing tools does the program have?
- How many colors does the program support?
- What is the image resolution (for paint programs only)?
- What kind of output devices, such as laser printers and color printers, does the program support?
- What file format does the program use? What file formats can be imported into and exported out of the program?
- What kind of personal computer do I need to run the software?
- How difficult is the program to learn and use?

To answer questions like these and other questions you may have, you can call the company and ask a customer service representative, ask a salesperson in a computer retail outlet, read the description of features on the software package, request a flier about the product from the company, and read reviews of paint and drawing software in computer magazines.

The following table gives specific recommendations for paint and drawing software based on a specific computer type, CPU, operating system, user interface, type of program, suggested retail price, and typical mail-order price.

Table 8.9
Paint and Drawing Software

Product			
	PC PaintBrush IV Plus 1.0	Corel Draw! 2.0	DeskPaint/DeskDraw 3.01
Company			
	ZSoft	Corel Systems	Zedcor
PC			
	IBM or compatible	IBM or compatible	Macintosh
CPU			
	8088 or greater	8088 or greater	68000 or greater
Operating system			
	PC-DOS/MS-DOS 4.01	PC-DOS/MS-DOS 4.01	System 6.0.6
User interface			
	Pull-down menus	Windows 3.0	Macintosh
Program type			
	Paint	Draw	Paint and Draw
Sugg. retail price			
	$199	$495	$200
Mail-order price			
	$130	$400	$125

continues

Table 8.9—*continued*
Paint and Drawing Software

Product			
	Adobe Illustrator 3.0	Deluxe Paint III	Professional Draw 2.0
Company			
	Adobe Systems	Electronic Arts	Gold Disk
PC			
	Macintosh	Amiga	Amiga
CPU			
	68000 or greater	68000 or greater	68000 or greater
Operating system			
	System 6.0.6	WorkBench 2.0	WorkBench 2.0
User interface			
	Macintosh	WorkBench	WorkBench
Program type			
	Draw	Paint	Draw
Sugg. retail price			
	$595	$150	N/A
Mail-order price			
	$360	$110	$140

All of these products offer a good blend of features for the price. However, you may consider other paint and draw packages. Any you do consider should be measured against the features and prices of the products listed in the table.

Music Sequencing and Notation Software

Music sequencing software enables a personal computer to act like a tape recorder to record one or more tracks of music information. Music is entered into a computer with an instrument such as a keyboard synthesizer. After the music is in RAM, the music can be manipulated with sequencing software. You can think of sequencers as word processors for music. After you edit, you can play the music out again through the synthesizer.

Music notation software translates music entered into the computer into standard music notation. Music can be entered into a computer through the computer's keyboard or an instrument such as a keyboard synthesizer. The programs produce sheet music on a printer.

Music sequencing and notation software normally are used in combination with a MIDI system such as the one shown in figure 8.1 (MIDI stands for Musical Instrument Digital Interface.) The figure shows a personal computer connected to a MIDI-compatible keyboard synthesizer, which is connected to an amplifier connected to speakers. If a personal computer has built-in MIDI circuits—and only the Atari ST and Mega do—you connect the keyboard to the MIDI port.

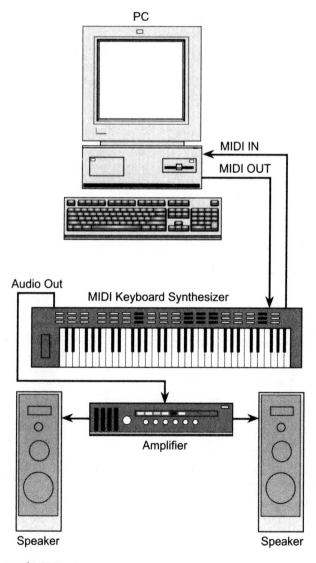

Fig. 8.1. A typical MIDI system.

For IBM compatibles, you can insert a MIDI adapter board into an expansion slot and connect the keyboard to the board's MIDI port. For Amigas and Macintoshes, you can place a MIDI interface box between the keyboard and the computer. The keyboard connects to the interface, and the interface connects to a serial port of the computer.

Music sequencing programs differ in the user interface, the method of displaying notes and tracks, the number of tracks supported, editing capabilities, and other features. Music notation programs differ in the user interface, the method of displaying notes, editing capabilities, number of pages per musical score, sequencing software supported, printers supported, and other features. Music sequencing and notation programs are targeted at professional musicians, although some companies offer apprentice versions of their products. Some music programs combine the capabilities of sequencing and notation software into one product.

Ask yourself the following questions when considering sequencing and notation software:

- What is the user interface? Is the program proprietary (only for IBM-compatible PCs) or does it follow the standards set by Windows 3.0 or the Macintosh?
- How does the program display musical notes and tracks?
- What editing features does the program have?
- How many tracks does the program support?
- What sequencing software does the notation software support?
- What is the maximum number of pages per musical score?
- What kind of dot-matrix, inkjet, and laser printers does the program support?
- What kind of personal computer do I need to run the software?
- How difficult is the program to learn and use?
- Is any technical support available with the program?

To answer questions like these and other questions you may have, you can call the company and ask a customer service representative, ask a salesperson in a computer retail outlet, read the description of features on the software package, request a flier about the product from the company, and read reviews of sequencing and notation software in computer and electronic music magazines.

Table 8.10 gives specific recommendations for music sequencing and notation software based on a specific computer type, CPU, operating system, user interface, and type of program.

Table 8.10
Music Sequencing and Notation Software

Product			
Cakewalk Professional 3.0	Copyist DTP	The Musicator	Performer 3.5

Company			
Twelve Tone Systems	Dr. T's Music Software	Musicator	Mark of the Unicorn

PC			
IBM or compatible	IBM or compatible	IBM or compatible	Macintosh

CPU			
8088 or greater	8088 or greater	8088 or greater	68000 or greater

Operating system			
PC-DOS/MS-DOS 4.01	PC-DOS/MS-DOS 4.01	PC-DOS/MS-DOS 4.01	System 6.0.6

User interface			
Pull-down menus	Pull-down menus	Pull-down menus	Macintosh

Program type			
Music sequencing	Music notation	Music sequencing and notation	Music sequencing

continues

Table 8.10—*continued*

Product		
Finale	Notator 3.0	Level II 3.0

Company		
Coda Music Software	Digidesign	Dr. T's Music Software

PC		
Macintosh	Atari	Amiga

CPU		
68000 or greater	68000	68000 or greater

Operating system		
System 6.0.6	GEM	WorkBench 2.0

User interface		
Macintosh	GEM	WorkBench

Program type		
Music notation	Music sequencing and notation	Music sequencing

All of these products offer a good blend of features for the price. However, you may consider other music sequencing and notation packages. Any you do consider should be measured against the features and prices of the products listed in the table.

Education and Game Programs

Game and education programs for personal computers fall into several categories. Most game programs can be classified as arcade, simulation, adventure, sports, board, game show, or casino games. Most education programs can be classified as arcade, simulation, role-play, adventure, interactive drill, and reference programs.

Game and education programs differ in graphics quality. If you have fairly sophisticated graphics available on your computer, such as a VGA adapter on an IBM-compatible computer, look for programs that support this feature. One of the most popular educational programs, Where in the World is Carmen San Diego?, recently was updated to include digitized photographs of various geographic locations taken from *National Geographic* magazine.

Another difference is the sound effects used by the program. Macintosh, Amiga, ST, Mega, and some IBM-compatible computers, such as the Tandy 1000 series, contain electronic circuits to produce synthesized sound. If you own or intend to buy one of these computers, look for programs that take advantage of this feature. Special sound boards, such as the Sound Blaster, can be inserted into an expansion slot of most IBM-compatible computers for sound capabilities.

Other differences to watch for are the level and content of the software. Educational programs are designed for different learning levels, from preschooler to adult. Game programs run the gamut of human experience; the packaging shows the subject matter of a game.

Like all other kinds of software, game and education programs differ in quality. Some games have a way of getting under your skin, and others are boring or difficult to play. Even the best games don't have the same effect on every player. Some education programs can do the job and some cannot.

For the most part, education and game programs are designed to run on low-end computers, although many support complete lines of computers. Many game and education programs have a version for different types of computers. Some programs demand a special piece of equipment. For example, an educational reference program, such as an electronic encyclopedia, usually requires a CD-ROM drive.

If you are interested in educational software developed by educators, check out software by MECC (Minnesota Educational Computing Corporation). Some of the company's products have won awards. For example, The Oregon Trail is a role-playing program that teaches decision-making and survival skills as you experience a pioneer lifestyle replete with hunting buffalo, rafting down rivers, visiting trading posts, acquiring supplies, and dealing with Indians and midnight robbers.

Ask yourself the following questions when considering education or games software:

- What category does the program fall into? For games, is the category arcade, simulation, adventure, sports, board, card, or casino game? For education, is the category arcade, simulation, role-play, adventure, or reference?
- What kind of graphics does the program support?
- Does the program have sound effects?
- If the program is an educational program, what is the subject and learning level?
- If the program is a game, what is the subject matter?
- What kind of personal computer do I need to run the software?
- Is any special equipment required?
- How difficult is the program to learn and use?
- Does the company provide customer support?

To answer questions like these and other questions you may have, you can call the company and ask a customer service representative, ask a salesperson in a computer retail outlet, read the description of features on the software package, request a flier about the product from the company, and read reviews of game and educational software in computer, educational, and electronic games magazines.

Too many game and educational programs exist to list even a small portion of them. Deciding on a game or educational program is to a great extent a matter of personal preference. Try out any programs you are considering at a retail store or at a friend's house and ask your friends for their recommendations.

Shareware

Shareware is software developed by independent programmers who let you try the program before you buy it. Shareware programs cover the whole spectrum of software, from word processors and spreadsheets to games and educational programs. Most shareware programs are significantly less expensive than commercial products.

The easiest way to obtain a shareware program is to send away for one through mail order. A shareware disk costs anywhere from $1 to $4. If you decide to buy the program after trying it, you send additional money to the author of the program (the program specifies the amount to pay). Paying the fee normally gives you some additional benefits, such as documentation, technical support, and notification of updates to the program. The whole concept of shareware is based on an honor system—no one forces you to pay the program's author.

Another way to obtain shareware is through on-line services and bulletin board systems. You use your modem to download any programs you want. If you like the program, you pay the author.

Some shareware programs are great, and others are awful. Because so many titles exist, you often have to find good programs by trial and error. You are unlikely to see reviews of shareware programs in computer magazines.

A related group of programs is public domain software. Any program or program file in the public domain is free. You pay only for obtaining the disk. You are not likely to find full-blown word processors and spreadsheets in the public domain, but you may find interesting utility programs, graphics, games, and educational programs.

Although you may have plenty of questions about various shareware and public domain programs, the system doesn't really lend itself to supplying answers. Try locating books or magazines dedicated to shareware, but these probably will not provide detailed up-to-date information. The following list gives one shareware program in each major category that you may find suitable for your needs.

Word processor:	PC Write 3.03
Spreadsheet:	As Easy As
Database:	PC-File 5.0
Communication:	ProComm
Accounting:	Painless Accounting
Educational:	PC FastType
Games:	Caddieshack (Golf)

This list certainly is not exhaustive, but the programs here can get you started on the right track with shareware. Although these programs are for IBM-compatible computers, shareware and public domain software is available for all types of computers.

Chapter Summary

This chapter provided an overview of different kinds of personal computer software you may consider. At the start of the chapter, you received suggestions about how to determine the correct computer configuration you need to run different kinds of software. This chapter continued with ways to analyze software in terms of the requirements you have. Then this chapter described various kinds of operating environments.

Finally, the chapter delved into a variety of software categories. For each category, this chapter defined the type of software, explained differences among products, gave a list of questions to consider, and provided a table of recommended products. These recommendations should provide a firm foundation for making software purchasing decisions.

In the Next Chapter

The next chapter explains how to install and maintain a personal computer. The chapter begins by showing you how to prepare your home or office for your new purchase, explaining how to set up the computer. Then the chapter gives you some advice about how to maintain your computer. Finally, the chapter supplies some troubleshooting tips that may help you avoid bringing your personal computer in for repair.

9

How Do I Install and Maintain My Computer?

After you decide which computer to purchase, you then must install and maintain your system. This chapter assists you in these areas.

This chapter also prepares you for the arrival of your new computer and assists you in selecting an appropriate place in your office or home for the system. This chapter suggests products that protect your hardware and software from such environmental factors as power surges, heat, static electricity, and magnetism.

The chapter guides you in setting up your system after you choose the right location for your PC and suggests items that make installation easy.

After your system is up, you want to keep it running smoothly. The chapter discusses products that will maintain your system unit, disk drives, keyboard, mouse, monitor, and printer in top condition.

The chapter tells you what to do when things go wrong. You can use troubleshooting tips to spot problems with your computer. Lastly the chapter suggests components you can use to correct problems in your system.

Preparing for Your New Computer

Unlike a television set, which sits in one corner of the room with only an antenna, or perhaps a connected cable, a personal computer requires a complex workspace. The location for your computer should be large enough to accommodate all system components and the printer. You also should consider such environmental issues as AC power, adequate workspace, and ventilation.

Ensuring Proper AC Power

The system unit, monitor, and printer have power cords; you need a sufficient number of power outlets, or you need a power strip. If you plan to use a modem or FAX, you also need a phone line. If you live in an area where the power is dependable, you need only an inexpensive power strip. You should know whether your power is good or bad by the success you have had with such electronic products as televisions, stereos, and VCRs. If lightning power surges have blown other appliances, you may have problems with your computer.

Two potential power problems to your computer are *brownouts* and *blackouts*. A brownout is a temporary drop in power. A blackout is a complete loss of power. When a computer has a drop in power or loses power completely, you lose everything in your computer's RAM. If you are writing a long letter and you get hit with a momentary loss of power, everything is lost in a flash. If you regularly save to disk, of course, you minimize your loss.

Some areas are susceptible to *power surges*, also called *power spikes*. Surges in power may be caused by momentary increases in electricity in your area or by lightning strikes. If you live in an area susceptible to power surges, you should invest in a quality power strip that offers power surge and spike protection. These surge/spike protectors reduce the increase in voltage caused by surges in your electrical line.

Different surge protectors are available from many manufacturers, and some guarantee the safety of your equipment. If you are creating an office in the home, don't inadvertently create power surge problems by connecting computer equipment to the same circuit breaker that services your refrigerator or washing machine. If you cannot determine which appliances are connected to which breakers, consult an electrician. If you regularly have trouble with other electronic equipment, you should consult an electrician to determine whether anything is wrong with your wiring.

If the power in your area is erratic and you regularly suffer from brownouts and blackouts, you should invest in a battery backup product, such as an uninterruptible power supply (UPS). Most UPS products sit between your computer and the power outlet. If the power goes out, your system remains in operation for several minutes, while you save whatever you are working on; some UPS models even save your work. The AccuCard, from Emerson Electric, fits into an expansion slot of IBM and compatible computers and sells for $249. If brownouts or blackouts occur at your site only during severe thunderstorms, avoid working on the computer at these times.

Ensuring Proper Ventilation

The area you choose for your computer should have sufficient space and ventilation to properly cool all components of the system. Most PCs have built-in fans or designs that promote proper cooling. Avoid placing the computer and other components in areas that would block the proper air-flow. Also, if your computer has a fan, make sure that the entrance of the airflow is easily accessible so that you may clean the dust build-up that occurs.

To avoid problems from heat, keep your workplace properly cooled. Computers need a room temperature of between 65 and 85 degrees when operating. Do not allow your computer to get too hot or cold when shut off. Temperature when the computer is off should generally not get below 50 degrees or above 110 degrees.

Working Environment

An important consideration is the working environment that you are in. A good work environment consists of several things: proper computer placement, proper lighting, a supportive chair, and adequate desk space. Your work environment should adapt to you, rather than forcing you to adapt to the environment.

Placement of your computer is important so that you easily can access the keyboard and disk drives and view the video display without becoming a contortionist. The video display should be at eye level and directly in front of you, which keep you from having those nagging neck pains. (Nothing is worse than a computer that is a pain in the neck.)

Lighting is very important. Although most offices may have overhead lights, a small room in your house may not. Many computer users prefer accent lighting—light that reflects off of a white ceiling. If you like accent lighting, make sure that you also have plenty of light around papers that you use near your computer.

The type of chair that you use can increase your productivity. Can you raise or lower the chair? Does it move easily on rollers, helping you access other materials by rolling to them rather than bending to reach them? Does the chair support your back? These are questions that you may want to ask yourself when deciding on a chair to use.

Finally, does your desk offer plenty of room for additional materials that you may need when working on your computer? Will your computer take up most of the desk space, forcing you to balance the materials in your lap while you bend forward to reach the computer? Computers are being designed smaller than they once were. Some computers are designed to set on the floor, so that only the keyboard and display take desk space. Products also may be purchased to place the display and keyboard on an arm that extends from the desk. This practice leaves desk space clear for materials that you may need.

Avoiding Static Electricity

Static electricity can cause havoc when mixed with computers. Discharging static electricity into your computer (that same zap you enjoyed annoying people with when you were a kid) generally cannot damage your computer but can cause the computer to lock up or restart itself. When your computer locks up or restarts, you possibly can lose data in RAM. If, however, you are handling a computer circuit board, and you discharge static electricity, you possibly can damage the circuit board.

One way to reduce static problems is to remove rugs from the area where you intend to set your computer. Rugs are a big source of static electricity, particularly when the weather is cool and dry.

In most cases, removing the rugs from your work area is just not feasible. You can use one of the following suggestions for decreasing or nearly eliminating static problems:

1. Install antistatic floormats.

2. Spray your carpets with antistatic sprays. You don't need to buy the expensive sprays found in electronics stores; Downy fabric softener diluted with water in a spray bottle works just fine. Spray the area

daily or as often as needed. Do not directly spray the computer. Lightly spray a rag and dust the computer.

3. Increase humidity by 35 to 65 percent by placing plants, aquariums, or humidifiers in your home or office.

4. Use antistatic wrist straps and mats when handling add-in components. You also should ground yourself by removing the power cord from the system unit and touching the case of the power supply before touching any circuit boards inside the computer. Touching the case of the power supply discharges any static from your body, without affecting the computer's components.

Avoiding Magnets

Magnetism is another environmental problem that can affect your computing. A magnet rubbed across a floppy disk or carelessly placed near a hard drive can do permanent damage to your valuable data.

To prevent magnetism problems with your personal computer, isolate or remove all magnets from the work area. Magnetic items include magnetic paper clip holders, electric pencil sharpeners, phones with clapper bells in the receiver, word processing stand magnets that hold paper in place, magnetic security badges, magnetic tools, and refrigerator magnets.

Notice that electric pencil sharpeners and phones with clapper bells were mentioned. These items work by the magnetic principle. Any equipment with an electric motor or that alternates to operate uses magnetic principles. Keep these a good distance from the computer.

Installing a Phone Line

If you plan to use a modem or a FAX board with your system, you need a phone line near your computer. Modems are as susceptible to power surges and spikes as other kinds of electronic equipment. As mentioned earlier, if you anticipate power problems, invest in a surge protector that fits into the phone jack.

If you work in an office that has a digital PBX, you cannot connect your modem; you must install a dedicated analog line. If you have a dedicated line, you can make calls with your modem, receive calls, and call your computer from a remote location.

Setting Up Your Computer

Setting up a personal computer system can be a simple task, if you prepare yourself well. The following steps are involved in setting up the computer:

1. Locating all the components delivered, especially the documentation
2. Unpacking the components
3. Positioning the computer
4. Attaching all cables
5. Making sure that the computer operates before storing all the boxes

The next few sections will help you get through what you must do.

Unpacking Your Equipment

After you first receive your equipment, check that all components were shipped. Remember that some of the items that you ordered—memory, hard disk, and video card—may reside inside the computer. Unless you open the computer to look for these items, you just have to trust the folks that you purchased the computer from and test for the components after you have completed the computer setup. Even if items have been installed in the computer, documentation should be available for the item. Make sure that you have all documentation available for the computer and the items that you purchase.

Follow these steps when setting up your computer:

1. Check that you have all the equipment you need. Cables sometimes are too short or are missing. If you purchase a floor-standing model, for example, ask about the length of the keyboard and monitor cables. If these cables are too short, you need extending cables. Ask whether your printer comes with a cable. If not, you must purchase one. Ask whether your modem comes with a cable to connect it to the computer and a wire to connect it to the phone line. If not, you must purchase these items.

2. When you unpack your video monitor, wipe the screen clean with a soft cloth. Video screens must be wiped frequently, because they attract dust. Special video screen wipes and video screen cleaning

fluids are available, but you can use ordinary window cleaner with a lint-free rag. If your screen has an antiglare coating, follow the manufacturer's instructions for cleaning.

3. Check the system unit for signs of damage: dents or cracks in the case, pieces that have been broken off—the pins in the connectors on the back of the machine, for example—and any other external signs of physical damage. Inspect all components. Send back the entire unit at the slightest sign of malfunction.

4. Save all packing materials for your system's components. You can use them if you need to return the component to the manufacturer for repair.

5. Look for a piece of cardboard in the slot of 5 1/4 inch floppy drives. The cardboard insert prevents damage to the disk drive during shipping and should be removed before you use the drive. Save this piece of cardboard. When you move your computer, insert the cardboard into the drive to prevent damage.

6. Printers usually arrive with a lot of packing material and tape to prevent parts from moving. Remove all this packing material and install the ribbon or ink cartridge before you use the printer.

7. Your computer system probably will arrive with a set of disks containing setup, utility, and diagnostic programs. After your computer is set up, duplicate these disks and keep the original disks in a safe place.

8. Fill out and return warranty cards for all components.

Setting Up Your System

Normally, dealers assemble your computer; format your hard disk, if you purchase one; and install the operating system and software for you. Even some mail-order companies perform this service for you. When selecting a vendor, check to make sure that they provide this service, even if this setup costs a little extra. The less you have to do to set up your computer, the less frustrating the experience will be.

Suppose that the computer you purchase does not come set up. You may have to open up the computer and insert any adapter cards and perhaps even disk drives. When installing the adapters, you may have to set switches so that one adapter does not conflict with another adapter. You then must format the hard disk, install the operating system, and install all software that you purchase.

Although all of this sounds difficult, carefully following the instructions that accompany each component will enable you to set up your computer easily. **Read all instructions.** Do not be afraid to call the technical support department where you purchased your computer to ask questions. Computer and adapter manufacturers also have technical support available. They usually are quite helpful when you are installing components into your computer.

After your computer has all of its components installed, you are ready to complete the computer setup. This final step involves attaching any external components to your computer system; attaching the monitor to the system unit by using a cable; attaching the keyboard (plugging its cable into the system); attaching the printer with the printer cable; attaching a mouse; attaching a modem with a phone cable; and attaching any other auxiliary devices to your computer. These final steps for setting up your computer also should be outlined in documentation that accompanies your computer.

After you connect all components — keyboard, mouse, monitor, printer, and modem—to the system unit with the appropriate cables, and you connect all components—system unit, video monitor, printer, and external modem—to an AC power outlet, you can turn on the computer system. Remember that all components that have a power cord also have a power switch; all switches must be turned on. If everything is connected properly, your computer starts. Several seconds later an operating system prompt should be displayed on the monitor. If the operating system has not been installed on the hard disk, and you do not have a disk in the drive, you may see an error message telling you to place a disk in the disk drive.

If you do not see anything on-screen, or if you see a message asking you to do something other than to insert a disk in the drive, you may have something attached incorrectly, or a component may not be plugged in tightly. Shut everything off, check all your connections, and turn on the system again. If the computer still does not start, check the troubleshooting section or the documentation that came with the computer system. Again, do not be afraid to call the technical support department where you purchased your computer.

Maintaining Your Computer

Like a car, your computer needs periodic maintenance. For your car, you must change the oil regularly, wash the body, have the brakes inspected, change the windshield wipers, and keep gas in the tank to keep the vehicle in good working order. If you do not perform this maintenance, you may have to pop for costly repairs.

You also should perform periodic *preventative maintenance* for your computer. Following a few procedures helps to keep the computer in tip-top performance and alleviates costly repair bills and expensive data loss.

System Unit Maintenance

The system unit requires little maintenance. If you work in a dusty environment, open the case every two months and vacuum the inside of the unit. Dust acts like a blanket on chips. Dust's insulating action causes chips to run at higher temperatures, which can lead to chip failure. Vacuum the dust with hand vacuums designed for electronic components or use canned compressed air. If you work in a normal environment, vacuum once a year.

Many systems contain batteries. IBM AT and compatible computers use the battery to power the part of RAM that holds setup information needed to operate the computer. When the battery dies, your computer does not start correctly. You must replace the battery and run a setup program to restore the information that your computer needs. The setup program is sometimes contained on a disk that you must use to boot your computer. After you turn on your computer, you may need to press a key combination to start the setup program. Normally, the computer determines the setup of the computer. If the setup program cannot determine the correct setup, you must supply information.

The life of batteries in a computer varies. Some batteries last ten years, but most last three years.

Disk Drive Maintenance

The floppy and hard disk drives, which reside in the system unit, also need occasional maintenance. Although the floppy disk drive requires physical maintenance, the hard disk drive requires only *software* maintenance, such as protecting data and reformatting. Performing maintenance to the drives preserves the usefulness of the drive, and more importantly, ensures the cabability of the drive to correctly record your data.

Floppy Disk Drives

The magnetic heads in the floppy drive should be cleaned every year. You easily can clean floppy drives with special cleaning disks. Companies that sell computer accessories, such as Curtis Manufacturing Co., sell cleaning kits for approximately $10 for 5 1/4-inch and 3 1/2-inch floppy disk drives. Cleaning kits also are available from computer retail stores. Make sure that the cleaning system of this type is a wet system rather than a dry system. Using the dry system for cleaning your disk drive heads actually may damage the recording heads.

A more laborious, yet efficient, way to clean the disk drive is to use a cotton swab and isopropyl alcohol. This method requires that you disassemble your computer to gain access to the disk drive heads.

Hard Disk Drives

Hard disks are the most vulnerable part of a personal computer system. If a hard disk crashes, you lose the use of your hard disk and the data on the disk. The term *crash* originally meant a hard disk head hit a hard disk platter, which caused irreparable damage to the disk and its data. Today, the term more loosely describes any problem that causes the hard disk to stop working. You can prepare for a crash by making backups of the hard disk on floppy disks. If anything happens to the hard disk, you have a duplicate copy of your programs and data.

PC Fullback+ 1.12, from West Lake Data, and Fastback Plus 2.1, from Fifth Generation Systems, are dedicated programs that back up hard disks for IBM and compatible computers. PC Tools Deluxe Version 6.0, created by Central Point Software, is a collection of useful disk utilities that also includes hard disk backup software. These programs generally are better than BACKUP that accompanies DOS. Not only are the third-party backup programs easier to use but also are faster and compress data—taking less disks to back up an entire hard disk.

Retrospect 1.1, from Dantz Development, is a good backup program for Macintosh computers, providing easy backup of the hard disk. A cousin product to Fastback Plus 2.1 for IBM and compatibles is Fastback Mac III 2.5. This program provides good backup capability for the Macintosh. From Central Point Software is Mactools Deluxe. This product, like PC Tools Deluxe mentioned earlier, provides many disk utilities, including hard disk backup capability.

Quarterback 4.0 from Central Coast Software is a good utility for backing up an Amiga hard disk.

Hard disk backups must be made regularly to be useful. Whether you make daily, weekly, or monthly backups depends on how much data you enter and how big the problem is if you lose the data. Hard disks are inherently reliable and work for many years, depending on how much you use your computer. Your backup strategy should reflect this level of dependability.

Several products for IBM and compatible computers are designed to prevent hard disk failure by examining the surface of the hard disk platter for defects. SpinRite II, from Gibson Research, is an example of a program that can aid in preventing hard disk disasters. This program scans the disk for correctable and uncorrectable errors. This program can even electronically realign certain hard disks.

Computer viruses have garnered a lot of press recently. A virus can be nondestructive and cause minor annoyances, such as messages appearing on your screen, or a virus can destroy some or all the data on your hard disk. If you download programs by modem from information services or bulletin-board systems, or if you exchange disks with someone who does, you are susceptible to a computer virus. If you want protection from computer viruses, purchase one of the following pieces of antiviral software: Symantec's Norton Antivirus or Microcom's Virex 1.1 for IBM and compatibles; AntiVirus for Mac, from Symantec, or Virex 2.71, from Microcom, for the Macintosh; Anti-Virus, from DevWare, for the Amiga.

The more you use a hard disk, the slower it operates because of *file fragmentation*. Fragmentation occurs when program and data files are broken into pieces and placed in available space on the hard disk. Disk-optimizing software connects the scattered pieces of a program or file in one block. Good choices for disk-optimizing software are: OPTune, from Gazelle Systems, and Norton Utilities 5.0, from Symantec, for IBM and compatibles; Disk Express II, from ALSoft, and Mac Tools Deluxe, from Central Point Software, for the Macintosh; and Quarterback Tools, from Central Coast Software, for the Amiga. Run a disk-optimizing program every two months.

No matter what the capacity of a hard disk, you eventually will fill it. Whether you fill your hard disk quickly or slowly depends on the number of software programs you install on the hard disk and the size of the files you create with those programs. You occasionally need to move some of the files from the hard disk to floppy disks for archival storage, or you need to erase files that you no longer use. If you use an IBM or compatible computer with MS-DOS only, these housekeeping chores can be very tedious, but a program like XTree Pro Gold, from XTree, enables you to complete this task quickly and effectively. If you use Windows 3.0 or a Macintosh or Amiga computer, removing files from the hard disk is not as tedious, and you don't need a special program to assist you. The frequency of this housekeeping depends upon the space available on your disk and the size and number of files you create daily.

Keyboard, Mouse, and Video Monitor Maintenance

The keyboard, mouse, and video monitor require little maintenance. The keyboard surface should be cleaned as needed with a damp cloth and a mild cleaning solvent. A mouse ball should be removed and cleaned with a mild solvent every six months. Inside the mouse, where the ball resides, are two rollers. These rollers can be cleaned with a cotton swab and a mild solvent. Clean the video monitor with ordinary glass cleaner, unless the screen is covered with an antiglare coating; the documentation tells you whether the screen is coated. For screens with antiglare coating, use a special screen cleaner, such as Clean Screen, from Curtis Manufacturing Co. Clean your screen once a week with the monitor turned off.

Printer Maintenance

Printers require periodic maintenance, primarily for replacing ribbons and cartridges. If you have a dot-matrix printer that uses a nylon ribbon, hang a page that was printed when the ribbon was new. As you use the ribbon, the print will become lighter. Use the page as a visual guide to tell you when to replace the ribbon.

Make it a habit to clean your dot-matrix printer when you change the printer ribbon. Paper dust tends to collect in the printer. Use a vacuum to suck out the dust. Periodically, perhaps every fifth time you change the ribbon, you may want to clean the printer head. Use a cotton swab and mild solvent to clean the printer head. Finally, use a soft cloth to clean the *platen*—the rubber-like cylinder against which the paper rests.

If you have a laser or inkjet printer, the printer signals you when replacement of a toner cartridge or an ink cartridge is necessary. Clean the inside of laser printers regularly, because the black toner powder spreads through the machine. Refer to the laser printer's documentation for the proper cleaning procedures.

As with a dot-matrix printer, clean your laser printer when you change the toner or ink cartridge.

Troubleshooting

Troubleshooting a personal computer system requires two phases. The first phase is the initial setup. Do all the related components work right out of the box? If they do not, you must follow some simple troubleshooting procedures. The second phase occurs after months or even years have passed. How do you deal with any problems that may arise after the system has been running for a period of time?

Troubleshooting the Initial Setup

When you connect the components of your computer system and turn on the power, you should see something on the display. If you don't see anything, or if you see an error message, do some basic troubleshooting before you call a dealer or technical support staff.

If nothing displays, check the power. Check that each component is plugged in and all power switches are turned on. If you are using a multiple-outlet power strip, check that its switch is turned on.

If a component seems to be on—a green or red indicator light is on—but nothing is happening, check that the cable connected to the system unit is secure. If the video monitor seems to be on, but nothing displays on-screen, adjust the contrast and brightness controls. If a printer or a modem isn't working, it may be connected to the wrong port. Some computers have more than one serial or parallel port. If a printer or modem is on but not responding, switch the printer or modem to a different port.

During shipment to your home or office, computer chips, batteries, and ribbon cables can come loose. To resolve most problems that occur during shipment, you must remove the cover of the system unit. If the computer works properly, you still can remove the cover and perform the following three spot checks to prevent related problems from developing.

1. Inspect all cables; they should be securely connected to such components as the disk drives and add-in boards.

2. Push down all add-in boards to verify that they are correctly seated in the expansion slots.

3. Push down any computer chips that are seated in, not soldered in, sockets.

Another problem may be with the computer's internal battery, if it has one. The battery probably is not dead. Perhaps the battery is unplugged, however, or has come loose in some way. Try removing the cover and reinserting the battery. If the battery is used to retain the computer's setup, you have to run the computer's setup program again.

If your computer still does not work, call your dealer or the technical support staff of the company from which you purchased your computer.

Long-Term Troubleshooting Strategies

After your system is up and running, you may not experience problems with components for several months or years. If you suspect a problem, run any diagnostic software that came with your computer. This software often pinpoints the problem for you. You may not be able to solve the problem, but you will have information to give your dealer or a technical support person.

The documentation that accompanied the computer should discuss how to operate the diagnostic software that came with the computer system.

If you have an IBM or compatible computer, you can purchase diagnostic software that is more thorough and easier to use than the software that comes with the system. A good choice is Check It, from TouchStone Software. Check It tests the system unit board, RAM, hard disk drive, floppy disk drives, video circuits, serial and parallel ports, keyboard, mouse, joy-stick, and printer. Check It also indicates whether the problem is caused by hardware or software.

Check It is manufactured by Touchstone Software. After you use Check It and find an error, you may use the information to repair the computer yourself or give the information to a repair person.

Computer problems are not always caused by system components. Problems can be the result of something foolish that you do, such as erasing a file or reformatting your hard disk. Problems like these can be devastating if you don't have software to get you out of these jams.

Utility software is designed to perform several important tasks: to recover erased files, to reverse problems caused by reformatting a hard disk, to reconstruct damaged files, and to repair a corrupted hard disk. When looking for utility programs, notice the features that they offer. Most utility programs offer many of the same features, mentioned previously; some may offer unique utilities or features. These unique utilities or features may make one utility program more important to you than another utility program.

Utility programs usually offer many other features that can be used for maintenance. Examples of this type of software for IBM and compatible computers are PC Tools Deluxe 6.0, from Central Point Software; Norton Utilities 5.0, from Symantec; and the Mace Utilities 1990, from Fifth Generation Systems. Examples of utility programs for Macintosh computers are Mac Tools Deluxe, from Central Point Software, and Norton Utilities for the Macintosh, from Peter Norton Computing. For the Amiga, choose Quarterback Tools, from Central Coast Software.

Chapter Summary

Chapter 9 began with advice concerning an appropriate place in your office or home to install a computer system. The chapter offered suggestions for protecting your system and software from problems caused by power surges, heat, static electricity, and magnetism.

The chapter continued with suggestions for setting up your system. The chapter told you what to expect from your dealer and gave you tips for a smooth installation.

The chapter suggested products for maintaining your PC in top condition. The chapter included product advice for the system unit, disk drives, keyboard, mouse, monitor, and printer and put special emphasis on maintaining the hard disk drive.

Chapter 9 lastly explained what to do when things go wrong. The chapter offered troubleshooting tips for spotting problems during setup and later in your computer's life. The chapter also suggested products that can assist you when hardware or software problems occur.

In the Next Chapter

Chapter 10 helps you prepare for the future. The next chapter describes different components you may want to add to your system. The chapter advises you on networking a future system to your current system. Chapter 10 lastly explains how to keep pace with new technology and how to upgrade your computer and software.

10

How Do I Plan for the Future?

The computer industry is continually changing. Technological advancements and improvements in hardware and software occur frequently. The system you purchase today may be outdated in a few years—unless you keep up with the changes manufacturers routinely make.

This chapter helps you know what to expect from a personal computer system you purchase today. Can the computer be maintained and repaired to keep it working in top condition? Can you upgrade your computer to keep it technologically competitive with newer systems?

Finally, the chapter describes some ways to keep track of what is going on in the personal computer industry and recommends some magazines and on-line sources of computing information that can keep you up to date with the latest developments in personal computing.

Repairing a Personal Computer System

Personal computer systems are inherently reliable and can give trouble-free service for many years. Nonetheless, electronic components still are susceptible to breakdown and in need of repair. While the computer is under warranty, you need only to return the computer to the dealer or contact the manufacturer for repair. When the computer and its components are out of warranty, you can make one of several choices.

In-Warranty Repairs

The warranty period differs from computer to computer and among components. Most computer manufacturers offer one-year warranties; however, a few offer longer warranties. If you buy additional components for your computer, such as a modem, the warranty period may be longer than for the computer. Keep accurate records as to purchase dates and warranty periods. Also make sure that you have copies of all your receipts showing the purchase date. You must prove that your computer is in warranty to obtain a warranty repair.

Keep a record of procedures that you must follow for a computer or component that breaks during warranty. If you purchased your computer or components from a dealer, you most likely need to return the computer to that dealer for repair. You generally get best service from the dealer that you purchased the equipment from.

Some computer manufacturers authorize dealers as a repair center. For example, IBM, Compaq, and Apple have authorized dealer repair centers. Generally, you may take your computer to one of these repair centers for a warranty repair. At an authorized service center, your warranty is honored.

In some cases, your warranty may provide on-site service for a period of time. The repairman comes to your home or business to repair your computer. This procedure saves you from unhooking and moving your computer. If you receive on-site service, verify the procedures that you must follow to get a repair person to your site.

Perhaps your dealer is not an authorized service center, and no authorized service centers are in your area. (You also may have purchased a computer through the mail, with no provision for on-site or carry-in service.) In this case, you need to mail the computer or component back to the manufacturer for repair.

While sending your computer away may sound intimidating, it often is quite easy. Many companies offer telephone support to aid you in verifying that your computer is really broken. After you determine that your computer needs to be repaired, you are instructed to return the computer. Make sure, however, that you have proper authorization from the company to return the computer.

Many companies return your computer to you in the same fashion that you sent it. Some companies return the system or components to you by air to expedite the return of your computer.

Ask your dealer or the manufacturer if a warranty repair extends the warranty. The replacement part may carry a warranty of its own. For example, suppose that your computer carries a one-year warranty. After six months, the disk drive needs repaired. If the new disk drive carries a warranty of its own, even when the computer is out of warranty, that replacement drive may still have another six months of coverage. Keep all paperwork involved with warranty repairs.

Out-of-Warranty Repairs

When the need for repair occurs after the warranty period, you may want to be more selective about your repair service. Although the dealer probably can fix your computer, you may pay a premium price for the repair. You may take two paths when dealing with an out-of-warranty repair. One is to decide on a good technical repair shop. The other is to consider making the repair yourself.

Finding a Reliable Repair Center

Your dealer, if an authorized service center, has the parts needed to fix your computer. The dealer from whom you purchased your system, however, is not the only reliable service center. Other repair shops are in business and may have better prices or offer other bonuses that your dealer does not; some repair shops may offer loaner or rental equipment while your computer or component is being repaired.

Where do you look for repair shops? First, ask a friend or someone else you trust. Word of mouth often is the best way to find reputable service centers. Second, check the yellow pages under *Computers & Computer Equipment—Service & Repair*. Most of the service centers in your area advertise this way. Their ads may tell you what computers and other products they service. Call several of the service centers near you to check prices and services available. Ask the following:

- Do you charge by the hour or by the job?
- Do you provide loaner or rental equipment?
- Do you use original replacement parts?
- Do you provide on-site service?

- Do you provide pick-up and delivery services?
- If on-site service or pick up and delivery are available, do you charge extra?
- How long will the repair take?
- Will you guarantee a time for completion?
- Do you offer a warranty on the repair?

Generally, when a repair is charged by the job, the cost is less, and the cost of the repair may be easier for you to budget. Loaner equipment, or even rental equipment may help you keep up your productivity, especially if the repair may take several days or a week.

Major computer manufacturers such as IBM, Apple, and Compaq have specially designed components in their systems. Often, the components are of a size or shape so that only original parts work well in the computers. The components that generally have to be replaced with original parts are the system board and power supply. Use your discretion and suggestions from the repair center to decide when to use components that are not original.

On-site service generally gets your computer fixed faster. Your travel time is cut, and computer downtime is kept to a minimum. You normally pay a premium price for this service. If the service center picks up and delivers, you also are saved travel time.

The question of how long the repair will take seems like an obvious one. The length of the repair, however, can help you make decisions, especially if the computer is used in a business setting. If the repair will take less than two days, you may not want to bother with borrowing or renting another computer. If your computer goes down in the middle of a time-essential task, however, you most likely will need another computer. You also may check with several repair facilities and send your computer to the service center who can repair the computer the quickest—even if the faster shop costs more for the repair.

Repairing Your Computer Yourself

Computers are very modular. Rather than intricate, difficult-to-understand wiring that you would have to wade through, a computer is made up of circuit cards. For example, the video generally is created on a video card. The disk drives are controlled by a card. If your computer is not displaying anything on-screen, the monitor is unplugged, not turned on, or faulty, or the video card is faulty. Suppose that you determine that the monitor is fine, how can you tell which of the cards in the computer is the video card? The video card has the cable from the monitor attached to it.

Opening the computer is quite simple. Normally, two to five screws on the rear of the computer hold the case on. Remove the screws, and the case slides off.

If you plan to perform some repairs yourself, seek initial help. You also can use a program that aids you in diagnosing computer problems. One such program is Check It Version 3.0 from Touchstone Software. For thorough help, consult *Upgrading and Repairing PCs*, written by Scott Mueller and published by Que Corporation.

Upgrading a Personal Computer System

If your personal computer lasts for five or more years, you may end up with a technologically deficient machine. Computers, however, usually can be upgraded to keep current with technological improvements. You should know about two kinds of upgrades: upgrades the manufacturer provides and upgrades you can provide for yourself. The following sections describe these upgrades.

Manufacturer's Hardware Upgrades

All personal computers have memory chips. ROM chips contain programs the computer needs to work properly. Manufacturers often change ROM programs when they announce new computer models. You should keep track of these changes. In most cases, you can take your computer back to your dealer and have the new ROM chips installed in your older model for a nominal fee. Your older model then is as up-to-date as the latest models offered by the manufacturer.

New ROM chips may be created if the manufacturer finds a small problem with one of the programs in an existing ROM chip. The manufacturer also may add a program in a later ROM chip to add support for a new device. To correct the problem or add support for the new device, the ROM chips in your computer also need to be replaced.

Manufacturer's Software Upgrades

Periodically, software developers upgrade software programs. As you probably have noticed, software recommended in this book often has a version number.

When you buy software, send in the warranty card so that the manufacturer has your name on file. If the software is upgraded, the manufacturer usually informs you of the upgrade and its cost.

Software is upgraded for one of two reasons: to correct program errors or to add new features. If the program is upgraded to correct errors, make sure that you upgrade your program. If, however, the program is upgraded to add new features, review the new features to see if the upgrade benefits you. If you can use at least one of the new features, you may want to upgrade your program. Weigh the cost of the upgrade and the cost in time that the upgrade may take verses the benefit of the upgrade.

Keep in mind that you can tell much by the version number of the new upgrade. Suppose that a program's version is 2.0. You receive in the mail information about the new 2.01 program. Because the increment is so small, the upgrade may not be worth your time (the exception, however, is if this new version fixes a problem, or you are required to keep current to get later upgrade information). Suppose that you see that the new version is 3.0. You should seriously consider this upgrade. With this large of a version change, the program may change significantly.

Other Upgrades

Most personal computers can be kept technologically competitive with newer models by upgrading components such as the memory, the hard disk, the graphics adapter, and even the system board. Sometimes an upgrade is necessary because your needs change; sometimes an upgrade is necessary because the technology changes.

Memory

Often, software programs can benefit through speed or additional capabilities with the more memory that you have. Upgrades to a program also may call for more memory. If you change operating systems, the new operating system may require more memory than the original operating system that you used.

When purchasing a computer with one megabyte of memory, you are not limited to that amount for the life of your system. When you need more memory, you can purchase memory chips from your dealer or through mail order. Increasing system memory is not a difficult task; you may want to install the memory yourself or ask a friend with some computer expertise to help. If you purchase memory from a dealer, installation may be included in the price of the memory.

Dynamic RAM costs about $75 per megabyte (depending on speed) through mail order but can cost significantly more through your dealer. Again, make sure that you specify your computer model when you order memory.

Hard Disk

If you buy a computer with a 40-megabyte hard disk, you are not limited to that capacity for the life of your system. Even if the drive is working fine, you may want to replace your hard disk with a model with more capacity. For example, you may want to switch from a 40-megabyte model to one that holds two or three times as much data.

Adding a larger hard disk does not mean that you throw away the old, smaller hard disk. Often, computers are equipped to handle more than one hard disk. You may just want to add the second hard disk to your system. You also may use the smaller hard disk to upgrade another computer with an even smaller hard disk, or no hard disk at all. If you do not need the hard disk that you are replacing, sell it.

Keep in mind that if the new hard disk does not use the same kind of controller as the old hard disk, you also have to buy a new controller. If you install a new hard disk yourself, the upgrade may cost much less than if you rely on your dealer. Prices of hard disk drives vary by capacity, manufacturer, controller technology, and speed. For more information about hard disk drives, see Chapter 3.

Monitor/Graphics Adapter

You may upgrade the video adapter on an IBM or compatible or on most of the Macintosh computers. Although upgrading the display may require purchasing only a monitor or adapter, you most likely will have to purchase both.

With an IBM or compatible computer, you can have different video standards, such as mono/graphics, CGA, EGA, VGA, and SuperVGA (also the new XGA that IBM introduced just prior to this writing). Switching from one of these standards to another requires purchasing a new monitor besides a new adapter. One exception is when moving from VGA to SuperVGA. Your video card may support SuperVGA, but your monitor does not, or your monitor may support SuperVGA, but your adapter does not. Consult the monitor and adapter documentation.

You may increase the resolution of your Macintosh display, except the portable or Classic, by purchasing a new monitor. Using the IIci or IIsi with built-in video or upgrading to a full-page display is supported.

You may increase the color capability and resolution of your Macintosh by purchasing a graphics adapter and a new monitor. For example, Apple offers a 24-bit color card that may be used in the IIsi and IIfx Macintoshes. The 24-bit color card increases color capabilities tremendously.

Prices of graphic adapters vary by company, graphics standard, resolution, and memory included on the board. For more information about graphics adapters, see Chapter 3.

System Board

You may upgrade the system board in most computers. Upgrading the system board is generally done to increase the speed of the CPU or to provide a more advanced CPU.

You may upgrade the system board in one of two ways. One way is to replace the system board entirely with another system board. This replacement may be done easily in most IBM-compatible computers. A second way is to add an adapter card that interfaces with your current system board. Adding an adapter card to the current system board is the way upgrading a Macintosh is most often done.

The cost involved in upgrading a computer using a new system board or adapter card varies according to the CPU that you are upgrading to. The actual cost of the system board may be as little as a few hundred dollars or as much as a few thousand dollars. One cost that must be factored in is the installation of the new system board or the CPU adapter card. You can upgrade the board or card yourself or use the dealer. Using the dealer may cost more, however, but the decrease in possible frustration may be worth the investment.

Depending on the cost of the upgrade, you may be better off purchasing a new computer—especially if upgrading the system board really shows just how slow the other components of the system are.

Suppose that you upgrade to a very fast system board but do not upgrade your hard disk. The speed of the system board may be degraded while it is waiting on your slow hard disk to transfer data. To increase the speed, you may purchase a faster hard disk and controller. Now, however, you have an old system board and hard disk and controller sitting around collecting dust. Weigh in the full cost of an upgrade versus a new computer.

Math Coprocessor

An upgrade that can enhance the numerical computing speed of a personal computer is a math coprocessor. System boards for IBM and compatible computers contain an empty socket for this chip. If you want spreadsheet, business graphics, accounting, statistical, and other such programs to run faster, purchase a math coprocessor. For Intel CPUs, the number of the coprocessor is one digit higher than the CPU number. For example, an 80386SX CPU uses an 80387SX coprocessor. For best performance, the speed of the coprocessor should match the speed of the CPU. For example, if you have a 25-MHz 80386 CPU, you should purchase a 25-MHz 80387 coprocessor. A coprocessor designed by Intel for its line of CPUs is a good choice.

The price of coprocessors for computers with 80386SX and 80386 CPUs range from $200 to $450. If you have an 80486 CPU, remember that the coprocessor already is built into the chip. The empty socket on many 80486 system boards is for a high-performance (and expensive) math coprocessor manufactured by Weitek. If you are using a computer for high-performance 3-D graphics and computer aided design work, consider this enhancement.

Installing a coprocessor on an IBM or compatible computer is just a matter of correctly seating the chip into its socket. Seating the chip is not difficult but must be done with extreme care so that none of the pins on the chip bend during insertion.

Some of the Macintosh computers include a coprocessor as a standard feature of the system board. Others do not even include an empty socket for one. The Macintosh IIx, IIci, and IIfx have coprocessors on the system board; whereas the Macintosh Classic and LC do not provide a coprocessor socket. To add a coprocessor to a Macintosh IIsi requires installing a special adapter board that includes a coprocessor. This upgrade is available from Apple Computer and costs approximately $200.

Printers

Upgrades are not limited to personal computers. You also can upgrade printers. Laser printers can be upgraded with more memory and with boards that add more features, such as PostScript printing. As with computers, the configuration you start with is not the configuration you are limited to for the lifetime of the printer.

You can find more information on upgrading a printer in *The Printer Bible*, written by Scott Foerster and published by Que Corporation.

Keeping Pace with New Developments

Buying a personal computer is different from buying any other piece of electronic equipment because of the computer's flexibility. For example, if you buy a personal computer for word processing, you could sell or give the computer to someone who wants to use it for spreadsheets. A personal computer is not limited to the purpose you originally plan. If you want to use the computer to manage your personal finances or to play games, you can. For this reason, you should keep abreast of new developments in personal computer components and software.

Computer magazines and on-line services are two good ways to keep current with developments in the personal computer industry.

Subscribing to Computer Magazines

A great number of computer magazines are devoted to different aspects of computing. If you are interested in comparative reviews, *PC Magazine* compares large numbers of similar products in each issue. This magazine, however, is geared toward the person who buys equipment and software for corporations, and the information may be overwhelming at first. One magazine that covers the mail-order industry is *Computer Shopper*. This magazine and others like it contain ads for hundreds of mail-order suppliers of personal computer systems and software.

Some magazines pay particular attention to a specific product. For example, *Lotus* magazine contains many articles about Lotus 1-2-3, and *WordPerfect* magazine contains many articles about the WordPerfect word processor. If you are interested in a specific area of computing, such as desktop publishing or music, you should look for magazines such as *Publish* and *Electronic Musician*.

When you consider buying or subscribing to a magazine, you should be aware of the readership the magazine addresses. For example, *Byte* magazine is for technically sophisticated people; whereas *PC Computing* is directed more toward the general reader.

Some magazines cover one kind of computer. For example, *PC Magazine* and *PC World* cover IBM and compatible computers; *Mac World* and *Mac User* cover the Macintosh computer; and *Amiga World* covers the Amiga computer.

These magazines are all good sources of information for using and buying products associated with a particular brand of personal computer.

Joining an On-Line Service

If you are using a personal computer daily, you may want to contact other people with similar computer systems and software to ask a question or discuss a particular topic. Consider signing up for an on-line service such as CompuServe or Genie. These services have hundreds of SIGs (special interest groups) where you can leave messages and get responses to questions about computing topics. You also can chat with other members while you are connected to the service.

To connect to an on-line service, you need a modem and communications software, and you are charged an hourly fee for using the service. Often, however, the information you receive is well worth the cost. Keep in mind the peak and off-peak hours for calling the service; peak rates can be two to three times the cost of off-peak rates.

Although Compuserve and Genie may be too expensive for you to justify, other on-line sources may interest you. One is Prodigy, sponsored by IBM and Sears. This on-line service charges a flat monthly fee, rather than on-line time. Another service is the local bulletin board service (BBS). Often computer user groups or other individuals leave their computer on-line for you to access. You may leave messages on this computer for others to read and respond to. Some BBSs cater to different needs—IBM and compatibles only, Macintosh only, and other special areas, even noncomputer related areas. Get in touch with your local user groups to find out about BBSs.

Chapter Summary

This chapter offered advice about planning for the future in two key areas: repairs and upgrades. The chapter explained considerations that you may make when your computer is in need of repair and how personal computers and software can be upgraded to keep pace with new technologies. Finally, the chapter described two ways to keep abreast of new products introduced for personal computers. Computer magazines and on-line services were recommended to help you keep up to date with computing, to help you get information about computing, and to help you locate people with interests similar to yours.

Index

1-2-3 Release 2.2, 190
1-2-3 Release 3.1, 190
101-key keyboards, 52
16-bit microprocessors, 40-41
24-pin dot-matrix printers, 155
3.5 inch floppy disks/disk drives, 30
3.5 inch hard disks/disk drives, 58-59
32-bit microprocessors, 40-41
4th Dimension 2.1, 193
5.25 inch floppy disks/disk drives, 30
5.25 inch hard disks/disk drives, 58-59
68000 microprocessor, 46-48
68020 microprocessor, 46-48
68030 microprocessor, 47-48
8-bit microprocessors, 40-41
80286 microprocessor, 43-44
80386 microprocessor, 44-45
80386SX microprocessor, 44-45
80486 microprocessors, 46
8086 microprocessor, 42-43
8088 microprocessor, 42-43
9-pin dot-matrix printers, 155

A

access speed (hard disks/disk drives), 60
accounting software, 194-195
  Business Sense, 195
  DacEasy Accounting 4.1, 195
  M.Y.O.B. 2.0, 195
  Pacioli 2000, 195
  Peachtree Complete III, 195
  printer considerations, 153
AccuCard, 219
Acer America, 79
Acius Incorporation
  4th Dimension 2.1, 193
Adobe Systems
  Illustrator 3.0, 208
  PostScript, 139
  PostScript laser printers
    Texas Instruments MicroLaser 35, 156
Adobe Illustrator 3.0, 208
Adobe PostScript, 139
Advanced Logic Research (ALR), 79-80

Aldus
  PageMaker 3.01, 200
  PageMaker 4.0, 200
ALR (Advanced Logic Research), 79-80
ALSoft
  Disk Express II, 227
Altec Technologies Corporation, 80
Amiga computers, 91-92
  computer magazines, 242
  floppy disks/disk drives, 31
  memory, 51
  MIDI software
    Level II 3.0, 211
  operating system, 36
  paint/drawing programs
    Deluxe Paint III, 208
    Professional Draw 2.0, 208
  speed, 93
  used computers, 127
  video system, 27
Amiga World computer magazine, 242
Anti-Virus, 227
AntiVirus for Mac, 227
Apple LaserWriter, 140
Apple LaserWriter II NTX PostScript laser printer, 156
Apple PostScript printers, 140
application software, 36, 37
  see also names of specific software packages
Ashton-Tate
  dBASE IV 1.1, 193
AST Research, 80
AT&T, 81
Atari computers
  floppy disks/disk drives, 31
  GEM operating system, 179
  Mega computer, 92
  memory, 51
  MIDI software
    Notator 3.0, 211
  operating systems, 34
  speed, 93
  ST computer, 92
  used computers, 127
  video system, 27
Austin Computer Systems, 81
authorized dealers, 160-161

B

backing up hard disks/disk drives, 226-227
banners, 149
benefits of personal computers, 6-8
Berkeley Software
  GEOWorks (Ensemble), 180
bits, 40-41
blackouts, 218
Borland
  Paradox 3.5, 193
  Quattro Pro 2.0, 190
brochures, 151
brownouts, 218
bus mouse, 53
buses
  EISA, 63
  ISA, 63
  MCA, 63
Business Sense, 195
ButtonWare
  PC-File 5.0, 193
Byte computer magazine, 242

C

cables, 222
CAD software
  example systems, 113
Cakewalk Professional 3.0, 211
Canon
  BJ-10e portable inkjet printer, 156

Index 247

capacity
    hard disks/disk drives, 59
CarbonCopy Mac, 204
case, 51, 52
Central Coast Software
    Quarterback 4.0, 226
    Quarterback Tools, 227, 230
Central Point Software
    Mac Tools Deluxe, 226, 227, 230
    PC Tools Deluxe 6.0, 230
    PC Tools Deluxe Version 6.0, 226
Color Graphics Adapter (CGA), 26
CGA video standard, 239
Check It, 230
chips, 24
Coda Music Software
    Finale, 211
color monitors, 55-56
color printers, 157
Commodore Business Machines
    see Amiga computers, 91
communications software
    CarbonCopy Mac, 204
    CompuServe Navigator 3.0, 204
    Microphone II 3.0, 203
    pcAnywhere III, 203
    ProComm Plus 1.1, 203
    purchasing considerations, 200-203
    SmartCom III 1.2, 203
    White Knight 11.6, 204
COMPAQ Computer, 81-82
comparing personal computers, 72
    graphical user interfaces, 73-75
    models, 96
    price, 76-77
    software availability, 73
    speed, 75-76
CompuAdd, 82, 161
CompuServe
    CompuServe Navigator 3.0, 204
CompuServe on-line service, 243

computer magazines
    Amiga World, 242
    Byte, 242
    Computer Shopper, 242
    Electronic Musician, 242
    Lotus, 242
    Mac User, 242
    Mac World, 242
    PC Computing, 242
    PC Magazine, 242
    Publish, 242
    WordPerfect, 242
Computer Shopper computer magazine, 242
connectors
    keyboard, 22-23
    ports, 143
    serial ports, 143
Copyist DTP, 211
Corel Draw! 2.0, 207
Corel Systems
    Corel Draw! 2.0, 207
CPU *see* microprocessors
Curtis Manufacturing, 225
cut-sheet feeders, 135

D

DacEasy Accounting 4.1, 195
DacEasy Incorporated
    DacEasy Accounting 4.1, 195
daisywheel printers, 137-138
Dantz Development
    Retrospect 1.1, 226
database programs
    4th Dimension 2.1, 193
    dBASE IV 1.1, 193
    File 2.0, 193
    FoxBASE II/Mac 2.01, 193
    FoxPro 1.02, 193
    Paradox 3.5, 193
    PC-File 5.0, 193

purchasing considerations, 191-193
    SuperBase 4, 193
databases, 11, 174
    example systems, 110-112
    flat-file, 191
    printer considerations, 152
    relational, 191
Datastorm Technologies
    ProComm Plus 1.1, 203
dBASE IV 1.1, 193
Dell Computer, 82-83
Deluxe Paint III, 208
DeskMate, 180
DeskPaint/DeskDraw 3.01, 207
desktop publishing, 10
    example systems, 115-116
    Express Publisher 1.0, 201
    FrameMaker 2.1, 200
    Interleaf Publisher 3.0, 201
    PageMaker 3.01, 200
    PFS: First Publisher 3.0, 201
    printer considerations, 153
    purchasing considerations, 198-199
    Springboard Publisher II 2.0, 200
    Ventura Publisher, 201
desktop publishing software, 174
    PageMaker 4.0, 200
    QuarkXpress 3.0, 200
DESQview, 179
DevWare
    Anti-Virus, 227
diagnostic software, 230
Digidesign
    Notator 3.0, 211
Digital Research
    GEM, 179
DIPs, 49-50
dirty power, 219
Disk Express II, 227
disk optimization, 227

display *see* video system, 25
document management, 186
DOS, 176, 177
dot-matrix printers, 132-135
    24-pin, 155
    9-pin, 155
    cut-sheet feeders, 135
    Epson
        LQ-510, 155
        LX810, 155
    manufacturers, 136
    operating costs, 147-148
    Panasonic
        KX-P1124, 155
        KX-P1180, 155
    paper parking, 135
    paper size, 147
    print modes, 135
    resolution, 145-146
    Seikosha
        SP1000, 155
    speed, 146
    Star Micronics
        NX-1000 Multifont II, 155
    tractor-feed mechanism, 135
dots per inch (dpi), 145-146
double density disks/disk drives, 31
DR DOS, 34
Dr. T's Music Software
    Copyist DTP, 211
    Level II 3.0, 211
drawing applications
    printer considerations, 154
drawing programs
    Adobe Illustrator 3.0, 208
    Corel Draw! 2.0, 207
    Deluxe Paint III, 208
    DeskPaint/DeskDraw 3.01, 207
    PC PaintBrush IV Plus 1.0, 207
    Professional Draw 2.0, 208
    purchasing consideration, 206-208

DTK Computer, 83
dual-in-line package memory chips
    see DIPs
Dynamic Microcomputer Association
    pcAnywhere III, 203
dynamic RAM, 49

E

education applications
    printer considerations, 154
educational software, 14
    example systems, 116-117
    purchasing considerations, 212-213
    shareware, 214-215
Enhanced Graphics Adapter (EGA), 26
EGA video standard, 239
EISA bus, 63
Electronic Arts
    Deluxe Paint III, 208
electronic mail, 11-12
Electronic Musician computer magazine, 242
elongated characters, 134
e-mail, 11-12
Emerson Electric
    AccuCard, 219
enhanced keyboards, 52
environments
    magnetism, 221
    multitasking operating
        DESQview, 179
        Windows, 178
    phone lines, 221
    single-tasking operating
        DOS, 176, 177
        System, 177
    static electricity, 220-221

Epson
    Epson LX810 dot-matrix printer, 155
Epson America
    computers, 83, 84
ESDI (enhanced small device interface) hard disks, 96
Everex Systems, 84
example systems
    CAD software, 113
    databases, 110-112
    desktop publishing, 115-116
    educational software, 116-117
    general-purpose, 118-119
    paint programs, 112-113
    presentation graphics, 112-113
    spreadsheets, 107-109
    telecommunications, 114
    word processing, 104-107
Excel 2.1, 190
Excel 2.2, 190
expanded memory, 50-51
expansion
    cards, 23-24
    slots, 23-24, 61-62
Express Publisher 1.0, 201
extended memory, 50

F

Fastback Mac III 2.5, 226
Fastback Plus 2.1, 226
Fifth Generation Systems
    Fastback Mac III 2.5, 226
    Fastback Plus 2.1, 226
    Mace Utilities 1990, 230
File 2.0, 193
file fragmentation, 227
Finale, 211
financial software, 11
Finder, 177

flat-file databases, 191
floppy disks/disk drives, 24-29
    3.5 inch, 30
    5.25 inch, 30
    Amiga, 31
    Atari, 31
    double density, 31
    high density, 31
    IBM-compatible computers, 31, 58
    Macintosh compters, 31
    maintenance, 225-226
fonts, 132
forms, 150
Fox Software
    FoxBASE II/Mac 2.01, 193
    FoxPro 1.02, 193
FoxBASE II/Mac 2.01, 193
FoxPro 1.02, 193
Frame Technology
    FrameMaker 2.1, 200
FreeSoft Microcomputer Products
    White Knight 11.6, 204

G

games, 13, 14
    purchasing considerations, 212-213
gas plasma screens, 121
Gateway 2000, 84
Gazelle Systems
    OPTune, 227
GCC PLP IIS page printer, 156
GEM operating system, 34, 179
Genie on-line service, 243
GEOWorks (Ensemble), 180
Gibson Research
    SpinRite II, 227
Gold Disk
    Professional Draw 2.0, 208
graphical user interfaces, 73-75
graphics applications
    printer considerations, 154

H

hard disk upgrades, 239
hard disks/disk drives, 24-32
    access speed, 60
    backing up, 226-227
    disk optimization, 227
    file fragmentation, 227
    hard cards, 61
    maintenance, 226-227
    removable hard disks, 61
    size, 58-59
    speed, 32
    storage capacity, 59
    transfer rate, 60-61
    types, 96
    upgrades, 239
    viruses, 227
hardware requirements
    software packages, 183-184
hardware upgrades, 237
Hayes
    SmartCom III 1.2, 203
Hewlett-Packard
    computers, 85
    LaserJet III printer, 139
    LaserJet Series III laser printer, 156
    PCL (Printer Control Language), 139
    Printer Control Language (PCL), 139
    Series II laser printer, 156
high density disks/disk drives, 31

I

IBM
    XGA video standard, 239
IBM compatibles
    video standards
        CGA, 26
        EGA, 26
        VGA, 27

IBM-compatible computers
  accounting programs
    DacEasy Accounting 4.1, 195
    Pacioli 2000, 195
  accounting software
    Peachtree Complete III, 195
  Canon BJ-10e portable inkjet printer, 156
  Centronics parallel port, 143
  color monitors, 55-56
  communications software
    pcAnywhere III, 203
    ProComm Plus 1.1, 203
    SmartCom III 1.2, 203
  computer magazines, 242
  database programs
    dBASE IV 1.1, 193
    FoxPro 1.02, 193
    Paradox 3.5, 193
    PC-File 5.0, 193
    SuperBase 4, 193
  desktop publishing
    Express Publisher 1.0, 201
    Interleaf Publisher 3.0, 201
    PageMaker 3.01, 200
    PFS: First Publisher 3.0, 201
    Ventura Publisher, 201
  dot-matrix printers, 132-135, 155
    24-pin, 155
    9-pin, 155
    cut-sheet feeders, 135
    dots per inch (dpi), 145-146
    manufacturers, 136
    operating costs, 147-148
    paper parking, 135
    paper size, 147
    print modes, 135
    resolution, 145-146
    speed, 146
    tractor-feed mechanisms, 135
  DR DOS operating system, 34
  example systems
    CAD software, 113
    databases, 110-111
    desktop publishing, 115-116
    educational, 116
    paint programs, 112
    presentation graphics, 112
    spreadsheets, 107-109
    word processing, 105-106
  floppy disks/disk drives, 31, 58
  Hewlett-Packard LaserJet Series III laser printer, 156
  Hewlett-Packard Series II laser printer, 156
  inkjet printers, 155
  integrated software packages
    PFS: First Choice 3.1, 205
    Symphony 2.2, 205
    Works 2.0, 205
  Kodak
    Dixonix 150 Plus portable inkjet printer, 156
  laser printers, 156
  manufacturers/dealers
    Acer America, 79
    ALR (Advanced Logic Research), 79-80
    Altec Technologies Corporation, 80
    AST Research, 80
    AT&T, 81
    Austin Computer Systems, 81
    Canon, 156
    COMPAQ Computer, 81-82
    CompuAdd, 82
    Dell Computer, 82-83
    DTK Computer, 83
    Epson America, 83-84
    Everex Systems, 84
    Gateway 2000, 84
    Hewlett-Packard, 85

IBM (International Business Machines), 77-78
Kaypro, 85
Kodak, 156
Leading Edge, 85-86
NEC (Nippon Electronics Corporation), 86
Northgate Computer Systems, 86
Packard Bell, 87
PC Brand, 87
Swan Technologies, 87
Tandon, 87-88
Tandy, 88-89
Texas Instruments, 89
Toshiba, 89
Wyse Technology, 90
Zenith, 90
ZEOS International, 90-91
memory, 50-51
MicroChannel architecture, 77
MIDI software
    Cakewalk Professional 3.0, 211
    Copyist DTP, 211
    The Musicator, 211
monochrome monitors, 54
MS-DOS operating system, 34
monitors
    mono/graphics, 239
    monochrome, 54
operating systems
    DeskMate, 180
    DESQview, 179
    DOS, 176, 177
    GEM, 179
    GEOWorks (Ensemble), 180
    OS/2, 181-182
    Windows, 178
paint/drawing programs
    Corel Draw! 2.0, 207
    PC PaintBrush IV Plus 1.0, 207

personal finance software
    Managing Your Money 7.0, 197
    Quicken 4.0, 197
portables
    Toshiba Model 3100SX, 121
printers, 155
    Canon BJ-10e, 156
    Kodak Dixonix 150 Plus, 156
PS/1, 98-99
PS/2, 97-98
repair centers, 234-235
speed, 93
spreadsheet programs
    1-2-3 Release 2.2, 190
    1-2-3 Release 3.1, 190
    Excel 2.1, 190
    Quattro Pro 2.0, 190
upgrades, 237
    graphics adapters, 239
    hardware, 237
    math coprocessors, 241
    memory, 238
    monitors, 239
    printers, 241
    software, 237
    system boards, 240
used computers, 124-126
    IBM PC, 125
    IBM PC AT, 125
    IBM PC XT, 125
    IBM PS/2, 125-126
video standards, 239
video systems, 94
Windows operating environment, 34-35
word processors
    LetterPerfect 1.0, 188
    Professional Write 2.2, 188
    Word for Windows, 188
    WordPerfect 5.1, 188

IBM used computers, 124-126
    IBM PC, 125
    IBM PC AT, 125
    IBM PC XT, 125
    IBM PS/2, 125-126
IDE (integrated device electronics)
    hard disks, 96
indicator lights, 22
Informix
    Wingz 1.1, 190
inkjet printers, 136
    features, 137
    fonts, 137
    manufacturers, 137
    paper size, 147
Inman Software
    Business Sense, 195
integrated device electronics (IDE)
    hard disks, 96
integrated software packages
    PFS: First Choice 3.1, 205
    purchasing considerations, 203-206
    Symphony 2.2, 205
    Works 2.0, 205
Intel microprocessors, 41-42
    80286, 43-44
    80386, 44-45
    80386SX, 44-45
    80486, 46
    8086, 42-43
    8088, 42-43
Interleaf Publisher 3.0, 201
Interleaf Software
    Interleaf Publisher 3.0, 201
internal reports, 148
Intuit
    Quicken 1.5, 197
    Quicken 4.0, 197
ISA bus, 63

K

Kaypro, 85
keyboard
    maintenance, 228
    connectors, 22-23
keyboards, 28-29
    101-key, 52
Kodak
    Diconix 150 Plus portable inkjet printer, 156
    Diconix 150M Plus portable inkjet printer, 156

L

laptop computers, 122
laser printers, 138, 141
    Adobe
        PostScript, 139
    Apple
        LaserWriter II NTX, 156
        LaserWriters, 140
    features, 140
    Hewlett-Packard
        LaserJet III, 139
        LaserJet Series III, 156
        Printer Control Language (PCL), 139
        Series II, 156
    manufacturers/dealers, 141
        Apple, 140
    operating costs, 147-148
    page description language, 139
    paper size, 147
    print language, 139
    printer engine, 141
    QuickDraw printers, 140
    speed, 146
Leading Edge, 85-86

letter-quality printers, 134
LetterPerfect 1.0, 188
letters, 149
Level II 3.0, 211
local bulletin board on-line
    services, 243
Lotus computer magazine, 242
Lotus Corporation
    1-2-3 Release 2.2, 190
    1-2-3 Release 3.1, 190
    Symphony 2.2, 205
luggables (portable computers),
    120-122

M

M-USA Business Systems
    Pacioli 2000, 195
M.Y.O.B. 2.0, 195
Mac Tools Deluxe, 227-230
Mac User computer
    magazine, 242
Mac World computer
    magazine, 242
Macintosh Computers
    Diconix 150M Plus portable
        inkjet printer, 156
Macintosh computers, 78
    accounting programs
        M.Y.O.B. 2.0, 195
    accounting software
        Business Sense, 195
    Apple
        Personal LaserWriter SC page
            printer, 156
    communications software
        CarbonCopy Mac, 204
        CompuServe
            Navigator 3.0, 204
        Microphone II 3.0, 203
        White Knight 11.6, 204
    database programs
        4th Dimension 2.1, 193
        FoxBASE II/Mac 2.01, 193

desktop publishing
    FrameMaker 2.1, 200
    QuarkXpress 3.0, 200
    Springboard
        Publisher II 2.0, 200
desktop publishing software
    PageMaker 4.0, 200
dot-matrix printers, 132-135, 155
    24-pin, 155
    9-pin, 155
    cut-sheet feeders, 135
    dots per inch (dpi), 145-146
    manufacturers, 136
    operating costs, 147-148
    paper parking, 135
    paper size, 147
    print modes, 135
    resolution, 145-146
    speed, 146
    tractor-feed mechanisms, 135
example systems
    databases, 110-112
    desktop publishing, 115
    educational, 116-117
    general purpose, 118-119
    paint programs, 113
    presentation graphics, 113
    spreadsheets, 108-109
    word processing, 105-107
Finder, 177
floppy disks/disk drives, 31
GCC PLP IIS page printer, 156
inkjet printers, 155
integrated software packages
    Works 2.0, 205
Macintosh Classic dot-matrix
    printer, 155
Macintosh Portable, 122
magazines
    see computer magazines
manufacturers/dealers
    Adobe, 138
    Apple, 156

Index

memory, 51
MIDI software
    Finale, 211
    Performer 3.5, 211
models available, 99-100
monochrome monitors, 54
multitasking operating system
    MultiFinder, 180
operating system, 36
    System 7, 182
paint/drawing programs
    Adobe Illustrator 3.0, 208
    DeskPaint/DeskDraw 3.01, 207
personal finance software
    Managing Your
      Money 3.0, 197
    Quicken 1.5, 197
printers
    QuickDraw, 140
    QuickDraw page printer, 156
    serial ports, 143
repair centers, 234, 235
Seikosha
    P1000 dot-matrix printer, 155
speed, 93
spreadsheet programs
    Excel 2.2, 190
    Wingz 1.1, 190
System, 177
upgrades, 237
    graphics adapters, 239
    hardware, 237
    math coprocessors, 241
    memory, 238
    monitors, 239
    printers, 241
    software, 237
    system boards, 240
used computers, 126-127
video standards, 239
video systems, 27, 95
word processors
    Word 4.0, 188
    WriteNow 2.2, 188

MacTools Deluxe, 226
magnetism, 221
mail order, 162-165
    finding vendors, 164
mailing labels, 149
maintenance
    floppy disks/disk drives, 225-226
    hard disks/disk drives, 226-227
    keyboard, 228
    magnetism, 221
    montiors, 228
    mouse, 228
    personal computers, 233
      warranty periods,
        234-236
    phone lines, 221
    power, 218-219
    printers, 228
    static electricity, 220-221
    system unit, 225
    ventilation, 219
    working environment, 219-220
Managing Your Money 3.0, 197
Managing Your Money 7.0, 197
manufacturers/dealers
    Adobe, 138
    Acer America, 79
    ALR (Advanced Logic
      Research), 79-80
    Altec Technologies
      Corporation, 80
    Apple, 156
    AST Research, 80
    AT&T, 81
    Austin Computer Systems, 81
    Canon, 156
    COMPAQ Computer, 81-82
    CompuAdd, 82
    Dell Computer, 82-83
    DTK Computer, 83
    Epson America, 83-84
    Everex Systems, 84
    Gateway 2000, 84
    Hewlett-Packard, 85

IBM (International Business Machines), 77-78
Kaypro, 85
Kodak, 156
Leading Edge, 85-86
NEC (Nippon Electronics Corporation), 86
Northgate Computer Systems, 86
Packard Bell, 87
PC Brand, 87
Swan Technologies, 87
Tandon, 87-88
Tandy, 88-89
Texas Instruments, 89
Toshiba, 89
Wyse Technology, 90
Zenith, 90
ZEOS International, 90-91
Mark of the Unicorn
    Performer 3.5, 211
MCA bus, 63
Meca Ventures
    Managing Your Money 3.0, 197
    Managing Your Money 7.0, 197
megahertz (MHz), 40
memory, 95-96, 144-145
    addressing, 40-41
    Amiga, 51
    Atari, 51
    expanded, 50-51
    extended, 50
    IBM-compatible computers, 50-51
    Macintosh, 51
    RAM, 49, 144-145
        dynamic, 49
        static, 49
    ROM, 33, 48
memory upgrades, 238
MFM (modified frequency modulation) hard disks, 96
MicroChannel architecture, 77
Microcom
    Virex 1.1, 227
    Virex 2.71, 227
Microcom Microcomputer Associates
    CarbonCopy Mac, 204
Microphone II 3.0, 203
microprocessors
    addressing, 40-41
    compatibility, 41
    Intel, 41-42
        80286, 43-44
        80386, 44-45
        80386SX, 44-45
        80486, 46
        8086, 42-43
        8088, 42-43
    Motorola
        68000, 46-48
        68020, 46-48
        68030, 47-48
    NEC, 43
    speed, 40, 93
Microsoft
    Excel 2.1, 190
    Excel 2.2, 190
    File 2.0, 193
    OS/2, 181-182
    Windows, 34-35, 178
    Word 4.0, 188
    Word for Windows, 188
    Works 2.0, 205
MIDI software, 13
    Cakewalk Professional 3.0, 211
    Copyist DTP, 211
    Finale, 211
    Level II 3.0, 211
    Notator 3.0, 211
    Performer 3.5, 211
    purchasing considerations, 208-212
    The Musicator, 211

Index

modems, 64-66, 114
monitors, 25-27
   colors, 55-56
   maintenance, 228
   monochrome, 26, 54
   multiscan, 27
   resolution, 26
   size, 56-57
monitors, *see also* video standards, 239
mono/graphics video standard, 239
monochrome monitors, 26, 54
motherboards, 24
Motorola microprocesors
   68000, 46-48
   68020, 46,-48
   68030, 47-48
mouse, 28-29, 52-53
   bus, 53
   maintenance, 228
   optical, 53
   opto-mechanical, 53
   ports, 53
MS-DOS, 34, 176-177
multi-tasking operating environments
   DESQview, 179
   Windows, 178
multi-tasking operating systems
   GEOWorks Ensemble, 180
   OS/2, 181-182
   System 7, 182
MultiFinder, 180
multiscan monitors, 27
Musicator
   The Musicator, 211

N

NEC (Nippon Electronics Corporation), 86
   V20 microprocessor, 43
   V30 microprocessor, 43
newsletters, 151
Northgate Computer Systems, 86
Norton Antivirus, 227
Norton Utilities 5.0, 227-230
Norton Utilities for the Macintosh, 230
Notator 3.0, 211
notebooks
   portable computers, 122-123

O

on-line services, 243
   CompuServe, 243
   Genie, 243
   local bulletin boards, 243
operating system software, 34
operating systems
   Amiga, 36
   DR DOS, 34
   GEM, 34
   Macintosh, 36
   MS-DOS, 34
   multitasking
      DESQview, 179
      GEOWorks Ensemble, 180
      MultiFinder, 180
      OS/2, 181-182
      System 7, 182
      Windows, 178
   single-tasking
      DeskMate, 180
      DOS, 176-177
      GEM, 179
      System, 177
   UNIX, 34
   Windows, 34-35
   XENIX, 34
optical mouse, 53
opto-mechanical mouse, 53
OPTune, 227
OS/2, 181-182

P

Pacioli 2000, 195
Packard Bell, 87
page description language, 139
page printers, 156
   Apple Personal
     LaserWriter SC, 156
   GCC PLP IIS, 156
PageMaker 3.01, 200
PageMaker 4.0, 200
paint programs
   Adobe Illustrator 3.0, 208
   Corel Draw! 2.0, 207
   Deluxe Paint III, 208
   DeskPaint/DeskDraw 3.01, 207
   example systems, 112-113
   PC PaintBrush IV Plus 1.0, 207
   Professional Draw 2.0, 208
   purchasing considerations,
     206-208
Panasonic
   KX-P1180 dot-matrix printer, 155
paper parking, 135
paper size, 147
Paradox 3.5, 193
parallel ports, 22-23, 63-64
PC Brand, 87
PC Computing computer
   magazine, 242
PC Fullback+ 1.12, 226
PC Magazine, 242
PC PaintBrush IV Plus 1.0, 207
PC Tools Deluxe 6.0, 230
PC Tools Deluxe Version 6.0, 226
PC-File 5.0, 193
pcAnywhere III, 203
Peachtree Complete III, 195
PeachTree Software
   Peachtree Complete III, 195
Performer 3.5, 211
personal computers
   benefits, 6-8

CAD systems, 113
comparisions, 72
   graphical user interfaces,
     73-75
   price, 76-77
   software availability, 73
   speed, 75-76
comparisons
   models, 96
database systems, 110-112
desktop publishing systems,
   115-116
educational systems, 116-117
general use systems, 118-119
hard disk upgrades, 239
hardware configurations,
   183-184
hardware upgrades, 237
maintenance, 233
   warranty periods,
     234-236
new developments, 242
on-line services, 243
paint program systems, 112-113
portables, 119-120
presentation graphics systems,
   112-113
purchasing considerations,
   166-169
   computer stores, 160-161
   department stores, 162
   electronics stores, 161-162
   mail order, 162-165
   superstores, 161
purchasing decisions, 14-16
ROM chips, 237
setting up, 166, 222-224
   unpacking equipment,
     222-223
spreadsheet systems, 107-109
system unit, 21-25
training, 166
upgrades, 237

hard disk, 239
hardware, 237
math coprocessors, 241
memory, 238
monitors, 239
software, 237
system boards, 240
used computers, 123-127
  Amiga computers, 127
  Atari computers, 127
  IBM PC, 125
  IBM PC AT, 125
  IBM PC XT, 125
  IBM PS/2, 125-126
  Macintosh computers, 126-127
  sources, 128-129
  warranty periods, 234-236
  word processing systems, 104-107
personal finance software
  purchasing considerations, 195-197
  Quicken 1.5, 197
  Quicken 4.0, 197
personal finances
  Managing Your Money 3.0, 197
  Managing Your Money 7.0, 197
Peter Norton Computing
  Norton Utilities 5.0, 227-230
  Norton Utilities for the Macintosh, 230
PFS: First Choice 3.1, 205
PFS: First Publisher 3.0, 201
phone lines, 221
picas, 134
portable computers, 119-120
  gas plasma screens, 121
  laptops, 122
  luggables, 120-122
  Macintosh Portable, 122
  notebooks, 122-123
  Toshiba
    Model 3100SX, 121
    T1000SE, 122

ports
  mouse, 53
  parallel, 22-23, 63-64
  printer, 143
  serial, 22-23, 63-64
PostScript laser printers
  Apple LaserWrite II NTX, 156
PostScript printers, 139
power
  blackouts, 218
  brownouts, 218
  power spikes, 218-219
  power surges, 218-219
power supply, 24-25
Power Up Software
  Express Publisher 1.0, 201
Precision Software
  SuperBase 4, 193
presentation graphics, 12-13
  example systems, 112-113
price of personal computers, 76-77
printer engines, 141
printers, 64, 131
  application considerations, 151
    accounting, 153
    databases, 152
    desktop publishing, 153
    drawing, 154
    educational, 154
    graphics, 154
    spreadsheets, 151-152
    word processing, 152-153
  Canon
    BJ-130 inkjet printer, 155
  color, 157
  daisywheel, 137-138
  determining needs, 154
  determining required output, 148
  dot-matrix, 132-135
    24-pin, 155
    9-pin, 155
    cut-sheet feeders, 135
    dots per inch (dpi), 145-146

manufacturers, 136
operating costs, 147-148
paper parking, 135
paper size, 147
print modes, 135
resolution, 145-146
speed, 146
tractor-feed mechanisms, 135
elongated characters, 134
Epson
   LQ-510 dot-matrix printer, 155
features, 142-143
fonts, 132
Hewlett-Packard
   DeskJet 500 inkjet printer, 155
inkjet, 136, 155
   features, 137
   fonts, 137
   manufacturers, 137
   paper size, 147
laser, 138-141
   engines, 141
   Hewlett-Packard LaserJet
     Series III, 156
   Hewlett-Packard Series III, 156
   operating costs, 147-148
   page description
     language, 139
   paper size, 147
   printer language, 139
   speed, 146
letter-quality, 134
letters, 149
maintenance, 228
manufacturers/dealers
   Apple, 140
memory, 144-145
   RAM, 144-145
operating costs, 147-148
Panasonic
   KX-P1124 dot-matrix printer,
     155

paper size, 147
pica, 134
ports, 143
PostScript, 139
print quality, 142-143
resolution, 141, 145-146
serial ports, 143
speed, 146
thermal transfer, 136
   features, 137
   fonts, 137
   manufacturers, 137
type faces, 132
upgrades, 241
printing
   accounting documents, 153
   banners, 149
   brochures, 151
   database programs, 152
   forms, 150
   high-quality documents, 151
   internal reports, 148
   mailing labels, 149
   newsletters, 151
   papers, 149
   resumes, 149
   spreadsheets, 150-152
ProComm Plus 1.1, 203
Professional Draw 2.0, 208
Professional Write 2.2, 188
programming languages, 14
PS/1 IBM-compatible computers,
   98-99
PS/2 computers
   used, 125-126
PS/2 IBM-compatible computers,
   97-98
Publish computer magazine, 242
purchasing considerations, 166-169
   accounting software, 194-195
   communications software,
     200-203

computer stores, 160-161
database programs, 191-193
department stores, 162
desktop publishing, 198-199
drawing programs, 206-208
educational software, 212-213
electronic stores, 161-162
games, 212-213
integrated software packages, 203-206
mail order, 162-165
MIDI software, 208-212
paint programs, 206-208
personal finance software, 195-197
shareware, 214-215
spreadsheet programs, 188-190
superstores, 161
word processors, 185-187
purchasing personal computers, 14-16

Q

Quark Software
   QuarkXpress 3.0, 200
QuarkXpress 3.0, 200
Quarterback 4.0, 226
Quarterback
   Tools, 227, 230
   Office Systems
      DESQview, 179
Quattro Pro 2.0, 190
Quicken 1.5, 197
Quicken 4.0, 197

R

RAM, 49, 144-145
   DIPs, 49-50
   dynamic, 49
   expanded memory, 50-51
   extended memory, 50

IBM-compatible computers, 50-51
   SIPPs, 49-50
   static, 49
random access memory
   see RAM
read only memory
   see ROM
relational databases, 191
removable hard disks, 61
resolution, 141
restocking fees, 163
resumes, 149
Retrospect 1.1, 226
RLL (run-length limited)
   hard disks/disk drives, 96
ROM, 33, 48
ROM chips, 237

S

scanners, 66
SCSI (small computer systems interface) hard disks, 96
security
   locks on system unit, 21-22
Seikosha
   SP1000 dot-matrix printer, 155
serial ports, 22-23, 63-64
setting up personal computers, 166, 222-224
   cables, 222
   unpacking equipment, 222-223
single-in-line memory modules
   see SIMMs, 49
single-tasking operating environments
   DOS, 176, 177
   System, 177
single-tasking operating sytems
   DeskMate, 180
   GEM, 179
SIPPs, 49-50
size of monitors, 56-57

SmartCom III 1.2, 203
Soft Warehouse computer
    store, 161
software
    accounting software, 194-195
    applications, 36-37
    availability, 73
    communications, 200-203
    database programs, 174, 191-193
    desktop publishing, 174, 198-199
    diagnostics, 230
    drawing programs, 206-208
    educational, 212-213
    games, 212-213
    hardware requirements,
        183-184
    integrated packages,
        203-206
    MIDI, 208-212
    operating systems, 34-36
    paint programs, 206-208
    personal finance software,
        195-197
    purchasing considerations,
        185-187
    shareware, 214-215
    spreadsheet programs, 173,
        188-190
    training, 182-183
    use, 172-173
    utilities, 230
Software Publishing Company
    PFS: First Choice 3.1, 205
    PFS: First Publisher 3.0, 201
    Professional Write 2.2, 188
software upgrades, 237
Software Ventures
    Microphone II 3.0, 203
speed, 75-76
    microprocessors
        Amiga computers, 93
        Atari computers, 93
        IBM-compatible
            computers, 93
        Macintosh computers, 93
spikes, 218-219
SpinRite II, 227
spreadsheet applications
    printer considerations,
        150-152
spreadsheet programs, 10, 173
    1-2-3 Release 2.2, 190
    1-2-3 Release 3.1, 190
    example systems, 107-109
    Excel 2.1, 190
    Excel 2.2, 190
    purchasing considerations,
        188-190
    Quattro Pro 2.0, 190
    Wingz 1.1, 190
Springboard Publisher II 2.0, 200
Springboard Software
    Springboard Publisher II 2.0, 200
Star Micronics
    NX-1000 Multifont II dot-matrix
        printer, 155
static electricity, 220-221
static RAM, 49
storage capacity
    hard disks/disk drives, 59
SuperBase 4, 193
Super VGA video standard, 239
surge protectors, 68, 218-219
surges, 218-219
Swan Technologies, 87
Symantec
    AntiVirus for Mac, 227
    Norton Antivirus, 227
    Norton Utilities 5.0, 227-230
Symphony 2.2, 205
System, 177
System 7, 182
system board upgrade, 240
system unit, 21-25

case, 51-52
chips, 24
expansion slots, 24, 61-62
hard disks, 24
indicator lights, 22
keyboard connector, 22-23
maintenance, 225
motherboard, 24
power supply, 24-25
system units
    expansion slots, 23
    locks, 21-22

T

T/Maker Company
    WriteNow 2.2, 188
Tandon, 87-88
Tandy, 88-89
    DeskMate, 180
telecommunications, 11-12
    modems, 64-66, 114
Teleware
    M.Y.O.B. 2.0, 195
Texas Instruments, 89
    MicroLaser 35 Postscript laser
        printer, 156
The Musicator, 211
thermal transfer printers, 136
    features, 137
    fonts, 137
    manufacturers, 137
Toshiba, 89
    Model 3100SX portable
        computer, 121
    T1000SE laptop computer, 122
TouchStone Software
    Check It, 230
trackballs, 53-54
tractor-feed mechanisms, 135
training

software, 182-183
    for personal computers, 166
transfer rate (hard disks/disk
    drives), 60-61
troubleshooting
    initial setup, 229
    long term, 230
Twelve Tone Systems
    Cakewalk Professional 3.0, 211
typefaces, 132
types of hard disks/disk drives, 96

U

uninterruptible power supplies
    (UPS), 219
UNIX, 34
upgrades, 237
    graphics adapters, 239
    hardware, 237
    math coprocessors, 241
    memory, 238
    monitors, 239
    printers, 241
    software, 237
    system boards, 240
UPS (uninterruptible power
    supply), 219
used computers, 123-124
    Amiga computers, 127
    Atari computers, 127
    IBM-compatible computers,
        124-126
        IBM PC, 125
        IBM PC AT, 125
        IBM PC XT, 125
        IBM PS/2, 125-126
    Macintosh computers, 126-127
    sources, 128-129
utiltity software, 230

V

V20 microprocessor, 43
V30 microprocessor, 43
ventilation, 219
Ventura Publisher, 201
Ventura Software
   Ventura Publisher, 201
VGA (Video Graphics Array), 27
VGA video standard, 239
video standards
   CGA, 239
   EGA, 239
   mono/graphics, 239
   SuperVGA, 239
   VGA, 239
   XGA, 239
video system
   CGA, 26
   monitor, 25-27
   VGA, 27
video systems
   adapters, 94-95
   Amiga, 27
   Atari, 27
   gas plasma screens, 121
   Macintosh, 27
   monitors, 94-95
      resolution, 26
Virex 1.1, 227
Virex 2.71, 227
viruses, 227

W

warranty periods, 234-236
West Lake Data
   PC Fullback+ 1.12, 226
What You See Is What You Get
   (WYSIWYG), 176
White Knight 11.6, 204
Windows, 34-35, 178
Wingz 1.1, 190
Word 4.0, 188
Word for Windows, 188
word processors
   document management, 186
   example systems, 104-107
   LetterPerfect 1.0, 188
   printer considerations, 152-153
   Professional Write 2.2, 188
   purchasing considerations,
      185-187
   Word 4.0, 188
   Word for Windows, 188
   WordPerfect 5.1, 188
   WriteNow 2.2, 188
WordPerfect 5.1, 188
WordPerfect computer
   magazine, 242
WordPerfect Corporation
   LetterPerfect 1.0, 188
   WordPerfect 5.1, 188
   WordPerfect computer
      magazine, 242
working environments, 219-220
   magnetism, 221
   phone lines, 221
   static electricity, 220-221
Works 2.0, 205
WriteNow 2.2, 188
Wyse Technolgy, 90
WYSIWYG (What You See Is What
   You Get), 176

X-Z

XENIX operating system, 34
XGA video standard, 239
Zedcor
   DeskPaint/DeskDraw 3.01, 207
Zenith, 90
ZEOS International, 90-91
ZSoft
   PC PaintBrush IV Plus 1.0, 207